ENCYCLOPEDIA OF LANGUAGE AND EDUCATION

Encyclopedia of Language and Education

VOLUME 2: LITERACY

The volume titles of this encyclopedia are listed at the end of this volume.

Encyclopedia of Language and Education

Volume 2

LITERACY

Edited by

VIV EDWARDS

*University of Reading
England*

and

DAVID CORSON

*The Ontario Institute for Studies in Education
University of Toronto
Canada*

KAP ARCHIEF

KLUWER ACADEMIC PUBLISHERS

DORDRECHT / BOSTON / LONDON

Library of Congress Cataloging-in-Publication Data

Literacy / edited by Viv Edwards and David Corson.
      p. cm. -- (Encyclopedia of language and education ; v. 2)
  Includes bibliographical references and index.
  ISBN 0-7923-4595-0 (alk. paper). -- ISBN 0-7923-4596-7 (set : alk.
paper)
  1. Language acquisition. 2. Literacy. I. Edwards, Viv.
II. Corson, David. III. Series.
P118.7.L584 1997
302.2'244--dc21
                    97-18842
                    CIP

ISBN 0-7923-4929-6 (PB)   ISBN 0-7923-4595-0 (HB)
ISBN 0-7923-4936-9 (PB-SET)   ISBN 0-7923-4596-7 (HB-SET)

Published by Kluwer Academic Publishers,
P.O. Box 17, 3300 AA Dordrecht, The Netherlands

Sold and distributed in the U.S.A. and Canada
by Kluwer Academic Publishers,
101 Philip Drive, Norwell, MA 02061, U.S.A.

In all other countries, sold and distributed
by Kluwer Academic Publishers Group,
P.O. Box 322, 3300 AH Dordrecht, The Netherlands

Printed in the Netherlands (on acid-free paper)

TABLE OF CONTENTS

VOLUME 2: LITERACY

Section 3: Focus on the Social Context of Literacy

Section 4: Focus on Selected Regions

GENERAL EDITOR'S INTRODUCTION

ENCYCLOPEDIA OF LANGUAGE AND EDUCATION

This is one of eight volumes of the Encyclopedia of Language and Education published by Kluwer Academic. The publication of this work signals the maturity of the field of 'language and education' as an international and interdisciplinary field of significance and cohesion. These volumes confirm that 'language and education' is much more than the preserve of any single discipline. In designing these volumes, we have tried to recognise the diversity of the field in our selection of contributors and in our choice of topics. The contributors come from every continent and from more than 40 countries. Their reviews discuss language and education issues affecting every country in the world.

We have also tried to recognise the diverse interdisciplinary nature of 'language and education' in the selection of the editorial personnel themselves. The major academic interests of the volume editors confirm this. As principal volume editor for Volume 1, Ruth Wodak has interests in critical linguistics, sociology of language, and language policy. For Volume 2, Viv Edwards has interests in policy and practice in multilingual classrooms and the sociology of language. For Volume 3, Bronwyn Davies has interests in the social psychology of language, the sociology of language, and interdisciplinary studies. For Volume 4, Richard Tucker has interests in language theory, applied linguistics, and the implementation and evaluation of innovative language education programs. For Volume 5, Jim Cummins has interests in the psychology of language and in critical linguistics. For Volume 6, Leo van Lier has interests in applied linguistics and in language theory. For Volume 7, Caroline Clapham has interests in research into second language acquisition and language measurement. And for Volume 8, Nancy Hornberger has interests in anthropological linguistics and in language policy. Finally, as general editor, I have interests in the philosophy and sociology of language, language policy, critical linguistics, and interdisciplinary studies. But the thing that unites us all, including all the contributors to this work, is an interest in the practice and theory of education itself.

People working in the applied and theoretical areas of education and language are often asked questions like the following: 'what is the latest research on such and such a problem?' or 'what do we know about such

V. Edwards and D. Corson (eds), Encyclopedia of Language and Education,
Volume 2: Literacy, vii–ix.
© *1997 Kluwer Academic Publishers. Printed in the Netherlands.*

and such an issue?' Questions like these are asked by many people: by policy makers and practitioners in education; by novice researchers; by publishers trying to relate to an issue; and above all by undergraduate and postgraduate students in the language disciplines. Each of the reviews that appears in this volume tries to anticipate and answer some of the more commonly asked questions about language and education. Taken together, the eight volumes of this Encyclopedia provide answers to more than 200 major questions of this type, and hundreds of subsidiary questions as well.

Each volume of the Encyclopedia of Language and Education deals with a single, substantial subject in the language and education field. The volume titles and their contents appear elsewhere in the pages of this work. Each book-length volume provides more than 20 state-of-the-art topical reviews of the literature. Taken together, these reviews attempt a complete coverage of the subject of the volume. Each review is written by one or more experts in the topic, or in a few cases by teams assembled by experts. As a collection, the Encyclopedia spans the range of subjects and topics normally falling within the scope of 'language and education'. Each volume, edited by an international expert in the subject of the volume, was designed and developed in close collaboration with the general editor of the Encyclopedia, who is a co-editor of each volume as well as general editor of the whole work.

The Encyclopedia has been planned as a necessary reference set for any university or college library that serves a faculty or school of education. Libraries serving academic departments in any of the language disciplines, especially applied linguistics, would also find this a valuable resource. It also seems very relevant to the needs of educational bureaucracies, policy agencies, and public libraries, particularly those serving multicultural or multilingual communities.

The Encyclopedia aims to speak to a prospective readership that is multinational, and to do so as unambiguously as possible. Because each book-size volume deals with a discrete and important subject in language and education, these state-of-the-art volumes also offer authoritative course textbooks in the areas suggested by their titles. This means that libraries will also catalogue these book-size individual volumes in relevant sections of their general collections. To meet this range of uses, the Encyclopedia is published in a hardback edition offering the durability needed for reference collections, and in a future student edition. The hardback edition is also available for single-volume purchase.

Each state-of-the-art review has about 3000 words of text and most follow a similar structure. A list of references to key works cited in each review supplements the information and authoritative opinion that the review contains. Many contributors survey early developments in their topic, major contributions, work in progress, problems and difficulties, and future directions for research and practice. The aim of the reviews, and of the Encyclopedia as a whole, is to give readers access to the international literature and research on each topic.

David Corson
General Editor Encyclopedia of Language and Education
Ontario Institute for Studies in Education of the University of Toronto
Canada

INTRODUCTION

The study of literacy is very much a multidisciplinary affair. Contributors to this volume acknowledge their debt of gratitude to anthropologists, archaeologists, calligraphers, computer scientists, curriculum workers, educational researchers, ethnographers, experimental and developmental psychologists, linguists, literary critics, medics, neurolinguists, occupational therapists, physiotherapists, psycholinguists, semioticians, sociolinguists, typographers as well as to those who study reading development and the teaching of reading. Unfortunately, each field has tended to work in isolation, using its own methodologies and only asking questions significant within its own discipline.

It is perhaps not surprising that such a diverse field should have generated very different models both of the reading process and of literacy itself. Our understanding of how literacy is acquired has been the focus for much debate. In Section 1 of this volume, various contributors consider issues and developments in what Kenneth Goodman in his review of the reading process has characterised as the 'word recognition' and the 'meaning construction' views of reading. G. Brian Thompson continues this theme in his review of the teaching of reading, from historical and contemporary perspectives. Bridie Raban considers the range of skills associated with emergent reading while William Tunmer focuses more specifically on the role of metalinguistic skills in reading development. Most children develop into competent readers with relatively little difficulty. However, in a small proportion of cases, discussed in this volume by Marie M. Clay, problems which emerge in the first year of school persist throughout formal education. Viv Edwards discusses another special situation, the teaching of reading in the multilingual classrooms which are now a feature of many city schools throughout the world.

In Section 2 of this volume, reviewers consider parallel issues in the acquisition of writing. Barbara Burnaby, for instance, discusses the advantages and disadvantages of different writing systems while Nigel Hall examines the development of young children as authors, and Gretchen Owocki and Yetta Goodman review the teaching of writing. These writers focus primarily on compositional rather than transcriptional aspects of writing. In contrast, Sandra Wilde looks at the development of spelling and punctuation, and Sue Walker at the development of handwriting skills. Finally, Viv Edwards provides an overview of issues relating to writing in multilingual classrooms. The emphasis in both the first and second parts of

V. Edwards and D. Corson (eds), Encyclopedia of Language and Education,
Volume 2: Literacy, xi–xvi.
© *1997 Kluwer Academic Publishers. Printed in the Netherlands.*

this volume, then, is not only on skills but also on social and developmental aspects of literacy.

Section 3 of this volume maintains the focus on social aspects of literacy. As John Edwards points out in his review of the social psychology of reading, teachers do not merely want to produce people who can read but people who are readers. As such we need to be concerned with questions such as what people read, the amount of reading done, the purposes and effects of reading. Ludo Verhoeven gives an overview of the functional model of literacy which emphasises the demands of literacy in a complex world, particularly in relation to employment and the economy. Brian Street critiques three current approaches to literacy: the autonomous model which emphasises cognitive skills and presents literacy as a neutral technique that can be universally applied; and the 'new literacy studies' and 'critical literacy' which emphasise social aspects of reading and writing. Allan Luke also focuses on critical approaches to literacy which have emerged in response to rapidly changing demographies, cultures, technologies and economies. Elsa Roberts Auerbach looks at the role of parents in children's literacy acquisition and academic achievement, while Alan Rogers examines the promotion of reading and writing skills among adults. The assumption that the move towards standard, national or official languages is a necessary condition for the spread of literacy is challenged by RK Agnihotri in his discussion of local literacies. Finally, Chris Abbott discusses the most recent social force in literacy development: information technology and the new avenues for communication between the literate peoples of the world.

Section 4 of this book looks at a range of very different geographical settings: three reviews – Danielle Béchennec and Liliane Sprenger-Charolles on France, Bente Hagtvet & Solveig-Alma Lyster on Norway and Pieter Reitsma on the Low Countries – describe literacy teaching in a European context. Contributions by RK Agnihotri on India and Benedicta Egbo on Nigeria, extend the geographical net, drawing attention not only to individual differences but to commonalities which unite literacy teaching in these very different settings.

The reviews, then, are organised in terms of reading, writing, social aspects of literacy and regional studies. This division, it should be stressed, is an organisational device rather than, for instance, an assumption of independence for different language skills. Thus Barbara Burnaby discusses the implications of different writing systems for learning to read; while Chris Abbott's overview of IT and literacy might have been placed just as comfortably with either reading or writing. In a similar vein, a number of themes, including the implications of theory for practice, and the impact of the political agenda on literacy teaching, recur throughout the volume.

THEORY INTO PRACTICE

Different theoretical models – whether of the reading process or of literacy itself – have wide reaching implications for pedagogy. As Alan Rogers points out in his review of adult literacy, the autonomous model often presents learning to read and write in terms of a one-off programme rather than a continuous, lifelong process. It also leads to a simple dichotomy between literate and illiterate, ignoring intermediate levels of competence. It is difficult to assess as yet the impact of the more recent 'social' or 'ideological' model of literacy which is only just beginning to influence pedagogy.

Brian Street suggests that the impact of theory on practice will be a major direction for research in the coming decade, as the ideas associated with different positions are applied to specific programmes and contexts. Elsa Roberts Auerbach also provides support for this position. She points out that, in spite of evidence for multiple literacies, teaching in family literacy programmes continues to be based on more traditional assumptions and concludes that the gap between research and practice continues to represent a stumbling block for work in this area. In a similar vein, Alan Rogers suggests that while research into literacy practices will almost certainly continue to grow, it is not clear how such research will lead to better learning programmes.

Similar debates are associated with the reading process. Kenneth S. Goodman characterises the two opposing positions as the Word Recognition (WR) view and the Meaning Construction (MR) view. He underlines the very different consequences for pedagogy of teachers working with word recognition and meaning construction models. He bemoans the fact that adherents of both positions tend to ignore research that does not fit their own paradigm and acknowledges that these very different views of reading will continue to drive research, theory and practice for some time to come.

Marie M. Clay underlines the dangers of oversimplistic extrapolation from theory to practice. For instance, if children selected for dyslexia programmes can be shown to have a deficit in phonological processing, it does not follow that this should form the sole focus for support at the expense of the many other factors which contribute to good reading and writing.

Bridie Raban also draws attention to the importance of a synthesis, arguing that children need to develop strategies for both word recognition and meaning construction. She points out that while this creates a problem for some researchers, who are unsure what advice to offer practitioners, for others it provides a starting point for creative and innovative observations.

POLITICAL ISSUES

As Alan Rogers observes, literacy has always been a political issue. The earliest religion-driven literacy campaigns, for instance, did not envisage that every adult would need to learn to read. On the contrary, there was concern that education would teach the labouring classes to despise their lot in life. When the concept of learning to read and write as a universal and compulsory 'good' emerged in the nineteenth century, this, too, was driven by political motives. Widespread literacy was viewed as essential for economic development; it also came to be seen as a human right, the denial of which would reflect badly on the state.

Bridie Raban and Kenneth S. Goodman both point to the heavy political overlay in discussions of reading in the popular press and elsewhere. Perceived falls in reading standards are very much an international concern, spanning a considerable period of time. Danielle Béchennec and Liliane Sprenger-Charolles, for instance, trace the French preoccupation with this issue from the beginning of the nineteenth century to the present day, in spite of evidence that overall standards have improved rather than declined.

As Brian Street points out, a major reason for continued concern lies in the fact that lay obervers continue to work within an autonomous model of literacy. The practical consequences of blind adherence to this model are clear to see. Allan Luke and Gretchen Owocki & Yetta Goodman, for example, draw attention to the impact of simplistic views of language instruction such as the multimillion dollar industry in standardized writing tests, spelling workbooks and handwriting kits which are promoted by politically motivated forces rather than a scientific understanding of how children develop written language.

Political agendas are apparent not only in school but in adult and family programmes. Thus Elsa Roberts Auerbach explains how some exponents of family literacy programmes attempt to deflect attention from the need for school reform by locating the source of educational problems in families. Marie M. Clay raises similar issues in relation to learners of low intelligence, and those who live in poverty. She argues that, while contemporary societies would like most of them to become literate, they have institutionalized practices which make this impossible.

The importance of the debate on standards lies in its destructive force. A significant obstacle to a convergence between exponents of the word recognition and the meaning construction models is a political agenda which targets allegedly left wing teachers and their trendy new ideas. In this context, it is interesting to note that the roots of many ideas currently enjoying popularity were in fact established in the past. In this volume, Nigel Hall identifies elements of current interest in children's authorship in John Rice's (1765) *Introduction to the art of reading with energy and propriety*; G. Brian Thompson traces holistic approaches to literacy teaching to the American 'Sentence Method' of teaching reading in the late nineteenth century United States, while Gretchen Owocki and Yetta Goodman draw attention to Hartog's (1907) publication on *The Writing of English*; several contributors refer to the importance of the work of Edmund Huey (1908) in challenging a purely mechanistic view of reading.

Anglocentricism

Another political issue concerns the all pervasive influence of standard official languages, in general, and English, in particular, in literacy teaching and research. With the development of new technologies, there is certainly a danger that this trend will continue. Chris Abbott, for instance, points to how very little is available in the languages of many of the smaller countries of the world.

A theme which runs through much of the present volume is the need to look critically at the impact of globalization on our understanding of literacy. Brian Street argues that close study of reading and writing in a range of social contexts forces us to suspend our own conceptions of 'literacy'. RK Agnihotri's review of 'Sustaining local literacies' is equally challenging. He questions the assumption that standardization is a necessary condition for development and the spread of literacy. He also argues that, if we wish to struggle for a socially just multiple literacy model, we have much to learn from multilingual societies such as India.

This more egalitarian perspective on literacy is, however, a relatively recent development. In her review of writing systems, Barbara Burnaby describes how ethnocentricity and faith in the power of English went largely unquestioned in Britain and North America for much of the twentieth century. This view led amongst other things to an idealization of phonemic orthographies, such as those used for European languages. It has also been associated with unsubstantiated casual links between alphabetic literacy and the rise of facets of Western civilization such as logic and history.

Efforts have been made in compiling this volume to guard against the worst excesses of Anglocentricism in two main ways. Firstly, as many contributors as possible have been identified outside the English-speaking world for the review of reading and writing and for discussions of the social aspects of literacy, as well as for the regional overviews of literacy teaching. Secondly, contributors have been asked to report as fully as possible on international research. The extent of English permeation of research on literacy has not always made this an easy task. None the less, many contributors discuss aspects of reading and writing in languages other than English.

Several contributors – most notably, Danielle Béchennec and Liliane Sprenger Charolles, and Bente Hagtvet and Solveig-Alma Lyster – point to the pressing need for more cross-language research. What are the implications for the acquisition of literacy in languages like French, Dutch or Norwegian where sound-symbol correspondences are more regular than in English?

Gender

Gender is another power related issue which receives attention from various contributors. Alan Rogers, for instance, draws attention to the gender gap in all forms of education and in the spread of literacy skills, despite several years of special attention to the literacy needs of women. In a similar vein, RK Agnihotri bemoans the fact that Indian women, particularly in the rural areas, have made such limited progress in learning to read and write. Benedicta Egbo, too, draws attention to the unfortunate consequences of persistently excluding women from access to literacy in rural Nigeria.

The interest in the relationship between gender and literacy is not, of course, restricted to third world contexts. Both Pieter Rietsma and John Edwards discuss gender differences in patterns of reading behaviour in the Netherlands and the English-speaking world respectively, while Allan Luke considers feminist approaches which set out to deconstruct patriarchal discourses and 'regimes of power' in everyday life.

Literacy, then, is a highly complex human behaviour. Our understanding of the reading process and the acquisition of literacy has rapidly expanded in recent years. The reviews which follow attempt to chart this progress at the same time as highlighting the controversies and likely directions for future development.

Section 1

Focus on Reading

KENNETH S. GOODMAN

THE READING PROCESS

Scholars from many disciplines are involved in studying reading. These include, but are not limited to psychologists, linguists, literary critics, psycholinguists, sociolinguists, semioticians, anthropologists, ethnographers, neurolinguists, educational researchers, curriculum workers, and those who study reading development and the teaching of reading. Except for occasional collaborations, each field has tended to work on its own, using its own methodologies and asking questions significant within the discipline. Sometimes attempting to bring these diverse vantage points together is like trying to construct an elephant from the descriptions of the blind men of Hindustan of their personal encounters with different portions of the elephant.

This situation is further complicated by the heavy political overlay in discussions of the reading process and the teaching and learning of reading in the popular press and in decision making groups such as legislative bodies and school boards. Attacks on schools on local, regional and national levels often focus on literacy instruction and on the views of reading that underlie them. Academics often find themselves and their views of reading drawn into this political maelstrom.

This review will attempt to present an inclusive and integrated view of the reading process, one which has achieved widespread acceptance particularly by teachers and other educational workers. At the same time, it will present alternate views and give some sense of the interests of groups of researchers and theoreticians working in different disciplines concerned with literacy.

HISTORY AND DEVELOPMENT

Attempts to understand the reading process began before the turn of the twentieth century. For instance, Huey (1908, 1968) argued that if we could understand reading we could understand the workings of the human brain. But it was not until the field of psycholinguistics came to prominence in the 1960s that attempts were made to articulate complete models of reading. Frank Smith (1982) synthesized the research in psychology and linguistics in his book *Understanding Reading*; Kenneth Goodman and his associates began publishing their work on miscue analysis culminating in Goodman's 1967 article, 'Reading: a Psycholinguistic Guessing Game'. This work stimulated others to make explicit the models that were the

V. Edwards and D. Corson (eds), Encyclopedia of Language and Education,
Volume 2: Literacy, 1–7.
© *1997 Kluwer Academic Publishers. Printed in the Netherlands.*

foundation for their research and theory. Development of these models has been represented in four editions of *Theoretical models and processes in reading*, published over three decades by the International Reading Association (Ruddell, Ruddell & Singer, 1994).

By the mid 1980s, those most centrally involved in the study of reading seemed to be converging on an integrated and unified model. A major trend among psychologists, particularly those at the Center for the Study of Reading at the University of Arizona at Tucson, was the study of comprehension of texts and schema theory (Spiro, Bruce & Brewer, 1980) In this view, people form schemas for organizing and interpreting texts, or indeed in making sense of any experience. Piagetian psychologists studying early literacy development were applying a psychogenetic view to study of how children learn to make sense of written language (Ferreiro & Teberosky, 1982; Goodman, 1991). In the field of literary criticism, reader response theory was laying out an active role for the reader of literature in constructing personal meaning (Rosenblatt, 1978). And ethnographers were looking at literacy in homes, communities and classrooms to examine literacy practices and uses (Bloome, 1989; Street, 1995).

In all these views, there was a central focus on an active reader constructing meaning. This was also the focus of the psycho-sociolinguistic transactional model of reading which grew out of miscue analysis, the study of the unexpected responses made by readers in the oral reading of unfamiliar texts (Goodman & Watson, 1987). It is this model of reading that has become widely accepted by teachers and incorporated into 'whole language' views of curriculum and literacy instruction (Goodman, 1996; see also reviews by Thompson and by Raban in this volume)

However, there has also been a resurgence of another view, one rooted strongly in experimental research and neo-behaviorism. In this view, reading is a matter of recognizing the words in a text rapidly and automatically (Adams, 1990; see also the review by Thompson, this volume). Advocates believe their research shows that readers must recognize every letter in every word and that they must go from print to sound – from written language to oral – before they can make sense of what they are reading.

These two opposing positions can be conveniently labelled the Word Recognition (WR) view and the Meaning Construction (MC) view. In the word recognition (WR) view, oral language is innate and easily comprehended; written language is a secondary representation of speech and access to meaning is via the lexicon by matching each written word to an oral word. The speed at which normal readers are able to read is explained as requiring this process of word recognition to become rapid, accurate and automatic.

In the MC view, proficient reading depends on both effectiveness and efficiency. Effectiveness is a matter of making sense. Since readers are constructing meaning based on what they know and believe, their interpretation can never be an exact match for the intentions of the writer, nor indeed for the interpretation of a third party like a teacher. Efficiency involves getting to meaning – or being effective – using minimal cues selectively, with the least amount of effort and time.

In the WR view, accuracy in recognizing (in some absolute sense) letters and words is essential to comprehension. In the MC view, accuracy is a by-product of proficient reading – all readers make miscues in the course of making sense of print. Proficient readers will make fewer miscues that disrupt meaning and will be likely to correct them when dealing with a comprehensible text, one to which they bring sufficient meaning.

READING AS CONSTRUCTION OF MEANING

The meaning construction view of reading is the one which has been most elaborated, most widely accepted by practitioners and is most consistent with continuing investigation of a wide range of contributory disciplines. With the qualification that there is a strongly advocated alternative word recognition view of reading, what follows is the elaboration of reading as meaning construction.

Strata or levels

Texts, according to Halliday (1985), have three strata or levels: signal, lexico-grammatical and semantic. In oral language, the signal level is phonology (the system of speech sounds) and, in written language, orthography (the system of spellings and punctuation). In alphabetically written language (see Burnaby's review in this volume), we also need to take into account phonics (the relationships between phonology and orthography). Phonics is not a system of letter-sound relationships but rather a set of relationships between the sound patterns of a reader and the spelling patterns of the language.

While the signal level can be derived directly from speech or writing, the other two levels must be inferred and constructed by the reader from cues in the text. The lexico-grammatical level encompasses the wording and syntactic patterns of the text. These features are interdependent: the form of words depends on the syntax and the syntax depends on the choice of words. In the semantic – or meaning – level, the reader focuses on constructing meaning from the published text. In doing so, cues from all three levels must be used simultaneously. When the process is going well, the reader has a sense of directly accessing meaning. When there are difficulties, the reader becomes more aware of the graphophonic and lexico-grammatical levels and the need to reprocess and gather more cues. None of this is automatic – the reader is making conscious choices – but, when reading is efficient, the choices are effective and meaning flows easily.

Cycles

There are four cycles during reading: the visual, the perceptual, the syntactic and the semantic. Reading begins with a visual cycle in which input is perceived by the brain. This is followed by the perceptual cycle, in which the brain uses schemas to assign value to the visual input. Perceptions, like meaning, are constructed. The perceptual cycle is followed by a syntactic cycle in which the reader uses cues to assign words to grammatical categories and, in the process, constructs a personal text parallel to the published text. In the semantic cycle the reader brings meaning to the text.

These cycles follow each other as the reading continues. Thus, as meaning is constructed, it is used by the reader to seek visual cues, to form perceptions, to assign word to grammatical categories and to construct further meaning.

Strategies

Readers are able to use strategies they have developed for making sense of print and for using the cues provided by the text. These psycholinguistic strategies are specialized forms of more generalized strategies which people use in making sense of their world.

Readers sample selectively from the print using their knowledge of the writing system. They do not process each feature of each letter of each word. Rather they use their experience to select the most useful information and infer the rest.

Prediction and inference are powerful strategies for using visual and perceptual information to get efficiently to meaning. We sample and select on the basis of predictions and inferences and we predict and infer on the basis of selected cues. Prediction involves using what is already known to anticipate what is coming in the text. Inference adds information in our meaning construction to what is explicit in the text. No text is ever complete in representing the author's meaning. All texts require readers to make inferences and supply implicit but unstated information. Again we predict on the basis of inferences and we make inferences on the basis of predictions. A whole genre of 'predictable books' for young people has grown out of our understanding that the more predictable a text is for a given reader, the easier it will be for the reader to make sense of it.

Reading is tentative. Readers, however proficient and confident, are always ready for the possibility that something may go wrong in their construction of meaning – some new cue or information may be inconsistent with what has been understood to that point. So readers develop strategies for confirming or disconfirming their constructions. This is a matter of self-monitoring, of using new information to check on the old. If there is confirmation, if things are as predicted, then the reader proceeds confidently but still tentatively. If not – if there is disconfirmation – then the reader employs correction strategies to reprocess, to gather more information and, if necessary, go back in the text so that the inconsistency can be resolved.

There are two more sets of strategies: initiation or what we do to begin reading, and termination or what we do when we decide, for a variety of reasons, to stop reading. Initiating reading is a deliberate strategy. We can look at print without treating it as a comprehensible text; only when we initiate reading do we begin to use the strategies we will need to make sense of it.

Termination happens when we decide we have finished reading a text, which is not necessarily at the end. We may decide to reread all or part of the text – for pleasure or to add to or reconfirm what we have understood. With a recipe for example, reading through to the end may only be preliminary to item by item reading as we cook. But we also stop reading for many other reasons. Terminating because we can't make sense of the text or we find its message distasteful, boring, or uninteresting are also common. In every case these decisions are deliberate, not automatic.

The Context of Reading

To understand reading fully, we need to put it into context. Reading, like all language, occurs in social situations. With oral language, we are dealing with speech acts. With literacy, we talk about literacy events, events in which readers, writers, or both, are using written language for some personal and/or social purpose.

Each literacy event can be considered an example of a particular genre. For instance, we can talk about a list genre and, more specifically, a shopping list genre. Or we can talk about a novel genre, a scientific report genre, or store front preacher genre and so forth. According to Halliday (1978), each speech act or literacy event has field, tenor and mode. The field relates to the content and the function of the text. The tenor is the set of relationships between the participants – newspaper reporter and reader, for example, or store clerk and customer. And the mode is the language form used – oral or written, list or paragraph, letter, short story, etc.

The context of the reading of any given text is social and cultural. Many writers (see Street's review in this volume) have questioned the traditional view of literacy as having an autonomous nature, quite apart from its use by particular groups within particular cultures. They also oppose the concomitant of this autonomous view that literacy makes possible a higher level of thought and therefore so-called oral cultures are more limited than literate ones. In fact, they question whether pre-literate societies exist at all. Much recent research deals instead with multiple social literacies, each rooted in a literacy practice of a given culture.

This view is critical of common school curricula and methodologies that treat reading as autonomous, teach it as a set of skills, and privilege a decontextualized literacy over social literacies which are often ignored in estimates of rates of literacy in communities and nations.

FUTURE DIRECTIONS IN RESEARCH AND PRACTICE

There is no doubt that at least two very different views of reading will continue for some time to come to drive research, theory and application to curriculum and methodology in schools. This situation would be beneficial if the adherents of each view tested their beliefs and conclusions against those of the other. The truth, of course, does not necessarily lie between these opposing views: a comfortable but unsustainable idea. There is, however, no rapprochement: adherents of both positions tend to ignore research that does not fit within their paradigm.

The ultimate test of any view of reading is perhaps how it is translated into practice by teachers and how it affects learners. There is certainly a sharp difference between the curriculum and practice growing out of the word recognition and meaning construction views. The former moves teachers toward focus on skills for recognizing words; the ability to comprehend texts is viewed as dependent on rapid automatic and accurate word recognition. Recently there has been a strong focus in such instruction on phonemic awareness – the ability to identify the speech sounds in a word or nonsense syllable and relate them to letters (Eastin, 1996).

The meaning construction view leads to earlier experiences with holistic reading and writing in authentic literacy events (see Owocki & Goodman's review, this volume). Children are encouraged to invent spellings as they write in journals, recording their messages to the world and comments on it. They are read to from a range of real children's literature, share the reading of big books, and learn to read and write by using reading and writing to learn. The curriculum shifts from focus on skills and words to making sense in and through written language.

Still more is being learned every year about the reading process, about development of literacy and about how to help learners become literate. School practice based on opposing paradigms yields new insights which should be useful to researchers and theoreticians. In the best of all worlds, there should eventually be convergence toward a consensus. But with the press and politicians imposing other agendas, this is not always easy.

University of Arizona, USA

REFERENCES

Adams, M.: 1990, *Beginning to Read*, MIT Press, Cambridge.

Bloome, D.: 1989, *Classrooms and Literacy*, Ablex, Norwood, NJ.

Eastin, D.: 1996, *Program Advisory*, California Department of Education, Sacramento, CA.

Ferreiro, E. & Teberosky. 1982, *Literacy Before Schooling*, translated by Karen Goodman, Heinemann, Portsmouth, NH.

Goodman, K.: 1967, 'Reading: A Psycholinguistic Guessing Game', *Journal of the Reading Specialist* 6(4), 126–135.

Goodman, K.: 1994, *Phonics Phacts*, Heinemann, Portsmouth, NH.

Goodman, K.: 1996, *On Reading*, Scholastic Canada, Toronto.

Goodman, Y. (Ed.): 1991, *How Children Construct Literacy*, International Reading Association, Newark, De.

Goodman, Y. & Watson D.: 1987, *Reading Miscue Inventory: Alternative Procedures*, Richard C. Owen, Katonah, NY.

Halliday, M.A.K.: 1978, *Language as Social Semiotic*, Edward Arnold, London.

Halliday, M.A.K.: 1985, *An Introduction to Functional Grammar*, Edward Arnold, London.

Huey, Edmund: 1908 (reprinted 1968), *The Psychology and Pedagogy of Reading*, MIT Press, Cambridge, MA.

Rosenblatt, L.: 1978, *The Reader, The Text, The Poem*, Southern Illinois University, Carbondale.

Ruddell, R., Ruddell, M. R., & Singer, H. (eds.): 1994, *Theoretical Models and Processes of Reading*, 4th Edition, International Reading Association: Newark, De.

Smith, F. (1982). *Understanding Reading*, third Edition, Holt, Rinehart and Winston, New York.

Spiro, R. J., Bruce, B. C., & Brewer, W. F.: 1980, *Theoretical Issues in Reading Comprehension*, Erlbaum Associates, Hillsdale, NJ.

Street, B.: 1995, *Social Literacies*, Longman, London.

G. BRIAN THOMPSON

THE TEACHING OF READING

Teaching has two principal aspects: the motivational and informational. The motivational aspect is concerned, for example, with promoting the learner's security and commitment to learning. The informational aspect is concerned with fostering the learner's knowledge and skill. This review of the teaching of reading considers the second aspect and offers historical and international perspectives on selected current research. The emphasis is on teaching normal progress children during the initial years of primary schooling. The influences of the family and society are considered elsewhere in this volume, as also are children's reading difficulties.

EARLY DEVELOPMENTS

The Alphabetic Method was the standard method of teaching reading for alphabetic orthographies (see Burnaby, this volume) for at least 3,000 years until the nineteenth century. In this method, the names of the individual letters of the alphabet were first taught to the child, then two-letter syllables such as *ab, eb, ib, ob, ub; ba, be, bi, bo, bu; ac,* ... These were spelt orally by naming the component letters and then pronouncing the syllable. The child later graduated to a similar procedure for short words, followed by brief texts which were selected for their significance to the educational aims of the times, for example, the Lord's prayer or the Creed. If children did not know a word, they spelt it orally before attempting to pronounce it (Davies, 1973).

By the second half of the nineteenth century the Alphabetic Method was losing its dominance (Smith, 1965). In the last decade of that century, in New Zealand, a country remote from the main centres of literate population, a book on teaching method was published (Farnie, 1895) which set out three alternatives to the Alphabetic Method. The first was a Phonic Method in which children were taught the most common sound for each letter, e.g. /buh/ for *b*. When they did not know a print word they were taught to pronounce the sound for each letter sequentially and then, by approximation, to blend these sounds into a recognisable word. The second alternative was the Look and Say Method. The children were taught to look at the word as a whole and respond to it without making any response to the individual letters. The third alternative, which Farnie recommended to teachers, was a combination of the 'best points' of the three Methods.

V. Edwards and D. Corson (eds), Encyclopedia of Language and Education,
Volume 2: Literacy, 9–17.
© *1997 Kluwer Academic Publishers. Printed in the Netherlands.*

In this alternative the alphabet was taught first, then the Look and Say Method, followed by teaching of the sounds of letters (Phonic Method) when this was considered necessary (Farnie, 1895).

Since the nineteenth century, there have been shifts to and fro between the more analytic Phonic Methods and the more global Look and Say. A Phonic Method had been advocated in the sixteenth century by Ickelsamer as more natural than the Alphabetic method for learning to read German, and by Hart for reading English. However, Phonic Methods were not widely adopted until the nineteenth century. This was also the case with Look and Say which had been advocated in Germany by Lubinus early in the seventeenth century and later carried out by Comenius (Davies, 1973; Hladczuk & Eller, 1992, Chapter 24).

Late in the nineteenth century, the Sentence Method, which was more global than Look and Say was advocated in the United States. The rationale of this method was that language is recognised in whole units that express thought. Hence the teaching of reading commenced with the meaningful reading of these whole units that are sentences rather than letters or words (Smith, 1965).

MAJOR CONTRIBUTIONS AND WORK IN PROGRESS

The integrity of literacy activities

From the turn of the century until the 1920s, the Story Method was a quite popular more global successor to the Sentence Method in the United States. The child commenced reading instruction by listening to complete stories, often from authentic literature, and did not attempt to read the print until familiar with the oral form (Smith, 1965). Subsequently, in the 1960s and 1970s the Language Experience Approach to teaching reading had some influence in several English-speaking countries. In this approach, reading was considered an extension of the language skills which a child had already acquired and the emphasis in teaching was on the purpose of reading as meaningful communication.

The current Whole Language Approach has evolved, in part, from Language Experience. Whole Language, however, has a stronger emphasis on wholeness and integrity of the literacy activities in which children engage, as well as on meaningful communication (see also reviews by Kenneth Goodman, and Gretchen Owocki and Yetta Goodman, this volume). Authentic literature for learners, including beginner readers, is advocated (Goodman, 1989). In fact, the emphasis on literature is such that 'Whole Literature' would seem a better label for the approach. Versions of the approach are currently influential in the United Kingdom, the United States,

Canada, and New Zealand (Hladczuk & Eller, 1992). In Russia an experimental reading programme has been developed which aims to educate readers in literature as art (Hladczuk & Eller, 1992, Chapter 20). From the United States perspective, Harris (1993) has reviewed issues that arise within the literature-based approaches to reading instruction.

Stahl and Miller (1989) have analysed numerous United States studies that compare the reading achievement outcomes of Language Experience and Whole Language programmes with 'basal reader' programmes which ostensibly use less authentic, graded, texts and more analytic teaching methods, such as lessons on phonics or on isolated words. An interesting finding was that the more rigorously conducted studies showed no trend favouring either type of teaching programme. However, these outcome comparisons did not include such matters as the readers' evaluations of the texts and response to literature as an art form.

A major issue here is whether in the years of primary schooling children are able to apply criteria to a reading experience in order to form an evaluation that justifies their personal reaction to a literary work. Do they have the ability to objectify their reading experience, and the ability to take multiple perspectives on their experience? Pinsent has reviewed the research literature on children's thinking about their reading experience, from the perspectives of the text, the author, and other readers. The evidence indicates that from 10 years of age children can begin engaging in the task of literary evaluation. From this age they would benefit from teaching which explicitly supports the development of their critical response to literature as an art form.

Word identification

In the twentieth century, there has been continuing debate about the relative merits of the analytic and global methods for teaching children to identify print words (see also the review by Kenneth Goodman, this volume). This has been an issue for alphabetic orthographies as diverse as the highly regular Serbo-Croatian and Hangul (of South Korea), the fairly regular German (Hladczuk & Eller, 1992) and Russian orthographies (Downing, 1988, Chapter 3), and English orthography which has some highly complex letter-phoneme relationships. It has also been an issue in teaching the reading of Chinese; whether to use an analytic method in which characters are grouped by similar visual structures and/or pronunciations, or a more global method in which characters are taught only in a meaningful language context such as a story text (Hladczuk & Eller, 1992, Chapter 4).

Alternative phonic methods have been introduced to provide ways for children to learn how to identify unfamiliar print words. By the 1920s in the United States letter-sound correspondences were sometimes taught by demonstrating common letter-sound components of words. For example, the words *sun, saw, sat* were presented in print and each pronounced by the teacher with prolongation of the initial sound that is common to the words. Spelling patterns larger than single phonemes were also used, the teacher presenting phonograms such as *-at* and showing how, by adding other letters, words such as *sat, bat, fat,* are produced. This type of Analytical Phonics was examined in studies by Gates (1928).

The effects on rate of learning of teaching programmes which include an emphasis on Phonics Methods continue to be compared with programmes such as Whole Language that have little or no such emphasis (e.g. Foorman, Francis, Novy & Liberman, 1991). Unfortunately such studies fail to take account of a complete set of potentially confounding variables, such as different vocabularies of print words in the programmes and their rate of introduction, teacher effects, teaching time, and learner levels on entry to instruction.

Recently, however, some studies have moved from consideration of outcome levels of achievement to examine whether the processes, or ways of learning, vary in the different teaching approaches when learners have reached the same level of reading achievement (Johnston, Thompson, Fletcher-Flinn & Holligan, 1995; Thompson, Tunmer & Nicholson, 1993, Chapter 3). For instance, Connelly, Johnston & Thompson found that when 5- and 6-year-old children taught with a mix of the Phonic Method and reading of story texts were compared with children in a Whole Language programme, the former were superior in reading totally unfamiliar items (regular pseudowords, e.g. *blum*) but poorer at reading ordinary words with irregular letter-sound correspondences (e.g. *sword*). The children taught phonics showed a small advantage in reading comprehension, probably due to their greater attention to word detail, as indicated by their much slower reading rate.

For identification of words, proponents of the Whole Language Approach usually advocate that the teacher encourage the child to give priority to predictions from the meaning provided by the context of the reading passage. Contrary to this, there is much research evidence showing that the context is little used by readers for identification of familiar words (Perfetti, 1995). For attempting unfamiliar words, context may provide some useful information, particularly for the beginning reader (Nicholson, 1991), but usually only in combination with the reader's use of information from letter-to-sound correspondences. There is evidence that this is the case in New Zealand for children taught by the Whole Language Approach (Tunmer & Chapman, 1997). Recommendations about the teaching of reading can now benefit from the accumulating evidence (Ehri, 1994) about the processes by which children learn to identify words as they develop reading skill.

The alphabetic principle

For beginning reading, Ickelsamer in Germany in the sixteenth century urged teachers to take account of how humans first learnt to read and to teach the child how spoken words can be mentally divided into constituent phonemes before teaching the letters (Davies, 1973). In the middle of last century Ushinsky in Russia advocated the Historic Method which was based on how the alphabetic writing system was supposedly invented (Downing, 1988, Chapters 3, 6, 22; see also the review by Burnaby, this volume). As this invention depended on discovery of the set of abstract sound segments which comprise the spoken words of a language, learning about this aspect of spoken words is the first step in teaching the child to read. For example, the child is taught to identify phonemes by selecting several spoken words which contain a particular initial sound, e.g. /k/; and to identify the first phoneme and the last phoneme of a presented spoken word. This Historic Method was not satisfactorily put into practice, although somewhat similar new methods of beginning reading instruction studied by Elkonin were developed in Russia in the 1960s and 1970s (Downing, 1973, Chapter 24; Downing, 1988, Chapter 22).

Knowledge of the alphabetic principle, that letters of words systematically map onto sounds in words, is more than knowledge of sound labels for letters. Children may learn, for example, that /buh/ is an appropriate sound label for the letter b. However, if they cannot identify the phoneme common in spoken words, e.g. /job/ and /crab/, they have not acquired the alphabetic principle. If for normal progress, implicit knowledge of this principle is necessary early in learning to read, then the teacher would need to ensure that knowledge of phoneme identities is acquired early in teaching. Does such knowledge have to await implicit spontaneous induction by the child or can it be fostered by explicit teaching? (See Tunmer, this volume).

Byrne & Fielding-Barnsley (1995) in Australia show that knowledge of phoneme identities can be taught to 4-year-olds over 12 weeks and prior to commencement of their school reading instruction. However, follow-up testing after two and three years of schooling, with some teaching of letter-sound correspondences, showed that these children then performed no better than a control group in reading individual words (although they did better on regularly spelt nonsense words). In contrast, Ball & Blachman (1991) show that seven weeks of teaching of phoneme identity, along with sound labels for letters, resulted in an advantage for 5-year-olds in their reading of simple regularly spelt words (constructed from the taught letter-sound labels). The children in this study were in a United States kindergarten programme which did not include systematic reading instruction. It is perhaps surprising that this reading advantage was achieved without also teaching the child how to apply knowledge of the alphabetic principle when attempting unfamiliar words. Teaching such strategies of application may well have facilitated a greater advantage. Tunmer & Chapman describe a Metacognitive Approach which considers the child's strategic knowledge for identification of unfamiliar words (Thompson & Nicholson, in press, Chapter 6).

Reading comprehension

Much of the child's skill which is often classified as reading comprehension is more properly considered language comprehension, which is not specific to reading (Thompson, Tunmer & Nicholson, 1993, Chapter 1). The principal issue here, however, is whether the development of the skill of understanding printed texts can benefit from explicit teaching. This has been an issue in several countries. For example in Japan some approaches to teaching reading comprehension have been more explicit and analytical, and others more global (Downing, 1973, Chapter 21). In the United States since the 1980s there has been much interest in a model of teaching reading comprehension in which the child is taught several strategies and when and why each should be used (Dole, Duffy, Roehler & Pearson, 1991; Pearson & Fielding, 1991). A number of researchers in the United States have attempted to determine whether such strategies can in fact be taught and whether the learner can apply them successfully to previously unseen texts in the same content area. There are, however, only a few research studies which come close to rigorous standards of methodology (Pressley et al., 1989). Raphael & Wonnacott (1985) found that 9-year-old students could be taught to recognize that the information for comprehension questions may be either explicit in the text, that it may be inferred by relating information from different locations in the text, or that it may have to be supplied from the reader's background knowledge. Dewitz, Carr & Patberg (1987) found that 10-year-old students could be taught to integrate their knowledge with the text information and (to a lesser extent) consider the structural organization of the text information.

There are objections to this approach to teaching reading comprehension. One is that teaching the strategies is unnecessary if students are motivated to read and are not attempting texts which exceed their level of understanding (Carver, 1987). Another objection is that the explanations about when and how to use the strategies will become more demanding for the reader than the comprehension activity itself (Pearson & Fielding, 1991). Yet another objection is that strategy instruction in the classroom has been too unidirectional, from teacher to students, and has not provided for teacher responsiveness to students or transactional teaching. Pressley et al. (1992) have reported on teaching which is intended to confront this particular objection and, rather than be limited to a concern with the extraction of ideas, also takes account of the readers' varied interpretations and emotional and aesthetic responses to the text.

FUTURE DIRECTIONS

There is now emerging a realization that the beginning reader can acquire and use the alphabetic principle in several different ways. The child may use sounds for letters as simple taught instances of the principle in order to 'sound out' unfamiliar print words. In another way, the beginning reader can acquire untaught instances of the alphabetic principle by self-teaching, or induction, of knowledge of patterns of letter-sound relations inherent in their accumulating reading vocabulary (e.g. the print words *sit, cat, not* have a common final letter and sound; *ball, fall, wall* have common letters and sounds). Such self-taught knowledge of letter-sound patterns can be used in the child's attempts to identify unfamiliar words (Thompson, Cottrell & Fletcher-Flinn, 1996; Thompson & Nicholson, in press, Chapter 4). There is yet a third way for using the alphabetic principle. The child may use an analogy word, e.g. *jump*, as a prompt in attempting to identify an unfamiliar word, e.g. *hump*. There has been recent research on the child's use of analogy prompts, which has led to the advocacy of teaching by analogies for beginning readers. Unfortunately, advocates have ignored longstanding evidence that teaching by analogies is less effective for initial learning than teaching by sounds of letters (Sullivan, Okada & Niedermeyer, 1971). To make effective spontaneous use of analogies for word identification requires the child to find an analogue word from an existing reading vocabulary. Unless this reading vocabulary is extensive enough, effective use of analogy will be very limited.

Phonics teaching provides the child with a limited number of taught instances of the alphabetic principle. It is not yet clear how much of such teaching is advantageous for the child's self-teaching of untaught instances of the principle. In a complex orthography such as English, explicit attention to each of the very large number of patterns of letter-sound relations would be overwhelming for both teacher and child. Some nonconscious self-teaching of knowledge of these patterns takes place. Future theory and research should provide the teacher with ways of monitoring when to provide explicit analytic teaching and when not, and how to determine how much is enough for particular students. Moreover, it should show how to effectively teach the child to apply the results of any such analytic teaching in literacy activities.

Victoria University of Wellington, New Zealand

REFERENCES

Ball, E.W. & Blachman, B.A.: 1991, 'Does Phoneme Awareness Training in Kindergarten Make a Difference in Early Word Recognition and Developmental Spelling?', *Reading Research Quarterly* 26, 49–66.

Byrne, B. & Fielding-Barnsley, R.: 1995, 'Evaluation of a Program to Teach Phonemic Awareness to Young Children: A 2- and 3-Year Follow-up and a New Preschool Trial', *Journal of Educational Psychology* 87, 488–503.

Carver, R.P.: 1987, 'Should Reading Comprehension Skills be Taught?', in J.E. Readance & R.S. Baldwin (eds.), *Research in Literacy: Merging Perspectives. Thirty-sixth Yearbook of The National Reading Conference*, National Reading Conference, Rochester NY, 1987, 115–126.

Davies, W.J.F.: 1973, *Teaching Reading in Early England*, Pitman, London UK.

Dewitz, P., Carr, E.M. & Patberg, J.P.: 1987, 'Effects of Inference Training on Comprehension and Comprehension Monitoring', *Reading Research Quarterly* 22, 99–121.

Dole, J.A., Duffy, G.G., Roehler, L.R. & Pearson, P.D.: 1991, 'Moving From the Old to the New: Research on Reading Comprehension Instruction', *Review of Educational Research* 61, 239–264.

Downing, J. (ed.): 1973, *Comparative Reading: Cross-National Studies of Behavior and Processes in Reading and Writing*, Macmillan, New York.

Downing, J.A. (ed.): 1988, *Cognitive Psychology and Reading in the U.S.S.R.*, North-Holland, Amsterdam. (Translation of Russian writings from the 1930s to 1980s.)

Ehri, L.C.: 1994, 'Development of the ability to Read Words: Update', in R.B. Ruddell, M.R. Ruddell & H. Singer (eds.), *Theoretical Models and Processes of Reading* (fourth edition), International Reading Association, Newark De, 1994, 323–358.

Farnie, T.C.: 1895, *Manual of School Method*, Whitcombe & Tombs, Christchurch New Zealand.

Foorman, B.R., Francis, D.J., Novy, D.M. & Liberman, D.: 1991, 'How Letter-Sound Instruction Mediates Progress in First-Grade Reading and Spelling', *Journal of Educational Psychology* 83, 456–469.

Gates, A.I.: 1928, *New Methods in Primary Reading*, Bureau of Publications, Teachers College, Columbia University, New York.

Goodman, Y.M.: 1989, 'Roots of the Whole Language Movement', *Elementary School Journal* 90, 113–127.

Harris, V.J.: 1993, 'Literature-Based Approaches to Reading Instruction', in L. Darling-Hammond (ed.), *Review of Research in Education*, Vol. 19, American Educational Research Association, Washington DC, 1995, 269–297.

Hladczuk, J. & Eller, W. (eds.): 1992, *International Handbook of Reading Education*, Greenwood Press, Westport Ct.

Johnston, R.S., Thompson, G.B., Fletcher-Flinn, C.F. & Holligan, C.: 1995, 'The functions of Phonology in the Acquisition of Reading: Lexical and Sentence Processing', *Memory & Cognition* 23, 749–766.

Nicholson, T.: 1991, 'Do Children Read Words Better in Context or in Lists? A classic Study Revisited', *Journal of Educational Psychology* 83, 444–450.

Pearson, P.D. & Fielding, L.: 1991, 'Comprehension Instruction', in R. Barr, M.L. Kamil, P.B. Mosenthal & P.D. Pearson (eds.), *Handbook of Reading Research Vol. 2*, Longman, White Plains NY, 1991, 815–860.

Perfetti, C.A.: 1995, 'Cognitive Research Can Inform Reading Education', *Journal of Research in Reading* 18, 106–115.

Pressley, M., Lysynchuk, L.M., d'Ailly, H., Smith, M. & Cake, H.: 1989, 'A Methodological Analysis of Experimental Studies of Comprehension Strategy Instruction', *Reading Research Quarterly* 24, 458–470.

Pressley, M., El-Dinary, P.B., Gaskins, I., Schuder, T., Bergman J.L., Almasi, J. & Brown,

R.: 1992, 'Beyond Direct Explanation: Transactional Instruction of Reading Comprehension Strategies', *Elementary School Journal* 92, 513–555.

Raphael, T.E. & Wonnacott, C.A.: 1985, 'Heightening Fourth-Grade Students' Sensitivity to Sources of Information for Answering Comprehension Questions', *Reading Research Quarterly* 20, 282–296.

Smith, N.B.: 1965, *American Reading Instruction*, International Reading Association, Newark De.

Stahl, S.A. & Miller, P.D.: 1989, 'Whole Language and Language Experience Approaches for Beginning Reading: A Quantitative Research Synthesis', *Review of Educational Research* 59, 87–116.

Sullivan, H.J., Okada, M. & Niedermeyer, F.C.: 1971, 'Learning and transfer under two methods of word-attack instruction', *American Educational Research Journal* 8, 227–239.

Thompson, G.B., Cottrell, D.S. & Fletcher-Flinn, C.M.: 1996, 'Sublexical Orthographic-Phonological Relations Early in the Acquisition of Reading: The Knowledge Sources Account', *Journal of Experimental Child Psychology* 62, 190–222.

Thompson, G.B., Tunmer, W.E. & Nicholson, T. (eds.): 1993, *Reading Acquisition Processes*, Multilingual Matters, Clevedon UK.

Tunmer, W.E. & Chapman, J.W.: in press, 'Language Prediction Skill, Phonological Recoding Ability, and Beginning Reading', in C. Hulme & R.M. Joshi (eds.), *Reading and Spelling: Development and Disorder*, Lawrence Erlbaum Associates, Hove UK.

READING SKILLS: EMERGENT LITERACY

Two of the continuingly intriguing aspects of literacy are how humans read and write seemingly so effortlessly and how they learn to do it in the first place. Huey (1908: 6) commented that 'to completely analyse what we do when we read would almost be the acme of a psychologist's achievements, for it would be to know very many of the most intricate workings of the human mind, as well as unravel the tangled story of the most remarkable specific performance that civilisation has learned in all its history.' Theorists and practitioners from many disciplines put forward their views and contribute to the debate concerning what skills and abilities involved in reading and writing are and how they are initially achieved. Everyone in a literate culture has an opinion. Each point of view will be coloured by a particular world view and research and theorising paradigms associated with their discipline of study and understanding and experience (see the review by Goodman, this volume).

This constant rehearsing and reviewing of literacy and learning to read and write has generated a diversity and perplexity of information which is difficult to analyse and synthesise. Professionals with responsibility for young children learning to read are now confused and intimidated by the volume of conflicting evidence and the associated political capital which is being generated at their expense: 'One third of 14 year olds have no literacy skills'; 'Lazy teachers waste children's time'; 'Standards are falling'; 'Return to basics before it is too late': these media headlines, and there are many more from across the world, give a sense of a lost purpose to the early years of schooling where literacy is typically taught (see also reviews by Clay, Street, Luke and Béchennec & Sprenger-Charolles, this volume). Parents and communities seek clarification while those responsible for preschool education and care skirt round the issue of children's developing literacy skills.

There are clear signs that confidence has been lost in the wealth of knowledge built up over time of how children learn about literacy and how to read and write. Much research evidence has been misinterpreted, misrepresented, left unreported and misunderstood. This has created a vacuum in both theory and practice which has allowed parents and others to develop expectations of children and their teachers which are not always appropriate.

V. Edwards and D. Corson (eds), Encyclopedia of Language and Education,
Volume 2: Literacy, 19–26.
© *1997 Kluwer Academic Publishers. Printed in the Netherlands.*

Some facts, however, are clearly understood:
- Children enter school for the first time at different ages across the different countries of the world.
- Children of the same age will exhibit different levels of development.
- Children's development across different domains will not be equivalent, eg. social and emotional development may be far in advance of intellectual and physical development.
- This developmental profile will vary over time.
- Children will differ in their experience of the world in general and literacy in particular as a result of their home, community and cultural environments.
- Expectations of children will vary across cultures, communities, homes and schools.
- Teachers' knowledge, beliefs and methods of teaching vary across classrooms.

All of these issues interweave with children's developing literacy skills, although they are rarely taken into account when discussions and debate occur outside the discourse of appropriate professional groupings. However, the distinctions listed above are critical to any argument concerning the teaching of reading, reading materials, books for children to read and books for teachers to use with children who are learning to read.

Much current debate focuses on the early stages of literacy development and the role of the adult (parent, prior-to-school provider and teacher) in respecting and promoting children's interest in the literate world around them (see also, Auerbach, this volume). How people react to children in these first stages will depend largely on what they believe about literacy development, and relevant information has only recently become more readily available.

EARLY DEVELOPMENTS

School failure during the 1920s was identified in 6–7 year old pupils (Grade 1) in American schools and in three studies this was seen to be related to poor reading achievement (summarized by Gray, 1956). As the start of schooling in Grade 1 was associated with the formal teaching of reading, reading problems came to be linked with premature instruction. With this link established in researchers' minds, they then postulated the notion of reading readiness and suggested that instruction be postponed until readiness was established.

Such views concerning readiness rested comfortably with the prevailing orthodoxy of that time which was characterised by developmental psychologists. Writers such as Gesell (1925) propounded a concept of human development which was predetermined in nature and which unfolded in stages. Accordingly, many professionals working with children learning to read associated the start of teaching children to read with a specific stage of development. If young children experienced difficulty with learning to read, then it was presumed that they had not reached the appropriate level of maturity. Similarly it was assumed that such maturity would be achieved with the passage of time.

During this time, the concept of mental age was associated with readiness and tests were devised to assess this aspect of development. The most prominent study (Morphett & Washburne, 1931) indicated a mental age of 6.5 to be a pre-requisite for beginning reading. This period prompted the development of reading readiness tests which were designed to assess a number of skills and abilities. They included assessment of visual and auditory discrimination, which were considered obvious skills associated with early reading. If children were deemed not ready for reading, they were given more time to mature.

There was a concurrent belief held by others (e.g. Hirsch, 1928) that the environment played a role in developing readiness. Because of these views, individual children's readiness tests were studied and areas of failure identified. Programs were then designed to make up for what were considered deficits in children's readiness profiles. It was believed that readiness would be hastened in this way.

What is remarkable is that these readiness tests and their associated programs involved no print items. Children looked at pictures of objects and identified similarities and differences and listened to real world sounds and noises, matching them with appropriate pictures. Shapes were copied and people drawn, but in none of these experiences were children invited to talk about or demonstrate their knowledge of print.

During the 1930s, Gates and his associates (Gates & Bond, 1936) concluded that the best time to begin the teaching of reading was not dependent on the child, but was in large measure determined by the nature of the reading program itself. Therefore, even before World War 2, significance was being credited to the kind and quality of program which young children received. It was beginning to be recognised that changes in teaching could influence a child's readiness, perhaps to a greater extent than mental age and maturation.

MAJOR CONTRIBUTIONS

During the 1960s new concepts of readiness emerged (Hunt 1961). These researchers emphasised the importance of early stimulation for learning and pointed up the significance of Bruner's statement 'any subject can be taught effectively in some intellectually honest form to any child at any stage of development' (Bruner, 1960). These views, in conjunction with those of Vygotsky (1962), which were just becoming known through translation, heralded the way forward to what we now understand as the social construction of knowledge. Vygotsky (1978: 87) provided the impetus for this through his statement: 'what a child can do with assistance today she will be able to do by herself tomorrow'.

These views extended the notion of the child as lone scientist hypothesising about the world and further exploring on their own. This position, in turn, was based on the interpretation of Piaget (1955): firstly that children were learning all the time and could be taught at any age; and secondly that they learned skills particularly by engaging in appropriate activities with more knowledgeable, significant others. This position was especially important for people working with children who experienced any difficulties in learning and groups of professionals emerged at this time who were dedicated to early intervention with least able children.

These developments in thinking had a profound impact during the 1970s. Researchers (Goodman, 1967; Clay, 1969, 1975) and others began to take notice of the activities of young children. They observed children learning, they observed them learning literacy. They reported the sophistication of very young children, how these learners drew on all kinds of information about print in their environment and meshed these experiences with what they already knew about language and ways of making sense of their world.

During the 1980s a great deal of interest was shown in how very young children construct literacy from their experience of literacy around them and others using literacy for their own purposes. Studies during this time (Bissex, 1980; Taylor, 1983) contributed further to this view of literacy as social construction. Ferreiro and Teborosky (1983: 12) gave their interpretation:

> The children we know are learners who actively try to understand
> the world around them, to answer questions the world poses.
> ... It is absurd to imagine that ... children growing up in an
> urban environment that displays print everywhere (on toys, on
> billboards and road signs, on their clothes, on TV) do not develop
> any ideas about this cultural object until they find themselves
> sitting in front of a teacher.

During the 1980s and 1990s the study of literacy has taken on a much broader perspective (Barton, 1994). Emerging literacy and its further development in young children is considered more inclusive of children's experiences of the world and their ability to make meaning from their environment (Hall, 1987). As Cairney (1995: 2) has emphasised, the meanings we build as we read and write are our experiences, our knowledge about the world, and also our reasons for developing them in the beginning:

> Types of discourse and the way we read and write them are the
> social constructs of specific groups. Individuals are enculturated
> into these practices and these meanings.

The development of literacy is a profoundly social process. McLane and MacNamee (1990) show how it is embedded in social relationships, especially in children's relationships with people in their immediate family, grandparents, friends, care givers and teachers. These are the more knowledgeable, significant others who act as models, provide the materials, offer support, establish expectations, instruct, encourage and reward effort. Through this perspective, literacy is seen to develop through children's relationships with their immediate care givers; it then broadens and is expressed and elaborated through the wider community – in the neighbourhood, the local community and other pre-school settings.

PROBLEMS AND DIFFICULTIES

Although young children appear to gain control over literacy in similar ways, there are differences in their rates of development because there are differences in the way that literacy is organised in different cultures and communities, and because literacy has different values and functions in peoples' daily lives. Children, therefore, experience different levels of purpose for their own literacy development. For example, some children have easy access to reading and writing materials while others do not; some children observe family members reading and writing regularly and others only occasionally; some children may experience support and interaction within the context of purposeful literacy experiences and others may not.

These variations in literacy experience have an impact on literacy development and will be profound when children start formal schooling which is typically precipitated by a single age of entry. Studies by Stanovich (1986) and others show that children who start school with less knowledge about literacy than others can soon begin to experience a sense of failure, especially as they are presented with increasingly difficult texts. Consequently they tend to read less and less and have less exposure to literacy experiences than other children who make accelerated progress. Children entering school at a single age of entry will span many months of birth dates. This means that the youngest children starting school will always vary greatly for reasons of maturity, experience and developmental profile.

The pioneer work of Edmund Huey (1908) at the turn of the century identified the challenge as one of understanding how the reader constructs meaning. He conducted experiments and gathered evidence demonstrating that even with an alphabetic writing system such as English, a mechanistic building block theory of reading was not merely inadequate, it was inaccurate. He determined, for example, that four letter and even eight letter words can be identified almost as rapidly as individual letters, thus suggesting that word identification does not ordinarily proceed from the identification of individual letters. Indeed, recent psycholinguistic research (Corson, 1995) suggests that that letter identification normally proceeds from the identification of words in fluent reading.

Unfortunately, as the century turns again we are still debating issues concerning holistic approaches and those which are atomistic and reductionist (see also reviews by Kenneth Goodman and Brian Thompson, this volume). To imply to teachers that literacy learning moves from parts to whole at the level of letters, or words or word parts is misleading. The picture is far more complex. Children do not learn what they do not understand and they do not learn the conventions of print without having them pointed out. For some researchers this provides a problem in their advice to practitioners; for others it provides a starting point for creative and innovative observations, experiments and support for professionals.

Literacy is a multi-faceted skill, and children learn to read and write at all levels at once. They do not learn one thing first and then another in any additive sense. Further work (Clay, 1991; Elster, 1994) illustrates that children learn to orchestrate information from a wide range of sources as literacy emerges. These sources will be related to spoken and written language and the ways in which these linguistic structures conventionally encode meanings. Children learn about print by interacting with print and not by practising pencil control, nor by talking about the pictures in a storybook, although these activities may well be part of more focused literacy events.

Both in Britain (Hannon & James, 1990) and in Australia (Raban & Ure, 1996), teachers of young children in pre-school settings are claiming that literacy is not part of their curriculum and that, where appropriate, they will engage children in pre-reading and pre-writing activities similar to those dictated by readiness tests from over sixty years ago. This means that children will have even fewer experiences of literacy as these activities include, for instance, matching and comparing objects other than print. What children need to know is the *b* and *B* are the same while *oo* in *book* and *choose* are not, and they acquire this information by interacting with print in meaningful contexts.

Parents express more interest in their children's literacy because they experience their children's reactions to living in a literate environment on a daily basis. They provide for and engage children in literate experiences in the ordinary weave of everyday and it is through experience of this kind that literacy emerges. There is an urgent need to incorporate the naturalness of written language into pre-school settings.

FUTURE DEVELOPMENTS

Longitudinal studies are beginning to yield more helpful directions in our understanding of young children's developing literacy. For instance, there is clear evidence that 7 year old children make more rapid progress with their reading if they are taught phonological skills which are integrated with their reading rather than teaching reading alone or phonology alone (Hatcher, Hulme et al., 1994).

Further work (Geekie & Raban, 1993; Geekie & Raban, 1994) illustrates the way in which one kindergaten teacher in New South Wales, Australia was a successful model, demonstrator, facilitator, provider and interactionist while supporting five year old children towards literacy achievements. This teacher structured her classroom environment so that print was an integral part of the room, not by merely labelling objects and furniture, but by marking them with phrases and sentences which were co-constructed with the children. She used patterns of predictable moments which allowed the children to follow her repeated models for incorporating print into various activities. This teacher provided predictable yet flexible interactional structures which made it easier for these children to learn. Reading and writing were not mysteries for these children.

More recent research (Reynolds, 1997) shows clearly the changes which can be made in one pre-school program to promote three to four year old children's literacy development. While maintaining her philosophy of child-centredness and a curriculum focus on children's interests, Reynolds has successfully supported and guided children towards reading and writing for themselves. She has fostered and responded to children's curiosity about written language and has used it as naturally as speech alongside all the activities which she and the children engage in. They leave each other messages, they look things up in books, they join in literacy events of a natural and wide variety.

These young children do not experience adult pressure, they do not stop exploring their lives through play, rather they use spoken and written language in their explorations and also explore spoken and written language through invention and through trial and error of their own imagination. None of this literacy learning would be possible without the constant provision of books, writing materials of all kinds and written language in all its forms. Beyond this, the role of the teacher as guide, supporter and conversational partner is critical. How to translate this into practice at the level of young children's environments and the training of teachers and other professionals is the next major question to be addressed.

The University of Melbourne, Australia

REFERENCES

Barton, D.: 1994, *Literacy: An Introduction to the Ecology of Written Language*, Blackwell, Oxford.

Bissex, G.: 1980, *Gnys at Wrk: A Child Learns to Write and Read*, Harvard University Press, Cambridge, Mass.

Bruner, J.S.: 1960, *The Process of Education*. Harvard University Press, Cambridge, Mass.

Cairney, T.H.: 1995, *Pathways to Literacy*. Cassell, London.

Clay, M.M.: 1969, 'Reading errors and self-correction behaviour', *British Journal of Education* 30, 47–56.

Clay, M.M.: 1975, *What Did I Write?* Heinemann, London.

Clay, M.M.: 1991, *Becoming Literate: The construction of inner control*, Heinemann, Auckland.

Corson, D.: 1995, *Using English Words*, Kluwer, Dordrecht.

Elster, C.: 1994, 'I Guess They do Listen: Young Children's Emergent Reading After Adult Read Alouds,' *Young children* March, 27–31.

Ferreiro, E. & Teborosky, A.: 1983, *Literacy Before Schooling*, Heinemann, London.

Gates, A. I. & Bond, G.: 1936, 'Reading readiness: A study of factors determining success and failure in beginning reading', *Teachers College Record* 37 (May), 679–685.

Geekie, P. & Raban, B.: 1993, *Learning to Read and Write Through Classroom Talk*, Trentham Books, Stoke-on-Trent.

Geekie, P. & Raban, B.: 1994, 'Language learning at home and at school', in C. Gallaway and B. Richards (eds.), *Input and Interaction in Language Acquisition*, Cambridge University Press, Cambridge, 153–180.

Gesell, A.: 1925, *The Mental Growth of the Preschool Child*, Macmillan, New York.

Goodman, K.S.: 1967, 'Reading: A psycholinguistic guessing game', *Journal of the Reading Specialist* 4, 126–135.

Gray, W.S.: 1956, *The Teaching of Reading and Writing*, UNESCO, Paris.

Hall, N.: 1987, *The Emergence of Literacy*, Hodder and Stoughton, Sevenoaks, Kent.

Hannon, P. & James, S.: 1990, 'Parents' and Teachers' Perspectives on Preschool Literacy Development', *British Educational Research Journal* 16(3), 259–272.

Hatcher, P., C. Hulme & Ellis, A.W.: 1994, 'Ameliorating Early Reading Failure by Integrating the Teaching of Reading and Phonological Skills: The Phonological Linkage Hypothesis', *Child Development* 65(1), 41–57.

Heath, S.B.: 1983, *Ways With Words*, Cambridge University Press, Cambridge.

Hirsch, N.D.M.: 1930, *Twins: Heredity and Environment*, Harvard University Press, Cambridge, Mass.

Huey, E.B.: 1908, *The Psychology and Pedogogy of Reading*, Macmillan, New York.

Hunt, J. McV.: 1961, *Intelligence and Experience*, Ronald, New York.

McLane, J. & McNamee, G.: 1990, *Early Literacy*, Harvard University Press, Cambridge.

Morphett, M.V. & Washburne, C.: 1931, 'When Should Children Begin to Read?', *Elementary School Journal* 31 (March), 496–508.

Piaget, J.: 1955, *The Child's Construction of Reality*, Routledge & Kegan Paul, London.

Raban, B. & Ure, C.: 1996, *Preschool Literacy Project, Faculty of Education*, The University of Melbourne, Melbourne.

Reynolds, B.: 1997, *Literacy in the Pre-School: The roles of teachers and parents*, Trentham Books, Stoke-on-Trent.

Stanovich, K.E.: 1986, 'Matthew Effects in Reading: Some Consequences of Individual Differences in the Acquisition of Literacy', *Reading Research Quarterly* 21(4), 360–406.

Taylor, D.: 1983, *Family Literacy: Young children learning to read and write*, Heinemann, Portsmouth, NH.

Vygotsky, L.: 1962, *Thought and Language*, MIT Press, New York.

Vygotsky, L.: 1978, *Mind and Society: The Development of Higher Psychological Processes*, Harvard University Press, Cambridge, MA.

WILLIAM E. TUNMER

METALINGUISTIC SKILLS IN READING DEVELOPMENT

In learning to read unfamiliar words, children are normally taught two general learning strategies: to use sentence context cues to narrow the possibilities of what the word might be, and to use mappings between sub-components of written and spoken words. The latter strategy is also used to produce preconventional (e.g., 'colour' spelled KLR) and conventional (e.g., 'dog' spelled dog) spellings of words. The ability to use sentence context cues to identify partially decoded words, which in turn increases word specific knowledge and knowledge of spelling-to-sound patterns, requires sensitivity to the semantic and syntactic constraints of sentence context (called syntactic awareness), and the ability to use mappings between letters and sounds to read and write unfamiliar words requires sensitivity to the subcomponents of spoken words (called phonological awareness). Syntactic and phonological awareness are two types of metalinguistic ability, where metalinguistic ability (or awareness) is defined as the ability to reflect on and manipulate the structural features of spoken language (i.e., phonemes, words, structural representations of sentences, and sets of in-terrelated propositions). In information processing terms metalinguistic operations can be described as mental operations performed on the outputs of the modular subsystems involved in sentence comprehension (Tunmer & Hoover, 1993). Accordingly, phonological awareness refers to the ability to perform mental operations on the output of the mechanism that converts the acoustic signal into a sequence of phonemes, and syntactic awareness refers to the ability to perform mental operations on the output of the mechanism that assigns intrasentential structural representations to groups of words.

EARLY DEVELOPMENTS

Because reading involves visual processes, it had long been thought that the major problem in learning to read was the failure to discriminate the visual representations of language – the letters and printed words. However, on the basis of several studies using a wide variety of tasks and procedures, it soon became clear that visual discrimination was not the central problem it was once thought to be, as there was little or no evidence to indicate that good and poor readers of the same intellectual ability differed in their basic visual information processing skills (Vellutino, 1979).

V. Edwards and D. Corson (eds), Encyclopedia of Language and Education,
Volume 2: Literacy, 27–36.
© 1997 Kluwer Academic Publishers. Printed in the Netherlands.

Rather, reading is now generally viewed as a derived skill that builds on spoken language. From this perspective reading can be defined as the translation from print to a form of code from which the reader can already derive meaning (Venezky, 1976). Thus, the fundamental task facing preliterate children is to discover how to map the printed text onto their existing language, which in an alphabetic orthography requires the ability to analyze the internal structure of spoken words.

In a seminal paper on the relation of metalinguistic skills to reading development, Mattingly (1972) claimed that 'speaking and listening are primary linguistic activities; reading is a secondary and rather special sort of activity that relies critically upon the reader's awareness of these primary activities' (p. 133). Mattingly referred to this awareness of primary linguistic activity as 'linguistic awareness', and argued that it varies considerably across speakers. He further observed that 'this variation contrasts markedly with the relative consistency from person to person with which primary linguistic activity is performed' (p. 140). Much of the early work stimulated by Mattingly's conceptual analysis is summarized in an edited volume by Downing and Valtin (1984).

MAJOR CONTRIBUTIONS

Most of the early work on the role of metalinguistic skills in reading development concentrated on phonological awareness (see Sawyer & Fox, 1991, for a review of this research). Beginning readers must be able to analyze the internal structure of spoken words to discover how phonemes are related to graphemes. However, many beginning readers find it extraordinarily difficult to detect the phonemic elements in spoken words, even though they are clearly capable of discriminating between speech sounds and using phonemic contrasts to signal meaning differences. The important distinction is that using a phonemic contrast to signal a meaning difference (e.g., *pig* vs. *big*), which is done intuitively and at a subconscious level, is not the same as the metalinguistic act of consciously reflecting on and manipulating the phonemic segments of speech. Examples of the latter include using counters to represent each phoneme in a word like *bat*; blending separate sounds together, such as *buh, ah, tuh*, to form a word; and indicating which of three orally presented words – like *sun, sea, rag* – does not begin with the same sound as the other two.

Performing such tasks is much more difficult for children because there is no simple physical basis for recognizing phonemes in speech. It is not possible to segment a speech signal such that each segment corresponds to one and only one phoneme (Liberman, Cooper, Shankweiler, & Studdert-Kennedy, 1967). Rather, the information necessary for identifying a particular phoneme often overlaps with that of another phoneme, a phenomenon referred to as parallel transmission of phonemic content. Because phonemic segments do not exist in the acoustic signal per se but must be constructed from it, children must develop an awareness of an entity that is inherently abstract. They must gain access to the products of the mental mechanism responsible for converting the speech signal into a sequence of phonemes.

These considerations help to explain why many children who have begun formal reading instruction fail to benefit from either letter-name knowledge or letter-sound knowledge in learning to recognize words. Because there is no one-to-one correspondence between phonemes and segments of the acoustic signal, it is not possible to pronounce in isolation the sound corresponding to most phonemes. Consequently, the strategy of simply 'sounding out' a word like *drag* will result in *duhruhahguh*, a nonsense word comprising four syllables (Liberman & Shankweiler, 1985). Letter sounds and letter names are only imprecise physical analogues of the phonemes in spoken words. Whether children learn to associate the sound 'duh' or the name 'dee' or both with the letter *d*, they must still be able to segment the sound or name to make the connection between the letter *d* and the phoneme /d/. In short, beginning readers must be phonologically aware.

Several studies provide support for the claim that at least some minimal level of explicit phonological awareness is necessary for children to discover the systematic correspondences between graphemes and phonemes. This research shows (1) that children's level of phonological awareness before they begin formal reading instruction predicts their later reading achievement even when those children showing any preschool reading ability are excluded (Bradley & Bryant, 1985) and when the influence of preschool reading ability is statistically controlled (Vellutino & Scanlon, 1987); (2) that phonological awareness influences reading comprehension indirectly through phonological recoding ability, which is the ability to translate letters and letter patterns into phonological forms (Juel, Griffith & Gough, 1986; Stanovich, Cunningham & Feeman, 1984; Tunmer & Nesdale, 1985; see also Béchennec & Sprenger-Charolles, this volume); and (3) that training in phonological awareness during or before reading instruction produces significant experimental group advantages in reading achievement (Ball & Blachman, 1991; Bryant & Bradley, 1985; Byrne & Fielding-Barnsley, 1995; Castle, Riach, & Nicholson, 1994; Lundberg, Frost & Petersen, 1988; Vellutino & Scanlon, 1987). Evidence that some minimal level of explicit phonological awareness is required to break the orthographic code comes from studies that have generated scatterplots of the relation of phonological awareness to phonological recoding ability, as measured by the ability to decode pseudowords; e.g. *tain* and *sark* (Juel et al., 1986; Tunmer & Nesdale, 1985). The scatterplots have shown that, although many children performed well on phoneme segmentation and poorly on pseudoword decoding, no children performed poorly on phoneme segmentation and well on pseudoword decoding. Explicit phonological awareness appears to be necessary, but not sufficient, for acquiring grapheme-phoneme correspondences.

WORK IN PROGRESS

Two metalinguistic skills that have more recently become the focus of attention in relation to reading development are onset/rime sensitivity and grammatical sensitivity (or syntactic awareness). Regarding the former, recent research suggests that there is a level of structure in spoken words that is intermediate in size between syllables and phonemes (see Treiman, 1992, for a review). Several studies reported by Treiman indicate that the ability to segment into phonemes is preceded by the ability to segment syllable units into the intrasyllabic units of onset and rime, where onset is the initial consonant or consonant cluster, and rime is the vowel and any following consonants. Research further indicates that for most children, sensitivity to the onset-rime division emerges spontaneously in development prior to exposure to reading instruction (Goswami & Bryant, 1990). In contrast, the ability to completely segment a word or syllable into its phonemic elements seems to develop only under certain learning conditions, such as when children are exposed to instruction in an alphabetic script or given specific training in phonemic segmentation skills.

These findings and the finding of a strong predictive relationship between preliterate onset-rime sensitivity and later reading achievement (Bradley & Bryant, 1985) have let to the hyphothesis that beginning readers may initially link elements of written and spoken language at the level of onsets and rimes (Goswami & Bryant, 1990; Treiman, 1992). Because preliterate children are generally incapable of fully analyzing spoken words into phonemes, they may have trouble discovering correspondences between single letters (or digraphs, e.g. *sh*) and single phonemes in the beginning stages of learning to read. In support of these suggestions is research by Goswami (see Goswami & Bryant, 1990) indicating that beginning readers can use multiletter units corresponding to onsets and rimes when reading new words. This research also shows that the ability to make analogies on the basis of onsets and rimes precedes the ability to make analogies that cut across the onset/rime boundary or constitute a part of an onset/rime unit.

Although Goswami's work has clearly shown that children are capable of using analogies as soon as they start to read, there remains the question of whether children spontaneously use analogies from the outset of reading acquisition without being prompted to do so and without the presence of trained 'clue' words. Opponents of Goswami's view argue that, although beginning readers have the potential to use analogies, they will not be able to use this strategy until they have developed a sufficiently large sight vocabulary on which to base analogical inferences. In addition, a significant amount of letter-sound knowledge may be needed to store the base (analog) words in memory in sufficient detail to recognize identical orthographic units in known and new words (Ehri & Robbins, 1992; Rack, Hulme, Snowling, & Wightman, 1994).

A third view, which is a combination of the two just described, proposes that there is a reciprocally facilitating relationship between the development of phonological recoding skills, sight word knowledge, and the ability to make use of rime-unit analogies. Some phonological recoding skills (especially knowledge of initial letter sounds in words) and basic sight word knowledge may be necessary to use rime-based analogies. However, the process of dividing words at the onset/rime boundary itself may help children to learn to isolate and recognize individual phonemes (Treiman, 1992). This in turn would enable children to utilize one-to-one correspondences between graphemes and phonemes *within* onsets and rimes. In support of this suggestion, Bowey and Hansen (1994) found that rime-unit knowledge and knowledge of grapheme-phoneme correspondences develop simultaneously during the first year of reading instruction. Further support for this view comes from a study by Goswami (1993) indicating that the use of vowel analogies emerges gradually as reading develops and follows an initial phase in which children's use of analogies is restricted to spelling patterns corresponding to onsets and rimes.

An increasing amount of attention has also been focused on the role of syntactic awareness in reading development. This metalinguistic skill enables beginning readers to combine knowledge of the constraints of sentence context with incomplete graphophonemic information to identify unfamiliar words (including irregularly spelled ones) and thus increase both their word-specific knowledge and their knowledge of grapheme-phoneme correspondences. The ability to use contextual information allows beginning readers to monitor accuracy in word identification by providing them with immediate feedback when their attempted responses to unfamiliar words in text fail to conform to the surrounding grammatical context, such as when a candidate word from the mental lexicon results in either a violation of a strict sub-categorization rule, which governs the syntactic structures into which a word can enter (e.g., The boy slept the bed), or a violation of a selectional restriction rule, which places constraints on how words of different form classes can be combined (e.g., The cage slept). Several studies using a variety of different tasks (e.g., judgement of grammaticality, correction of word order violations or morpheme deletions, oral cloze) have demonstrated that syntactic awareness is related to beginning reading achievement (see Ryan & Ledger, 1984, for a review). For example, Willows and Ryan (1986) found that measures of syntactic awareness were related to beginning reading achievement even when cognitive ability and vocabulary level were controlled.

There are two ways in which syntactic awareness may influence reading development. One is by enabling readers to monitor their ongoing comprehension processes more effectively (Bowey, 1986). The second way, as noted previously, is by helping children to acquire phonological recoding skill. In support of the latter claim, research has shown (1) that syntactic awareness typically correlates more strongly with context free word identification ability than with reading comprehension ability, and (2) that when measures of both word identification and phonological recoding are included in a study, syntactic awareness usually correlates more highly with phonological recoding (see Tunmer & Hoover, 1993). Siegal and Ryan (1988), for example, found that each of three measures of syntactic awareness correlated more strongly with phonological recoding (as measured by pseudoword decoding) than with real word recognition.

PROBLEMS AND DIFFICULTIES

In a recently reported longitudinal study, Bryant, Maclean and Bradley (1990) found strong predictive correlations between measures of phonological and syntactic awareness and later reading achievement. However, in a multiple regression analysis that included three extraneous variables (age, mother's educational level, IQ), four linguistic variables (vocabulary, expressive language, receptive language, sentence imitation) and two measures of phonological awareness (rhyme and alliteration oddity tasks), syntactic awareness failed to make an independent contribution to future reading achievement. The two phonological awareness measures, however, did make independent contributions to reading. It is possible that the strong relationships observed between syntactic awareness and reading simply reflect the indirect contribution of some third factor such as phonological awareness, which has been shown to be related to both syntactic awareness and reading ability. Syntactic awareness, like phonological awareness, is a metalinguistic ability and therefore shares in common with phonological awareness many of the same component operations (invoking control processing, performing mental operations on the outputs of the modular subsystems involved in sentence comprehension, etc.).

An alternative explanation of Bryant et al.'s (1990) findings is that, unlike phonological awareness, syntactic awareness, as noted previously, also influences the development of listening comprehension ability by enabling children to monitor their ongoing comprehension processes more effectively and to make intelligent guesses about the meanings of unfamiliar words. Syntactic awareness would therefore be expected to be related to aspects of general language development. In the Bryant et al. (1990)

study, syntactic awareness did, in fact, correlate much more highly with the four language measures than did either of the phonological awareness measures. This would account for the pattern of results obtained by Bryant and colleagues. Consistent with this interpretation, Tunmer (1989) found in a longitudinal study that syntactic awareness was related to later achievement in real word recognition, pseudoword decoding, listening comprehension, and reading comprehension. The same was true for phonological awareness with the exception of listening comprehension, where there was no relationship ($r = 0.04$). If syntactic awareness facilitates the development of word recognition skill by enabling beginning readers to use context to identify unfamiliar words which, in turn, increases their word-specific knowledge and knowledge of grapheme-phoneme correspondences, then syntactic awareness should make a contribution to the development of word recognition ability that is distinct from that made by phonological awareness. In support of this claim, a path analysis of the data, which included measures of verbal intelligence and decentration ability, showed that phonological and syntactic awareness in first grade each made an independent and approximately equal contribution to phonological recoding ability in second grade. Only syntactic awareness made an independent contribution to listening comprehension ability in second grade.

FUTURE DIRECTIONS

The available evidence suggests that syntactic awareness plays an important role in early reading development. However, unlike the large amount of research that has been reported on the positive effects of phonological awareness training on reading development, there is as yet little evidence demonstrating that training in syntactic awareness during or before reading instruction produces significant experimental group advantages in reading achievement. More work is needed before researchers can recommend that syntactic awareness training be incorporated into beginning reading programmes with the same degree of confidence as phonological awareness training (Bowey, 1994). Further research is also needed to determine whether some combination of phonological and syntactic awareness training is more effective than training in either type of metalinguistic skill alone.

A more theoretical question that has yet to be resolved is why some beginning readers encounter considerable difficulty in performing metalinguistic operations despite having had access to appropriate linguistic and environmental opportunities. Two general views have emerged in the literature (see Tunmer & Hoover, 1993). The first focuses on differences in the phonological storage and processing component of working memory. If some beginning readers are less able to maintain phonological material in working memory, or if their phonological representations in working memory are poorly differentiated, they would be expected to experience difficulty in reflecting on spoken words and sentence contexts to discover letter-sound patterns and identify partially decoded words. In contrast, the second view ascribes greater importance to differences in the limited capacity central executive that is used to operate control processes in working memory. According to this view metalinguistic development is related to a more general change in information processing capability that occurs during middle childhood, which is the development of metacognitive control over the information processing system. During middle childhood children become increasingly aware of how they can control their intellectual processes in a wide range of situations and tasks, including those requiring metalinguistic skills. Metalinguistic operations, unlike normal language operations, require control processing. When comprehending or producing an utterance, speakers are normally unaware of the individual phonemes and words comprising the utterance and the grouping relationships among the utterance's constituent words unless they deliberately reflect on the structural features of the utterance; that is, unless they invoke control processing. Children with a delay or deficit in the development of control processing ability would therefore be expected to have difficulty in gaining access to and performing mental operations on the products of the mental mechanisms involved in sentence processing. It is possible, of course, that both views are correct; deficits in the ability to perform metalinguistic operations may be due to more than one factor.

Massey University, New Zealand

REFERENCES

Ball, E. & Blachman, B.: 1991, 'Does Phoneme Awareness Training in Kindergarten Make a Difference in Early Word Recognition and Developing Spelling?', *Reading Research Quarterly* 26, 46–66.

Bowey, J.A.: 1986, 'Syntactic Awareness in Relation to Reading Skill and Ongoing Reading Comprehension Monitoring', *Journal of Experimental Child Psychology* 41, 282–299.

Bowey, J.A.: 1994, 'Grammatical Awareness and Learning to Read: A Critique', in E.M.H. Assink (ed.), *Literacy Acquisition and Social Context*, Harvester-Wheatsheaf, London, 1994, 1–28.

Bowey, J.A., & Hansen, J.: 1994, 'The Development of Orthographic Rimes as Units of Word Recognition', *Journal of Experimental Child Psychology* 58, 465–488.

Bradley, L. & Bryant, P.E.: 1985, *Rhyme and Reason in Reading and Spelling*, University of Michigan Press, Ann Arbor.

Bryant, P., MacLean, M. & Bradley, L.: 1990, 'Rhyme, Language, and Children's Reading,' *Applied Psycholinguistics* 11, 237–252.

Byrne, B. & Fielding-Barnsley, R.: 1995, 'Evaluation of a Program to Teach Phonemic Awareness to Young Children: A 2-, and 3-Year Follow-up and a New Preschool Trial', *Journal of Educational Psychology* 87, 488–503.

Castle, J.M., Riach, J. & Nicholson, T.: 1994, 'Getting Off to a Better Start in Reading and Spelling: The Effects of Phonemic Awareness Instruction Within a Whole Language Program', *Journal of Educational Psychology* 86, 350–359.

Downing, J. & Valtin, R. (eds.): 1984, *Language Awareness and Learning to Read*, Springer-Verlag, New York.

Ehri, L.C. & Robbins, C.: 1992, 'Beginners Need Some Decoding Skill to Read by Analogy', *Reading Research Quarterly* 27, 13–26.

Goswami, U.: 1993, 'Toward an Interactive Analogy Model of Reading Development: Decoding Vowel Graphemes in Beginning Reading', *Journal of Experimental Child Psychology* 56, 443–475.

Goswami, U. & Bryant, P.E.: 1990, *Phonological Skills and Learning to Read*, Lawrence Erlbaum Associates, Hillsdale NJ.

Juel, C., Griffith, P.L. & Gough, P.B.: 1986, 'Acquisition of Literacy: A Longitudinal Study of Children in First and Second Grade', *Journal of Educational Psychology* 78, 243–255.

Liberman, A., Cooper, F., Shankweiler, D. & Studdert-Kennedy, M.: 1967, 'Perception of the Speech Code', *Psychological Review* 74, 431–461.

Liberman, I. & Shankweiler, D.: 1985, 'Phonology and the Problem of Learning to Read and Write', *Remedial and Special Education* 6, 8–17.

Lundberg, I., Frost, J. & Petersen, O.P.: 1988, 'Effects of an Extensive Program for Stimulating Phonological Awareness in Preschool Children', *Reading Research Quarterly* 23, 267–284.

Mattingly, I.G.: 1972, 'Reading, the Linguistic Process, and Linguistic Awareness', in J.F. Kavanagh & I.G. Mattingly (eds.), *Language by Ear and by Eye*, MIT Press, Cambridge, Ma, 1972, 133–147.

Rack, J., Hulme, C., Snowling, M. & Wightman, J.: 1994, 'The Role of Phonology in Young Children Learning to Read Words: The Direct-Mapping Hypothesis', *Journal of Experimental Child Psychology* 57, 42–71.

Ryan, E.B. & Ledger, G.W.: 1984, 'Learning to Attend to Sentence Structure: Links between Metalinguistic Development and Reading', in J. Downing & R. Valtin (eds.), *Language Awareness and Learning to Read*, Springer-Verlag, New York, 1984, 149–171.

Sawyer, D.J. & Fox, B.J. (eds.): 1991, *Phonological Awareness in Reading: The Evolution of Current Perspectives*, Springer-Verlag, New York.

Siegel, L. & Ryan, E.: 1988, 'Development of Grammatical-sensitivity, Phonological and Short-term Memory Skills in Normally Achieving and Learning Disabled Children', *Developmental Psychology* 24, 28–37.

Stanovich, K.E., Cunningham, A.E. & Feeman, D.J.: 1984, 'Intelligence cognitive, skills and early reading progress', *Reading Research Quarterly* 19, 278–303.

Treiman, R.: 1992, 'The Role of Intrasyllabic Units in Learning to Read and Spell', in P.B. Gough, L. Ehri & R. Treiman (eds.), *Reading Acquisition*, Lawrence Erlbaum Associates, Hillsdale, NJ, 1992, 65–106.

Tunmer, W.E.: 1989, 'The Role of Language-related Factors in Reading Disability', in D. Shankweiler & I. Liberman (eds.), *Phonology and Reading Disability: Solving the Reading Puzzle*, University of Michigan Press, Ann Arbor, 1989, 91–131.

Tunmer, W.E. & Hoover, W.: 1993, 'Components of Variance Models of Language-related factors in reading disability: A Conceptual Overview', in M. Joshi & C.K. Leong (eds.), *Reading Disabilities: Diagnosis and Component Processes*, Kluwer Academic Publishers, Dordrecht, 1993, 135–173.

Tunmer, W.E. & Nesdale, A.R.: 1985, 'Phonemic Segmentation Skill and Beginning Reading', *Journal of Educational Psychology* 77, 417–427.

Vellutino, F.R.: 1979, *Dyslexia: Theory and Research*, MIT Press, Cambridge, Ma.

Vellutino, F.R. & Scanlon, D.M.: 1987, 'Phonological Coding, Phonological Awareness, and Reading Ability: Evidence from a Longitudinal and Experimental Study', *Merrill-Palmer Quarterly* 33, 321–363.

Venezky, R.L.: 1976, *Theoretical and Experimental Bases for Teaching Reading*, Mouton, The Hague.

Willows, D. & Ryan, E.: 1986, 'The Development of Grammatical Sensitivity and its Relationship to Early Reading Achievement', *Reading Research Quarterly* 21, 253–266.

MARIE M. CLAY

THE DEVELOPMENT OF LITERACY DIFFICULTIES

Literacy difficulties emerge during the first year of school, persist in some form throughout education, and affect adult adjustment and work potential. As classmates pull ahead the slow pace of some children's progress is apparent to teachers, parents, psychologists, medical practitioners, and special educators. Well-designed interventions delivered *individually* and *early* can reverse that slow progress and bring many children into the average band for their class. Such outcomes rarely occur with older children even when they get extended, individual, tutorial help.

Adults who read and spell poorly throughout their lifetime frequently have language problems which involve far more than phonology and decoding (Johnston, 1985). Sustained, quality instruction for as long as it takes is the recommended treatment to move learners from where they are to where they want or need to be.

The knowledge bases of printed language – the symbols, sound-to-symbol relationships, the structure of words, the structure of phrases, sentences and texts, and the meanings of words singly or in sequences – are common to reading and writing and both are usually affected.

EARLY DEVELOPMENTS

Educators have searched for a beginning curriculum that will minimize literacy difficulties and too often see this as a sufficient prevention strategy (Ogilvy, 1994).

Analyses of reading difficulties were historically driven by three searches (Robinson, 1977): the first was for remedial approaches that teachers could use to determine the difficulties of pupils who fell below some standard of performance (Fernald, 1943; Strang, 1964); the second was for clinical identification of causative factors impeding an individual's progress (Robinson, 1946); and the third for research-based investigations of reading processes (from Huey, 1901 to Ruddell, Ruddell & Singer, 1994).

Gradual shifts in academic and practical theories have led to different emphases in recent research. Children with different IQ's are expected to learn at different rates and this has led to institutionalized provisions for some children to progress slowly (Shepard, 1991). Slow progress has also become linked through research on poverty to a false expectation that children of the poor will necessarily fall behind in literacy learning. These

V. Edwards and D. Corson (eds), Encyclopedia of Language and Education,
Volume 2: Literacy, 37–46.
© *1997 Kluwer Academic Publishers. Printed in the Netherlands.*

two groups – those of low intelligence, and those who live in poverty – have missed 'opportunities to learn' as preschoolers and yet the expectations held for their school progress has led to providing them with fewer rather than more opportunities to learn in school. They have been called the 'generally backward' or the 'garden variety' group in research studies. Contemporary societies would like most of them to become literate but have institutionalized practices which do not achieve this.

Research-based investigation of specific literacy difficulties shifted from theorizing about reading processes to the role played by neurological variations in literacy difficulties. Concepts of minimal brain damage and brain dysfunction were explored (Strauss & Kephart, 1955) and the term 'dyslexia', previously used to describe the loss of the ability to read following central nervous system damage or dysfunction, came to include a new hypothesis about a pre-existing condition in children with pronounced difficulty in literacy learning, called 'developmental dyslexia.' It could be congenital, perhaps hereditary, and mild to severe. It was diagnosed after excluding most other causes such as sensory impairment, emotional disorders, lack of motivation, or faulty instruction. To eliminate low intelligence as a factor, diagnoses established a discrepancy between achievement and intellectual potential. Only learners with average or better scores on intelligence tests were included in most dyslexia research samples. Dyslexia, specific learning disability or retardation, and severe literacy learning difficulties are almost synonyms applied to literacy difficulties which have no other apparent explanation.

Historically, spelling and writing problems were studied separately (Robinson, 1977) although early treatment programmes worked with both reading and writing (Fernald, 1943; Strauss & Kephart, 1955). They are studied together only by those researchers who see that the mastery of alphabetic writing requires facility in decomposing words into phonemes and morphemes, and that writing could encourage such exploration in reading (Ehri, in press; Treiman, 1993).

MAJOR CONTRIBUTIONS

Widespread support exists for a clinical syndrome related to phonemic awareness and phonological coding (Hulme & Snowling, 1994), as a single/major cause of difficulties. Learning about phonology begins before school entry. It is extended in school literacy activities as children attend to the sounds of their own speech paired with the same messages in print. They read aloud slowly, solve new words, and write down their own speech. In diverse programmes children articulate speech in ways that sharpen their visual attention to print. It was hypothesized that, if children of average or higher intelligence could hear these sounds but had literacy problems, possibly the auditory centres in the brain could not process these phonemes. This limitation was extensively studied in several alphabetic languages (Hulme & Snowling, 1994).

Despite some consensus, a gulf exists between what researchers report and what teachers might do in group lessons, or individual treatments. The academic guidance goes little beyond 'stress rhyming,' 'teach phonemic awareness,' or 'teach phonics,' and ignores a classical early analysis of the psychological challenges to young children by Elkonin (1973), who stressed the hearing of 'the sound sequence in words,' the importance of slow articulation by the student of that sound sequence, and in the extreme case the additional use of a small mirror to allow the child to see how he is making the sounds. It is not clear what precise classroom performance academics would consider evidence of becoming phonemically aware. Experimental treatments have trained the hearing of rhymes, or the hearing of phonemes by elongating hard-to-hear sounds and making them louder (Tallal et al., 1995), and educators have delivered lessons using pseudo-linguistic analyses of letter-sound relationships in English popularly known as 'phonics,' in prescribed sequences (Hatcher, 1994). Williams (1995) advised teachers to help children acquire phonemic awareness by providing practice in segmenting spoken words through games for this enhances concurrent or subsequent phonics instruction or other reading instruction.

When researchers assume that reading and writing are as complex as brain activity gets, then multiple causation of difficulties becomes a competing hypothesis. Different parts or processes of the brain could be involved, neurological networks would be forming across the brain, and the relationship of such development to beginning instruction would become a critical issue. Deficits may not be specific to vision or language alone, but to the linking of more than one process, and how articulated language becomes integrated with fast visual processing resurfaces as an exciting question.

If reading processes are complex then learners could use many strategies on multiple sources of information to become good readers, including word knowledge, phonological analysis, grammar and sentence meaning, and knowledge of the world; and individual literacy difficulties could arise at different times in the acquisition process.

Questions are raised by comparison studies of older learning disabled with regular students about the distinctiveness of these groups. Both groups may display deficiencies in spelling and in decoding that overlap in their scoring range. One illustrative example from Grade 9–10 students in USA found both groups recognized most common words in print but lacked the linguistic sophistication that would permit them to attain higher levels of orthographic knowledge and apply it. This included a lack of knowledge of word derivations and English spelling conventions which could be fostered by class teachers (Shankweiler, Lundquist, Dreyer and Dickenson, 1996). Stated another way, this means that children with aptitude/achievement discrepancies have been found to have achievement profiles that are surprisingly similar to children who do not.

WORK IN PROGRESS

While research continues with the phonological hypothesis, theoretical discussions are now more open to the implications of interactions among processes (Goswami, 1993) and deficits among the interactions. The organic emphasis of specific brain damage or dysfunction is tempered by recognition that genetic and environmental factors have interactive influences on how the brain develops. What was complex becomes more complex.

In Seymour's (1993) programmatic research which explores multiple causation in dyslexia, cases show large degrees of heterogeneity, no syndromes or patterns, phonological problems affecting letter-sound translation, and morphemic problems affecting direct word recognition. He attributes the problems to grapheme processing and morpheme processing and not to some underlying deficit. He acknowledges the reciprocity of knowledge sources in reading and writing, and concludes that children use both word recognition and alphabetic processing from the start, although use is strongly biassed by emphases in instruction. He suggests that orthographic analysis must be considered a third process which may appear quite early as soon as children begin to attend to clusters of letters rather than only to single phonemes.

Recent work in neuroscience has provided some refined answers to age-old questions. The imaging of individual variations in the brain is possible and quantitative methods for identifying cerebral anomalies on magnetic resonance images (MRI's) of subjects with language learning disabilities are being studied. High-resolution magnetic images can reveal functionally relevant variations and anomalies in cerebral structure and further refinement of these techniques may improve the diagnosis, classification, and treatment of language learning disabilities (Leonard et al., 1993). An old ghost in clinical child psychology may impede this progress: knowledge about normal variability in brain morphology and its relationship to cognitive and behavioural development is sorely needed as background for the study of anomalies and such research is rarely funded.

The high visibility of attention deficit disorders (ADD) led to questions about their relationship to literacy difficulties. One study, Hynd et al. (1995), illustrates an apparent trend in other findings. When children with reading disability (RD) were compared with subjects with attention deficit hyperactivity disorder (ADHD) on neurolinguistic and phonological measures, group comparisons revealed the RD group to have relative deficits in phonological coding, expressive language, elision, and vocabulary. Regardless of the presence of co-occurring psychopathology, children with

RD suffered primary deficits in language and phonological processes that were specific to the presence of reading disabilities. The report points to mounting evidence on the relative independence of reading disability and ADHD. Either disorder may, however, develop secondarily to the manifestation of a primary disorder or occur as a truly comorbid familial-genetic disorder.

If reading is one of the most complex tasks we undertake then it may lead us to a better understanding of other cognitive systems. A renewed interest in visual processes is apparent. The eye fixations of both dyslexic and non-dyslexic readers reflect the difficulties that both groups have with successfully identifying words in a text. Researchers have found subjects with poor visual temporal processing among both their dyslexic and their backward reader groups concluding that both are poor readers because reading requires fast, sequential processing (Eden, Stein, Wood & Wood, 1995). Phonological processing may also be implicated in this result and knowing more about it may make it easier to study elusive visual processing functions. While current cognitive research directs attention to questions of brain processing in literacy tasks, and what can be done if the brain fails to process effectively, a seemingly unrelated field of activity arose from studying literacy learners in classrooms developmentally as they pass through the first three years of school. Early intervention directed to those with low achievement, irrespective of cause, has been widely reported. Reading Recovery (Hobsbaum, Peters & Sylva, 1996) is an early intervention which operates in a model of three phases:

Phase 1: Children who enter school with different intelligence and different experiences have a year in a good classroom programme and most begin literacy learning.

Phase 2: Then the lowest achievers irrespective of causation are selected for individually designed and efficiently delivered instruction for the shortest time necessary (within half a school year) to bring all aspects of reading and writing processing to the level of the average band in the classroom. The intervention adapts to individual needs and most children can shrug off the risk of literacy problems by the end of their second school year.

Phase 3: Diagnostically, not succeeding in Reading Recovery enhances the chance of getting appropriate long-term help in a special prgrogamme as numbers may be reduced to as low as one per cent of the age group. The pragmatic value of this to educators is that it reduces literacy problems, and identifies those who need continuing help. For the few who are not yet within the average band, a specialist report is then sought, and the supplementary help or placement changed to provide instructional support for as long as it takes (which fits well with the British Code of Practice for special education referrals). Multiple causation is still involved in the literacy difficulties at Phase 3 for it would include children with poor school experiences, children of low intelligence who need more help for longer, other children with missed opportunities who need more teaching, and children who need more expert teaching to build neurological networks which bypass brain processing problems.

The outcomes of early intervention and/or individual tutoring treatments should be subjected to careful analysis for they are fashionable but of varying qualility. Evaluative questions include
- Who is selected for supplementary help, and why?
- What specialist teaching is given?
- What are the outcome criteria of success?
- Who and how many become adequate readers and writers?
- What benefits and continuing adaptations are made after a pre-referral programme for the small group requiring continuing help?

PROBLEMS AND DIFFICULTIES

When more research effort is directed to literacy difficulties than to theories of reading well, administrators run the risk of allowing research on problems to dominate change in classroom practices. This could be avoided if research plotted how both normal and abnormal functioning change over that period of time when basic literacy processing skills are being established. Farnham-Diggory (1994) criticized most studies of classroom instruction with failing to present information about actual instruction. If instruction is treated as randomized variation (which makes statistical sense) are researchers saying that rigorous educational research can be conducted only if major treatments (school training) and avowed objectives (improvements in school training) are defined as random errors? She suspects that it is difficult to map classroom instruction onto the theories that drive laboratory research. The translation of experimental results into classroom practice suffers from underdeveloped 'researcher awareness' and a lack of educationally relevant studies.

Without clear mapping of how the cognitive and other psychological processes are assembled, and collectively and reciprocally change in the first two years of literacy learning (Stanovich, 1986), we can derive little guidance about treatments for older learners from studies of those who have been building poor processing circuits for five to ten years. A defective foundation in print processing will continue to generate confusions which will show up even in silent reading comprehension, and the answer is not merely to teach phonemic awareness to the older silent reader expecting that key to open the door. The phonemic awareness must be embedded in, and integrated with the word recognition and language comprehension from the beginning.

In the academic search for the cause(s) of literacy difficulties large numbers of children have been excluded from the samples studied, those with missed opportunities to learn, with poor instruction and low intelligence. Educational solutions for these groups are currently far from satisfactory; although they learn they fall further and further behind their successful classmates (Aman & Singh, 1983).

Additionally the numbers of children diagnosed with severe reading difficulties and referred for treatment have increased as laws acknowledge the labels, as funding is allocated for educational solutions (Carrier, 1984), and as society demands higher achievements. A specified set of defining characteristics by etiology, diagnosis, treatment or prognosis does not exist, and problems of identification are embedded in a definition debate. A 1996 survey sent to professionals in the USA asked them to nominate definitive/diagnostic behaviours indicative of specific learning disabilities. This approach is circular.

The limited and relatively unsuccessful search for improved remediation of dyslexia is unsatisfactory. There is no evidence of strong later remediation programmes; published reports of success are rare and results minimal in terms of effective change (Gittleman, 1983). The concept of stepped interventions which follow the learner's construction of literacy processes and adapt as needed deserves our attention.

Stanovich (1986) has critically reviewed commonly accepted concepts. His 'neglect' hypothesis predicts that poor readers practice what they do easily and well, and attend less to their weaker processes. He explains how recognizing reciprocal relationships between reading ability and cognitive processes makes the design and interpretation of research more difficult. He clarifies how differentially advantaged organisms are exposed to non-random distributions of environmental quality, producing strong environmental effects. These mechanisms create the 'rich get richer' and 'poor get poorer' patterns in reading achievement which he calls 'the Matthew effects.' Educational practices then contribute to slowing the progress of the poor readers. Early reversal of such trends is critical. More recently Stanovich (1991) challenged the use of the discrepancy between reading achievement and measured intelligence (used in dyslexia research) because of the evidence that the acquisition of literacy fosters the very cognitive skills that are assessed by aptitude measures.

FUTURE DIRECTIONS

In an information society people need to be literate if they are not to be closed out of participation: they need to be enabled to make choices and make their contributions. Many now believe that every child could become literate, but educators have some areas of concern.

The literacy debate about classroom programmes continues. Instruction brings roughly 80 per cent of children to success in literacy learning in any programme and education systems strive for higher average scores. We can expect literacy problems to persist as no classroom delivery system will be perfect for individual learners. Retaining the quality aspects of current programmes and empowering teachers to accommodate their modes of class instruction to individual differences will serve all students well, particularly when policies are adopted to include students with special needs in mainstream classrooms.

Two groups of children – those of low intelligence and those from poverty backgrounds – are expected to become 'slow learners' and school practices produce this result (see also the review by Street, this volume). This runs counter to current concerns for higher literacy levels in 'the information society'. As both groups bring less prior experience to school learning, they need extra experience on entry to school as make-up for success in literacy learning, but schools do not provide for such acceleration. Phase 2 of the Reading Recovery model (described above) achieves accelerated learning for many children in these groups, in addition to serving a third group. This third group for whom expectations are low are children with severe literacy learning difficulties, and several hypotheses suggest that an effectively delivered intervention may shorten the time they need in continuing help.

Theorists, researchers, or remediation/support groups select children for dyslexia programmes because they demonstrate general competence and specific disability, and then they receive instruction narrowly focussed on phonological aspects of reading. An important question is whether that analysis of how to teach dyslexic children is correct. Even if it became accepted that phonological processing were the deficit of this group it does not follow that this is what should receive direct instruction. If decoding is hard for these intelligent children to learn, then why would we make it the sole scaffold or dominating process in all reading? Weaving the weak decoding into the strong mental processing fabric of these learners is surely the challenge. Foregrounding phonological processing as the major variable causing literacy difficulties leads to neglect of the rich variety of other factors that contribute to good reading and writing.

Policy makers need to distinguish between advocacies for particular approaches to literacy learning which apply to classrooms and those which apply to the three groups predicted to encounter difficulty learning. Dyslexia programmes derived for intelligent children have been used by schools which wanted to raise scores generally; one of the early learning areas of school programmes (sound to letter relationships) has become a major focus in some literacy instruction, and is sometimes seen as 'all you need to know to be a reader.' That emphasis instantly deprives all the groups having difficulty with learning of the very enrichment and make-up opportunities they need, perhaps limiting the progress of 20–40 per cent of children. More intelligent children will hopefully fight their way past this error.

For children who are trying to build neurological networks to overcome processing problems, research in the dyslexia area may well follow Seymour's assumptions and reveal many different kinds of processing problems requiring idiosyncratic instructional solutions. It may also be the case that treatment of phonological processing difficulties will come to be seen as a dilemma: if a difficulty with phonological processing is treated with a heavy emphases on this aspect of instruction such that learners are encouraged to neglect the use of the remaining rich sources of information in print, then the learners have been tutored to neglect precisely what they need in order to reach advanced levels of literacy learning.

University of Auckland, New Zealand

REFERENCES

Aman, M.G. & Singh, M.M.: 1983, 'Specific reading disorders: concepts of etiology reconsidered', in K.D. Gadow & I. Bailer, (eds.), *Advances in Learning and Behavioral Disabilities* 3, JAI Press, Greenwich, Connecticut, 1–47.

Carrier, J.G.: 1984, 'Comparative special education: ideology, differentiation and allocation in England and the United States', in L. Barton & S. Tomlinson (eds.), *Special Education and Social Interests*, Croom Helm, Beckenham, 1984, 35–64.

Eden, G.F., Stein, J.F., Wood, H.M. & Wood, F.B.: 1995, 'Temporal and spatial processing in reading disabled and normal children', *Cortex* 3, 451–468.

Ehri, L.C.: (in press), 'The unobtrusive role of words in reading text', in A. Watson, A. Badenhop & L. Giorcelli (eds.), *Accepting the Literacy Challenge*, Scholastic, Australia.

Elkonin, D.B.: 1973, 'USSR', in J. Downing (ed.), *Comparative Reading*, Macmillan, New York.

Farnham-Diggory, S.: 1994, 'Paradigms of knowledge and instruction', *Review of Educational Research* 64, 463–477.

Fernald, G.M.: 1943, *Remedial Techniques in Basic School Subjects*, McGraw-Hill, New York.

Gittleman, R. & Feingold, I.: 1983, 'Children with reading disorders-11: Efficacy of reading remediation', *Journal of Child Psychology and Child Psychiatry* 24, 167–192.

Goswami, U.: 1993, 'Phonological skills and learning to read,' in P. Tallal, A.M. Galaburda, R.R. Llinas, & C. von Euler (eds.), *Temporal Information Processing in the Nervous System: special Ref erence to Dyslexia and Dysphasia*, Annals of the New York Academy of Sciences 682, New York, 296–311.

Hatcher, P.: 1994, 'An integrated approach to encouraging the development of phonological awareness, reading and writing', in C. Hulme and M. Snowling (eds.).

Hobsbaum, A., Peters, S., & Sylva, K.: 1996, 'Scaffolding in Reading Recovery,' *Oxford Review of Education*, 22(1), 17–35.

Huey, E.B.: 1901, 'On the psychology and physiology of reading', *American Journal of Psychology* 12, 292–313.

Hulme, C. & Snowling, M. (eds.): 1994, *Reading Development and Dyslexia*. Whurr Publishers, London.

Hynd, G.W., Morgan, A.E., Edmonds, J.E., Black, K.,Riccio, C.A., & Lombardino, L.: 1995, 'Reading disabilities, comorbid pathology, and the specificity of neurolinguistic deficits', *Developmental Neuropsychology* 11, 311–322.

46 MARIE M. CLAY

Johnston, P.H.: 1985, 'Understanding reading disability: a case study approach', *Harvard Educational Review* 55, 153–177.

Leonard, C.M., Voeller, K.K.S., Lombardino, L.J., Morris, M.K., Hynd, G.W., Alexander, A.W., Andersen, H.G., Garofalakis, M., Honeyman, J.C. Jington, M., Agee, F. & Staab, E.V.: 1993, 'Anomalous cerebral structure in dyslexia revealed with magnetic resonance imaging', *Archives of Neurology* 50, 461–469.

Ogilvy, C.M.: 1994, 'What is the diagnostic significance of specific learning disabilities?', *School Psychology International* 15, 55–68.

Robinson, H.A. (ed.): 1977, *Reading and Writing Instruction in the United States: Historical Trends*, International Reading Association, Newark, Delaware.

Robinson, H.M.: 1946, *Why Pupils Fail in Reading*, The University of Chicago Press, Chicago.

Ruddell, R. B., Ruddell, M.R. & Singer, H.: 1994, *Theoretical Models and Processes of Reading* (fourth edition), International Reading Association, Newark, Delaware.

Seymour, P.H. & Evans, H.M.: 1993, 'The visual (orthographic) processor and developmental dyslexia', in D.M. Willows, R.S. Kruk, E. Corcos (eds.), *Visual Processes in Reading and Reading Disabilities*, Lawrence Erlbaum Associates, Hillsdale, NJ.

Shankweiler, D., Lundquist, E., Dreyer, L.G. & Dickenson, C.C.: 1996, 'Reading and spelling difficulties in high school students: Causes and consequences', *Reading and Writing: An Interdisciplinary Journal* 8, 1–28.

Shepard, L.: 1991, 'Negative policies for dealing with diversity: When does assessment and diagnosis turn into sorting and segregation', in E. Hiebert (ed.), *Literacy for a Diverse Society: Perspectives, Practices, and Policies*, New York: Teachers College Press: 279–298.

Stanovich, K.E.: 1986, 'Matthew effects in reading: Some consequences of individual differences in the acquisition of literacy', *Reading Research Quarterly* 21, 360–407.

Stanovich, K.E.: 1991, 'Discrepancy definitions of reading disability: Has intelligence led us astray?', *Reading Research Quarterly*, 26(1), 7–29.

Strang, R.: 1964, *Diagnostic Teaching of Reading*, McGraw-Hill, New York.

Strauss, A.A. & Kephart, N.C.: 1955, *Psychopathology and Education of the Brain-Injured Child*, Vol. 2, Grune & Stratton, New York.

Tallal, P., Galaburda, A.M., Llinas,R.R., von Euler, C. (eds.): 1993, *Temporal Information Processing in the Nervous System: Special reference to Dyslexia and Dysphasia*, Annals of the New York Academy of Sciences 682, New York, 296–311.

Treiman, R.: 1993, *Beginning to Spell: A Study of First-Grade Children*, Oxford University Press, New York.

Williams, J.: 1995, 'Phonemic Awareness', in T.L Harris & R.C. Hodges (eds.), *The Literacy Dictionary: The Vocabulary of Reading and Writing*, International Reading Association, Newark, Delaware, 185–186.

READING IN MULTILINGUAL CLASSROOMS

One of the consequences of the unprecedented scale of population move-ment in the last fifty years is that multilingual classrooms have become the norm in many cities throughout the English-speaking world and continen-tal Europe. The extent of this linguistic diversity is staggering. In 1990, a third of the largest school districts in the USA had over 50 per cent ethnic and language minority students (National Center for Education Statistics, 1993). According to the Canadian Ethnocultural Council (1988), 72 school boards in Ontario were offering 4,364 classes in 58 different languages to over 90,000 students. By the late 1980s, close to 200 different languages were spoken in the schools of London, UK (MRC, 1995). Meanwhile in Australia, Horvath & Vaughan (1991) document some fifty eight different community or heritage languages.

The focus for the present review is reading in multilingual classrooms, an educational setting quite distinct from the bilingual programmes de-scribed in volume five. In bilingual programmes, children are educated through the medium of the minority language in addition to the (official or unofficial) national language. In contrast, in multilingual classrooms, varying proportions of children for whom the national language is a second language learn mainly or exclusively through the medium of the national language.

EARLY DEVELOPMENTS

A number of early developments provided a stimulus for research on reading in multilingual classrooms, including the psycholinguistic study of the reading process; the emergence of language experience approaches to the teaching of reading; and the recognition of the intellectual and social benefits of bilingualism.

The insights into fluent reader behaviour offered by the analysis of miscues – or departures from the text in oral reading – from the late 1960s onwards (see Goodman's review, this volume), offered an invaluable framework for examining the ways in which second language learners and dialect speakers interacted with text.

The emergence of language experience approaches to the teaching of literacy (see Thompson's review this volume) also helped promote our understanding of reading in a second language. Two charismatic teachers

V. Edwards and D. Corson (eds), Encyclopedia of Language and Education,
Volume 2: Literacy, 47–56.
© *1997 Kluwer Academic Publishers. Printed in the Netherlands.*

– Paolo Freire, working with adult learners in Brazil, and Sylvia Ashton-Warner, working with Maori children in New Zealand – came independently to the conclusion that traditional learning materials were unsuitable for their purposes (Freire, 1973; Ashton-Warner, 1963). Although there were obvious differences between the two settings, the approaches of these teachers had much in common. Both set out to link the content of the reading materials with cultural practices or emotions that were important in the communities where they were based. Both believed that students should actively control their own learning and that teachers were mediators of new knowledge, a bridge between home and school.

The third influence which can be detected in current discussions of reading in multilingual classrooms are the more positive attitudes towards bilingualism which first emerged in the 1960s. For many years, the prevailing view was that bilingualism placed speakers at an social and intellectual disadvantage. The early research on bilingualism, however, has been shown to suffer singly and cumulatively from many methodological flaws (Baker, 1996). More recently, the notion of a common underlying proficency (Cummins, 1979) has offered an alternative model of bilingualism which has, in turn, stimulated research in many new directions. In this view, various cognitive and intellectual skills are transferred from one language to another; they do not have to be relearned. Children who are already literate in their own languages will, for instance, know that print carries meaning and that the stream of print is broken into words. They understand conventions, such as the direction of the print. Fluent readers also know that it is possible to skip inessential words, that unknown words can be guessed from context, and that you can read ahead when you don't know a word.

MAJOR CONTRIBUTIONS

Research on reading in multilingual classrooms has been undertaken by ethnographers, sociolinguists, anthropologists and psycholinguists, as well as by a growing number of teacher-researchers. Several books for teachers offer overviews of this research including Wallace (1985), Edwards (1995) and Gregory (1996) in the UK; Gibbons (1991) in Australia; and Williams & Snipper (1990) and Spangenberg-Urbschat & Pritchard (1994) in the USA. Research findings tend to cluster around three main themes: an exploration of the reading behaviours of second language and dialect readers and the ways in which teachers respond to these behaviours; the description and analysis of literacy practices in different cultural contexts; and discussions of ways in which children's biliterate development can be supported in the mainstream school.

Reading behaviours in multilingual classrooms

Goodman & Goodman (1978) were pioneers in this area, conducting miscue analyses of Spanish, Arabic, Navajo and Samoan children. They report that interlingual errors are more common in the very early stages of second language learning, and when the reader's first language is very different from the target language.

Of particular concern is the evidence provided by a range of writers of the ways in which teachers respond differentially to children of different levels of reading ability. The miscues of poor readers tend to be 'corrected' immediately rather than waiting until the end of a phrase or a clause boundary (Allington, 1980), a practice which has been criticized on the grounds that it increases dependence on the teacher rather than progress towards self-correction (McNaughton & Glynn, 1980). There is also evidence that teachers pay more attention to decoding than to meaning in poor readers (Allington, 1980; McDermott, 1978; Gumperz, 1970). The significance of these findings for the present discussion lies in the fact that disproportionate numbers of children from non-standard and other language backgrounds are found among low achieving readers (Cazden, 1988). Some studies focus specifically on these last two groups: Cunningham (1976–7), for instance, reports that dialect miscues are corrected more often than non-dialect errors, while Moll et al. (1980) found that non-native pronunciations are often mistaken for erroneous decoding.

The conclusion drawn by many writers is that teacher intervention in children's oral reading is desirable only when their miscues change the meaning of the text; constant 'correction' disturbs the flow and sends a message to the children that reading is concerned with word-for-word accuracy rather than meaning making (Wallace, 1985; Edwards, 1995). In the case of second language learners, this outcome is particularly undesirable. Because they cannot use the structures and meanings of texts to predict as effectively as native speakers, second language learners often read mechanically: they make a low number of errors and tend to hypercorrect; but they also have a greater tendency to make grapho-phonic miscues and to tolerate substitutions that change the meaning of the text. The imperative is therefore to provide children with strategies for prediction rather than word-by-word decoding.

Gregory (1996) offers the most comprehensive recent discussion of miscue analysis with second language learners, assessing both the strengths which second language learners may bring and the particular problems which they may experience in relation to different cueing systems.

Another area which has been identified as causing particular difficulties for second language readers is textual cohesion (Gibbons, 1991; Wallace, 1985). Grammatical relations exist not only within the sentence, but between sentences in the form of deictic devices such as *it* and *this* which refer back to the subject of previous sentences, and also in the form of connectives, such as *thus*. Without an understanding of the connective tissue of texts, it very difficult for second language learners to follow what they are reading.

Different experiences of literacy

A great deal of research activity is currently focused in the area of 'multiple literacies'. For many years, it was believed that becoming literate involved the acquisition of certain text-related skills. More recently, the social dimension in literacy learning has been acknowledged and many researchers have sought to document the range of relationships with print which exist in different communities (see Street, this volume).

The work of Shirley Brice Heath (1983) on the different relationships with the written word of three communities in South Carolina has been particularly influential. For instance, in the African-American community of Trackton, children have no books and emphasis is put on reading to learn rather than learning to read. Encounters with print tend to be functional: picking out the relevant parts of instruction booklets in order to assemble or modify a piece of equipment, or reading the price tags in the local store to identify bargains. In Trackton, anyone who chooses to read alone is dismissed as lacking social skills: reading is considered a social activity. The evening newspaper, circulars and other letters of general interest are usually read aloud on the front porch and generate a great deal of discussion. Heath (1983: 200–1) describes this approach to the written word as 'a new synthesis of information from the text and the joint experience of community members'.

Various other researchers have built on the foundations of Brice Heath's painstaking ethnographic descriptions of literacy events in the eastern USA. Vogt et al. (1987), for instance, describe how knowledge about different discourse structures led to changes in teacher behaviour around reading in the Kamehameha Early Education Program (KEEP) in Hawaii. When children were discussing books which they had read, turn-taking rules were relaxed in order to allow them to speak without being called on by the teacher and even to overlap with other students' contributions, a pattern characteristic of much Polynesian speech. Teachers replaced praise for individuals with more indirect praise or praise intended for the group; and children were organised 'vertically' so that more advanced students could more easily help less experienced peers. Using this approach, children were able to demonstrate a much better understanding of what they had read. Teachers also began to change their views of children as lacking in motivation or difficult to manage.

Brian Street (1984) describes approaches to the written word in traditional Moslem religious schools or 'maktabs' where children learn, among other things, to recite by heart whole passages of the Qu'rān. Maktab literacy often produces children who recognise passages they have memorized by their position on the page, layout and style rather than by 'cracking the phonemic code'. Yet, despite the differences between maktab and school literacy, Moslem children acquire many skills in mosque classes which can be easily transferred to reading in English. They understand the concept of 'word,' directionality and different ways of breaking up the page. Maktab literacy also helps develop skills for non-sequential reading. In order to find specific passages to justify an argument, students learn to thumb their way around the Qu'rān and other texts using, for example, headings and contents pages.

Gregory (1996) also explores maktab literacy, pointing to the definite boundaries between 'work' and 'play' which make Qur'ānic schools very different from mainstream education. The same principles often spill over from Qu'rānic to voluntary community language classes including Urdu, Bengali and Gujarati. Children are clear that they 'read and write' in Bengali school and 'play' in English school. In classes which often last for two hours without a break, children remain seated on the floor or at the table and all talk is directed to the task in hand. Tuition is exact and direct. The child answers and will be told either, 'Yes' or 'Not like that, like this.'

The Chinese experience of literacy has much in common with maktab literacy (Gregory, 1996; Wong, 1992). Great importance is attached to the values of Confucianism which include respect for parents and achievement in education. There is a strict division between work and play. Children sit in rows and do as the teacher directs them. They practise characters over and over until they are perfect. If they forget or misplace a single stroke, they may completely change the meaning of the character, so close attention to detail is essential. Like in the maktab, children who attend Chinese community classes recite words in chorus after the teacher. They learn through repetition, memorization and careful copying.

Books are held in very high esteem but parents believe that children must prove themselves worthy through hard work. In much the same way that Moslem children are given the Qu'rān when they have worked their way through Arabic primers, many Chinese children are rewarded with books only when they have learned to read.

Support for biliteracy

The realisation that a firm foundation in the home language is important for literacy development in the language of the school has important implications for educators. The level of support for literacy in community languages in mainstream schools is constrained by both political will and the availability of trained bilingual teachers. However, growing attention is being paid to initiatives which acknowledge the value of bilingualism.

The provision of bilingual support teachers has received some attention in the UK (Bourne, 1989; Edwards & Redfern, 1992; Edwards, 1995; Martin-Jones & Saxena, 1997). Teachers and classroom aides who speak the same language as the children are able to offer invaluable support: by asking questions in the common language, they determine if children have understood what they are reading and the exact meaning of any unknown word. They can also encourage inference and help children to 'read between the lines'. Even when there is no bilingual teacher, it is possible to enlist the help of other bilinguals – parents, grandparents, older siblings and even peers (Gregory, 1996; MRC, 1995). In many cases, support of this kind is designed to accelerate children's progress in English rather than to promote biliteracy. When sensitively handled, however, the presence of bilingual support teachers has the potential to both enhance the status of second language learners and increase monolingual children's 'knowledge about language' (DES, 1988).

Another response to linguistic diversity has been the introduction of books in other languages into growing numbers of schools. The earliest arrivals were imported books, most of which were destined for the rapidly burgeoning networks of community schools. More common, however, are dual language texts in English and a range of other languages which were seized upon as something very exciting by monolingual teachers (MRC, 1995; Feuerverger, 1994). Bilingual teachers, however, often felt more cautious. They were better placed to judge features such as the quality of translation. They were also concerned that, as long as there was an English text, bilingual children would have little motivation to read the other language. There were also status issues. For instance, because of problems of access to typesetting or word-processing in non-latin scripts, the second language was all too often handwritten, looking very much the poor relation next to the typeset English text.

PROBLEMS AND DIFFICULTIES

Children from minority cultures clearly have to negotiate a complex course between very different approaches to the written word. A number of areas have emerged as requiring careful thought on the part of those working in multilingual classrooms.

The growing awareness of different literacies, for instance, has important implications for teacher's attitudes towards parents. Traditionally, parents were seen as having little or no part to play in the formal education of their children. More recently, parents who failed to provide the same kinds of literacy experience as the school have been blamed for their children's underachievement and attempts made to train them in school practices. This response is overly simplistic. There is a growing consensus that we need to draw on parents' knowledge and experience to transform what is offered in school rather than trying to transfer school practices to the home.

While our understanding of how this can be achieved is very imprecise, there can be little doubt as to the value of parental involvement. In Britain, Topping & Wolfendale (1985) point to the positive impact of teacher co-operation with parents on children's performance in school. In the USA, Chall & Snow (1982) come to a similar conclusion in a study of more and less successful working class children in grades 2–7. They show how parental involvement in schooling – whether initiated by parents or by teachers – correlated significantly with children's gains in reading over the school year (see also, the review by Auerbach, this volume, of family literacy).

Tizard, Schofield & Hewison (1982) also point to the importance of parental involvement in reading. Half the children chosen at random from two inner city schools in the London borough of Haringey were given books to read to their parents at home. This extra practice produced highly significant improvements in reading, even when their parents were unable to speak English.

More recently, Gregory (1998) argues for the need to move beyond the paradigm of parental involvement in reading. A study of the Bangladeshi community in London suggests that, while many parents may be only minimally involved in reading at home, older siblings often provide finely tuned scaffolding which closely mirrors the reading ability of individual children, combining elements of school and Qur'ānic literacy events.

The knowledge that the school's interpretation of reading is only one among many carries heavy responsibilities for the teacher. When children start school, they bring with them a picture of themselves as learners, based on all that has happened up to this point. It is critical that teachers find ways to acknowledge this pre-school experience. In order to do this, they need to create opportunities for discussing previous activities with children, their parents and others with the same background as the children.

It is useful for the teacher to know, for example, if the child has previously experienced scripts which run from right to left, or left to right; whether the script hangs down from or rests on a real or imaginary line; or whether they are currently learning to read and write the home language in community classes. The importance attached to consulting children and parents not only provides useful information for the school; it also indicates that the teacher appreciates and understands the knowledge which children bring with them to formal education.

If parents and teachers are to work together, teachers must also find ways of making explicit to parents the school's view of what counts as reading. The practices which have evolved over the last thirty years and which reflect our greater understanding of the reading process are not always clear to white middle class parents. Parents who have grown up in different traditions find these practices even more confusing.

FUTURE DIRECTIONS

For many years, the assumption that literacy development consisted simply of acquiring a set of skills – and that this process remains essentially the same from one cultural context to the next – has blinded teachers and researchers to the enormous range of literacy practices and their implications for what takes place in multilingual classrooms. The recent growth in research on social literacies marks a long overdue awakening to the possibilities, and activity in this area is likely to increase for some time to come.

The other hopeful trend lies in the mapping of the practices at home to literacy events in the classroom. As yet we have a very partial view of the ways in which home literacy practices affect children's strategies in learning to read in school, or of the extent to which home learning strategies can be transferred to school.

Research in multilingual classrooms is taking place within a rapidly changing social context. The political agenda in many parts of the world in recent years has shifted the focus from children's biliterate development to the acquisition of the national language. In such an atmosphere, researchers, ability to focus on questions concerning the relationship between children's literacy development in their first and subsequent languages is seriously compromised. Future developments will necessarily be prescribed to some extent by the prevailing political climate.

University of Reading, England

REFERENCES

Allington, R.: 1980, 'Teacher interruption behaviors in primary grade oral reading', *Journal of Educational Psychology* 72, 1–377.
Ashton-Warner, S.: 1963, *Teacher*, Penguin, London (reprinted by Virago, London, 1980).
Baker, C.: 1996, *Foundations of Bilingual Education and Bilingualism*, Multilingual Matters, Clevedon, Avon.
Bourne, J.: 1989, *Moving Into the Mainstream: LEA Provision for Bilingual Pupils*, Windsor: NFER-Nelson.
Canadian Ethnocultural Council: 1988, *The Other Canadian Languages: A Report on the State of Heritage Languages Across Canada*, Canadian Ethnocultural Council, Ottowa.
Cazden, C.: 1988, *Classroom Discourse: The Language of Teaching and Learming*, Heinemann, Portsmouth, New Hampshire.
Chall, J. & Snow, C.: 1982, 'Families and literacy: The contributions of out of school experiences to children's acquisition of literacy', A final report to the National Institution of Education.

Cummins, J.: 1979, 'Linguistic interdependence and the educational development of bilingual children', *Review of Educational Research* 49, 222–251.

Cunningham, P.: 1976–77, 'Teachers' correction responses to black dialect miscues which are non-meaning changing', *Reading Research Quarterly* 12, 637–653.

Department of Education and Science: 1988, *Report of the Committee of Inquiry into the Teaching of English Language* (The Kingman Report), HMSO: London.

Edwards, V.: 1995, *Reading in Multilingual Classrooms*, Reading: Reading and Language Information Centre, University of Reading.

Freire, P.: 1973, *Education: The Practice of Freedom*, Writers and Readers Publishing Co-op, London.

Feuerverger, G.: 1994, 'A multilingual literacy intervention for minority language students', *Language and Education* 8(3), 123–146.

Gibbons, P.: 1991, *Learning to Learn in a Second Language*, Primary English Teaching Association, Newtown, New South Wales.

Goodman, K. & Goodman, Y.: 1978, 'Reading of American children whose language is a stable rural dialect of a language other than English', ERIC ED, pp. 173–754.

Gregory, E.: 1993a, 'Reading between the lines', *Times Educational Supplement*.

Gregory, E.: 1993b, 'Sweet and sour: learning to read in a British and Chinese school', *English in Education* 27(3), 53–59.

Gregory, E.: 1996, *Making Sense of a New World: Learning to Read in a Second Language*, Paul Chapman, London.

Gregory, E.: in press, 'Siblings as mediators of literacy in linguistic minority communities', *Language and Education* 12, 33–54.

Gumperz, J.: 1970, 'Verbal strategies in multilingual communication', in J. Alatis (ed.), *Round-table on Languages and Linguistics 1970*, Georgetown University Press, Washington DC.

Heath, S.B.: 1983, *Ways with words*, Cambridge: Cambridge University Press.

Horvath, B. & Vaughan, P.: 1991, *Community Languages: A Handbook*, Multilingual Matters, Clevedon, Avon.

Martin-Jones, M. & Daxena, M. (eds.): 1997, *Bilingual Support in the Mainstream Classroom*, Multilingual Matters, Clevedon, Avon.

McDermott, R.: 1978, 'Pirandello in the classroom: on the possibility of equal educational opportunity in American culture', in M. Reynolds (ed.), *Futures of Exceptional Children: Emerging Structures*, Council for Exceptional Children, Reston, Va.

McNaughton, S. & Glynn, T.: 1980, 'Behavioural analysis of educational settings', *Current research trends in New Zealand*, New Zealand Association for Research in Education, Delta Research Monographs, no 3.

Moll, L., Estrada, E., Diaz, E. & Lopes, L.: 1980, 'The organisation of bilingual lessons: Implications for Schooling', *Quarterly Newsletter of the Laboratory of Comparative Human Cognition* 2, 53–58.

Multilingual Resources for Children Project (MRC): 1995, *Building Bridges: Multilingual Resources for Children*, Multilingual Matters, Clevedon, Avon.

National Center for Education Statistics: 1993, *The condition of Education, Department of Education*, Office of Educational Research and Improvement, Washington DC.

Spangenberg-Urbschat, K. & Pritchard, R. (eds): 1994, *Kids Come in All Languages: Reading Instruction for ESL Students*, International Reading Association, Newark, Delaware.

Street, B.: 1984, *Literacy in Theory and Practice.* Cambridge: Cambridge University Press.

Tizard, J. Schofield, W. & Hewison, J.: 1982, 'Symposium: reading collaboration between teachers and parents in assisting children's reading', *British Journal of Educational Psychology* 52: 1–15.

Topping, K. & Wolfendale, S. (eds): 1985, *Parental Involvement in Children's Reading*, New York: Nichols.

Wallace, C.: 1985, *Learning to Read in a Multicultural Society: The Social Context of Second Language Literacy*, Pergamon, Oxford.

Williams, J. & Snipper, G.: 1990, *Literacy and Bilingualism*, Longman, New York and London.

Wong, L.Y.-F.: 1991, *The Education of Chinese Children in Britain and the USA*, Multilingual Matters, Clevedon, Avon.

Section 2

Focus on Writing

BARBARA BURNABY

WRITING SYSTEMS AND ORTHOGRAPHIES

Academic discussion of writing systems (grammatology) extends to both detailed descriptions of the mechanics of particular systems and visceral theoretical debates involving linguistics, anthropology, archaeology, sociology, history and psychology. Issues are raised concerning competing views of reality (e.g. Street, 1984, p. 130) and the power of Western thought in relation to non-Western knowledge and its dissemination (e.g. DeFrancis, 1989, p. xi). This review of literature leans towards cross-national and comparative studies, although it is biassed by the writer's limitation to works in English. Under the headings of definitions, typologies, values, first and second language literacy learning, and other factors, it touches the surface of a massive body of work.

WHAT IS A WRITING SYSTEM?

Authors generally agree with Gelb (1963, p. 12) that writing is 'a system of human intercommunication by means of conventional visible marks'. If one construes 'marks' liberally, body sign languages (as in sign languages used by the Deaf) can be included, and the definition encompasses systems such as musical notation and those that indicate kinesics (e.g. Basso & Anderson, 1977). Gauer (1984, p. 14), equating writing with information storage, takes this stance. Many others (e.g. Coulmas, 1989, p. 17) consider as writing only those systems with 'conventional [unambiguous] relation to language' (De Francis, 1989, p. 7). Beneath these distinctions lies debate not only on the primacy of oracy versus literacy, but also on the importance of literacy as 'social practices' (see Street's review, this volume; Stubbs, 1980).

Gelb (1963), followed by Coulmas (1989), DeFrancis (1989) and others, distinguishes 'full writing' systems from their 'forerunners' as having gone beyond pictures/icons and mnemonic devices to a firm relation between symbol and sound.

> A primitive [picture/icon] writing can develop into a full system only if it succeeds in attaching to a sign a phonetic value independent of the meaning which the sign has as a word. This is phonetization, the most important single step in the history of writing. In modern usage this device is called 'rebus writing' (Gelb, 1963, pp. 193–194).

V. Edwards and D. Corson (eds), Encyclopedia of Language and Education,
Volume 2: Literacy, 59–68.
© 1997 Kluwer Academic Publishers. Printed in the Netherlands.

Gelb attaches a developmental directionality to writing systems (p. 210) starting from picture writing through 'word-syllabic' and 'syllabic' to 'alphabetic' systems. With racist overtones, he considers alphabetic writing to have 'conquered the world' (pp. 183–189). Challenges to this position as Euro-centric are discussed below.

Coulmas (1989, pp. 38–39) makes the distinction between: a 'writing system', which 'makes a selection of the linguistic units to be graphically represented' (e.g. syllable writing or phonetic writing); a 'script', which 'makes a specific selection of the possibilities of a given system in accordance with the structural conditions of a given language' (e.g. Chinese script or Arabic script); and 'orthography', which 'makes a specific selection of the possibilities of a script for writing a particular language in a uniform and standardized way' (e.g. Standard German/Swiss German orthography).

DIFFERENT TYPES OF WRITING SYSTEM

Mountford (1996, pp. 627–628) divides writing systems functionally into orthographies, stenographies (shorthands), cryptographies (for concealment), pedographies (for ease of learning a standard orthography), and technographies (scientific tools). However, the bulk of academic discussion (in English at least) on writing systems focusses on the relationship between spoken language and sets of written symbols. Gray (1956, p. 31) uses a typology of characters in writing established in the nineteenth century (Daniels, 1996a, p. 6), arranged 'in order of their historical development'.

1. Word-concept characters, commonly called ideographs (more properly called logographs), as in Chinese. Each character used in writing represents an idea or concept, more strictly a morpheme, i.e. a meaningful linguistic form, rather than a sound. (e.g., 'cheated' has two morphemes, 'cheat' and '-ed', each with its separate meaning)
2. Syllable-sound characters, often called syllabaries, as in Cherokee Indian or Japanese. Each character used represents the sound of a syllable, which may consist of a single phoneme or a group of phonemes. (e.g. 'cheated' has two syllables, each with its own beat in the rhythm of the utterance)
3. Letter-sound characters, as in all alphabetic languages (see also the review by Thompson, this volume). Each letter represents the sound of one, or sometimes more, phonemes or a combination of letters can represent one phoneme, e.g. 'cheated' has five phonemes in English, represented as 'ch', 'ea', 't', 'e', and 'd').

This typology is frequently used but is also frequently disputed. As Gelb (1963, p. 199) notes, 'There are no pure systems of writing just as there are no pure races in anthropology and no pure languages in linguistics'.

Indeed, many authors start with a typology such as that quoted from Gray and then discuss at length why a certain writing system/script does not fit the pattern. For example, Sampson (1985, p. 143) has suggested that the Hangul system for Korean marks features that are finer sound distinctions than phonemes (see also Taylor & Olson, 1995, p. 2).

Concepts in Western literature about non-Western writing systems, specifically Chinese, led DeFrancis (1989, pp. xi–xii, pp. 220ff.) to write a book to correct 'misrepresentations' which, he claims, have created misunderstandings about the nature of all writing systems. He goes to some length to demonstrate the fact that Chinese characters generally convey significant sound-based information and the impact of that fact on writing system theory. Academic literature in English has benefitted enormously by increasing numbers of publications on non-Western writing systems by native speakers (e.g. various authors in Taylor and Olson, 1995). A well-known example of international exchange began with a quote from Halle (1969, p. 18) to the effect that learning Chinese characters is like learning so many telephone numbers. Wang (1980, p. 200) suggested that Halle's comparison was 'to compliment the Chinese for memory feats of which few mortals are capable!'

Taylor & Taylor's (1983, p. 115) solution to such classification problems seems to make sense in light of disputes over (mis)typing of writing systems. They provide a chart on which various writing systems are described as strongly coded, weakly coded or not coded at all for each of the language unit levels of phoneme, syllable, morpheme, word, meaning, and function/content.

WHAT IS A GOOD WRITING SYSTEM?

Hairsplitting over typologies pales in contentiousness beside attempts to assess the value of writing systems. Earlier in this century, reverence for positivism, ethnocentricity, and faith in the power of English were largely unquestioned in Britain and North America. Therefore, it is not surprising that phoneme-oriented orthographies based on linguistic analysis of speech were idealized. As a linguist struggling with the priority society placed on written language over spoken, Bloomfield (1933, p. 21) 'scientifically' pronounced that 'writing is not language, but merely a way of recording language by means of visible marks.' He, along with other would-be reformers of English spelling such as Charles Darwin and William James, 'assume[d] that the deleterious effects of orthographic irregularities on learning to read are obvious and without need of demonstration' (Venezky, 1980, p. 2). Authors more closely involved with designing practical writing systems for 'exotic' languages espoused basic adherence to phonemically based systems (e.g. Lado, 1957, p. 96), but Pike in 1947 encouraged a distinction between technical, practical and scientific orthographies, and

Nida in 1963 indicated that phonemic orthographies should be altered to preserve the forms of morphemes and to reflect as much as possible the orthography of the dominant language of the area (discussed in Stubbs, 1980, p. 95). In 1964, Smalley provides five criteria for an optimal new writing system.

1. maximum motivation for the learner;
2. maximum representation of speech;
3. maximum ease of learning;
4. maximum transfer;
5. maximum ease of reproduction (in Coulmas, 1989, p. 226).

Still, in this intellectual climate where, as Gaur (1995, p. 29) says, 'universal literacy and the alphabet were seen as the panacea for all social, economic and (in countries under colonial rule) political ills', we can again pick up the thread of Gelb's claim that all development in writing systems was in the direction of greater 'phonetization' so that 'the development of a full Greek alphabet, expressing single sounds of language by means of consonant and vowel signs, is the last important step in the history of writing' (1963, p. 184). Also, in the middle of this century, anthropologists were wrestling with a perceived dichotomy between modern and primitive societies (e.g. Lévi-Strauss, 1964). This dichotomy has been variously called the Grand Dichotomy or the Great Divide, and Gelb (1963), for example, devoted a chapter to discussion of 'Modern Writing among Primitives'.

Diringer (1948), McLuhan (1962), Havelock (1976), and Goody & Watt (1968) make links between alphabetic literacy in ancient Greece, popular literacy, democracy, and the rise of major facets of Western civilization such as logic and history; according to Goody & Watt (1968, p. 67) 'it was only when the simplicity and flexibility of later alphabetic writing made widespread literacy possible that for the first time there began to take shape in the Greek world of the seventh century B.C. a society that was essentially literate and that soon established many of the institutions that became characteristic of all later literate societies'. In response to criticisms, Goody (1977) later explicitly distanced himself from the Grand Dichotomy and tried to loosen causal links in his argument between (alphabetic) writing (which he described as a technology of the intellect) and characteristics of modern civilization. Also in this vein, Olson (1977) claimed that (alphabetic) literacy permits a kind of logical competence that is in some way autonomous from the ordinary interpersonal functions of language.

Responses to these various claims about the supposed qualities of alphabetic writing include Graff's 1979 historical study showing that such democratic and economic benefits claimed for literacy do not necessarily follow when lower class people, especially, become literate. Others (e.g., Daniels 1996b, p. 27) point out that an alphabetic system is not the best for some languages because of their structures. Scribner & Cole (1981) teased out distinctions between schooling and literacy to show that literacy has some impact on the intellectual skills of those who are literate but not schooled, but that these skills are not necessarily the kind of logical, autonomous ones predicted by writers such as Olson. Street took Goody and others head on and proposed an 'ideological' model of literacy as grounded in social practice as opposed to the 'autonomous model' which posits an objective capacity of thought as a consequence of literacy. He calls particularly for cross-cultural research rather than attempts at universal theorizing to inform teaching practice (see Street's review, this volume). Finally, Bernal (1987) makes the elaborate case that northern Europeans from the eighteenth century on basically rewrote the history of cultural, intellectual, and linguistic relationships between the Greeks and their Asian and African neighbours of the second millennium B.C. He argues that racism and positivism required Europeans to conceptualize the roots of their civilization in 'Aryan' Greece rather than in Egypt or the Near East. The main thread to his argument rests on Western claims that alphabetic literacy arose in Greece.

HOW DO WRITING SYSTEMS AFFECT LEARNING TO READ IN THE FIRST LANGUAGE?

Oceans of ink have been spilled on issues concerning learning to read (among children especially). Malmquist & Grundin (1980, p. 121) note that research on learning to read is extremely unevenly distributed among different geographical regions of the world; and that very few cross-national studies have been accomplished. For the purposes of this review only cross-orthography studies will be discussed.

Gray's (1956) study of eye-movements of adult readers of fourteen widely different languages/scripts was ground-breaking since, as first of its scope, it helped to dispel unfounded conjecture about differences in reading various writing systems. His conclusion was simple: '(these) studies demonstrate that the general nature of the reading act is essentially the same among all mature readers' (p. 50).

Gillooly (1973) reported on a review of various cross-orthography and Initial Teaching Alphabet (i.t.a., a more phonemic writing system for English than regular English orthography) reading studies. Its conclusions have been borne out in many respects in subsequent research.

1. In the early stages of learning to read (i.e. in the first grade), phonetic writing systems have an advantage over traditional English orthography in terms of greater word recognition skills ...

2. At the intermediate levels (grades four to six) children reading traditional English orthography (rather than a writing system with more simple, direct grapheme-phoneme correspondences) seem to have an advantage in terms of reading speed. This is most likely so because

characteristics of our traditional English orthography (such as the use of graphemic and lexical units) probably encourage children to read larger 'chunks' of printed material (higher-order units) at an earlier age than is so in countries employing a more phonetic writing system.

3. Once reading skill has been acquired (i.e. among mature readers), writing system characteristics no longer seem to exert any appreciable influence on the act of reading.

4. To the extent that reading disabilities are related to writing-system characteristics in the first place, they seem to be more a function of the base of a writing system (i.e., whether it is a syllabary, etc.) than of the writing system's rules of correspondence.

5. Our traditional English writing system seems to be a near-optimal one [sic] for learning to read and, therefore, no basis has been found for the claim by spelling reformers that our traditional English orthography should be modified. (Gillooly, 1973, p. 194)

Downing's (1973) book was a landmark in that it provided English speakers the opportunity to learn about how reading was taught to children in thirteen countries. However, the data in the descriptions were not organized so that direct comparisons of factors could readily be made. His discussion of studies of experiments in teaching reading using the i.t.a. (pp. 221–227) indicate that it seemed to be an advantage to the children using it in *the early grades*.

Kavanagh & Venezky's (1980) collection of articles on orthography, reading and dyslexia had similar drawbacks to Downing's with respect to drawing comparative conclusions about the impact of writing systems on learning to read. The article on Finland by Kyöstiö (1980) confirms earlier findings that regularity of phoneme-grapheme correspondence (for which the writing system for Finnish is famous) is an advantage to the beginning reader but not to the more mature reader.

... the answer to the question of easiness in reading the Finnish language is affirmative as far as mechanical reading is concerned. But if by reading we mean higher level skill, the answer might be the same as in other languages: children have difficulties in comprehension and other more developed skills (p. 49).

In the same volume, Grimes & Gordon (1980) consider the design of new orthographies and conclude that '... [although] orthographies ought to approach some optimum ... an orthography could be considered optimal in terms of one kind of linguistic encoding, without necessarily being optimal in terms of another, or from the standpoint of learnability' (p. 103). An interesting finding, reported by Lukatela and Turvey (1980), indicates that Serbo-Croatian speakers who learn both the Roman and Cyrillic scripts for the language are profoundly influenced by the script they learned first even after many years of using both.

Finally, a collection edited by Taylor & Olson (1995) includes separate discussions of a range of languages and writing systems as well as direct comparisons across orthographies. Major conclusions are generally consistent with those already discussed here. It is noted that children's performance differs according to the script in word recognition and in types of errors, but that they tend to perform similarly when reading text, whatever the orthography. Stevenson (1987, p. 148), from his study comparing U.S., Taiwanese, and Japanese children learning alphabetic, 'logographic', and syllabic scripts, stated 'it is difficult to accept the hypothesis that problems in reading are closely linked to different writing systems.'

The more orthographies tend to reflect language sound rather than meaning, the more disadvantageous they are to speakers of (non-standard) dialects. However, there is some agreement that, while such dialect speakers are somewhat disadvantaged in the early stages of learning to read sound-based orthographies, causes of reading failure are more likely found in other, sociolinguistic issues such as racism or classism (Downing, 1973, ch. 10; Stubbs, 1980, pp. 132–135; Taylor & Taylor, 1983, pp. 365–368). Less comparative attention has been paid to the fact that children's ability to attend to phonemes rather than syllables, as well as other aspects of their language, are not necessarily developed by early school age (Stubbs, 1980, pp. 8–9).

HOW DO WRITING SYSTEMS AFFECT LEARNING TO READ IN A SECOND LANGUAGE?

With respect to learning to read and write in a second language, there seems to be little grounds for concern that learning a different writing system will cause major problems (see also reviews by Viv Edwards, Wilde and Walker, this volume). Venezky (1977) outlines three levels of skills to attend to in transfer to the orthography of a second language: (1) the function of an orthography; (2) types of relationships in the writing system; and (3) specific correspondences for letters. He cites no reasons for serious concern at any of these levels (pp. 48–49). Hornberger (1989, p. 288) created a multidimensional model for the study and description of biliteracy. One of the nine continua that form the model is the 'convergent-divergent scripts continuum'. Reviewing research on this factor, she notes studies in which similarity and difference between the first and second orthography created advantages and disadvantages. She cites Fishman, et al.'s (1985) study of four ethnolinguistic schools in New York which found no significant effects of the different orthographies involved.

WHAT ABOUT EVERYTHING ELSE?

Space limitations have precluded discussion of many other interesting factors relating writing systems to education. For example, the ability to organize written material into 'alphabetical order' is a cornerstone of information processing (O'Connor, 1996). Handwriting and the variations in orthographic symbols (such as capital and lower case letters in Roman alphabets) are widely considered in the literature (see also Walker's review, this volume). These relate in turn to discussion of tools and materials used for writing (e.g. Sirat, 1994). This leads to matters of printing, typewriters, and now computing, all strongly favouring alphabetic systems because of their relatively small numbers of symbols (Daniels, 1996c). We generally fail to appreciate the importance of our writing system(s) in our lives as fish fail to appreciate the role of the water they swim in.

The Ontario Institute for Studies in Education, Canada

REFERENCES

Basso, K.H. & Anderson, N.: 1977, 'A western Apache writing system: The symbols of Silas John', in J.A. Fishman (ed.), *Advances in the Creation and Revision of Writing Systems*, Mouton, The Hague and Paris, 77–104.

Bernal, M.: 1987, *Black Athena: The Afroasiatic Roots of Classical Civilization*, Rutgers University Press, New Brunswick, New Jersey.

Bloomfield, L.: 1933, *Language*, Holt, New York.

Coulmas, F.: 1989, *The Writing Systems of the World*, Basil Blackwell, Oxford.

Daniels, P.T.: 1996a, 'The study of writing systems', in P.T. Daniels & W. Bright (eds.), *The World's Writing Systems*, Oxford University Press, New York, Oxford, pp. 3–17.

Daniels, P.T.: 1996b, 'The first civilizations', in P.T. Daniels & W. Bright (eds), *The World's Writing Systems*, Oxford University Press, New York, Oxford, pp. 21–32.

Daniels, P.T.: 1996c, 'Analog and digital writing', in P.T. Daniels & W. Bright (eds.), *The World's Writing Systems*, Oxford University Press, New York, Oxford, pp. 883–892.

DeFrancis, J.: 1989, *Visible Speech: The Diverse Oneness of Writing Systems*, University of Hawaii Press, Honolulu.

Diringer, D.: 1948, *The Alphabet: A Key to the History of Mankind*, Hutchinson, London and New York.

Downing, J.: 1973, *Comparative Reading: Cross-National Studies of Behavior and Processes in Reading and Writing*, The Macmillan Company, New York and Collier-Macmillan Limited, London.

Gaur, A.: 1995, 'Scripts and writing systems: A historical perspective', in I. Taylor & D.R. Olson (eds.), *Scripts and Literacy: Reading and Learning to Read Alphabets, Syllabaries and Characters*, Kluwer Academic Publishers, Dordrecht, Boston, and London, 19–30.

Gelb, I.J.: 1963, *A Study of Writing* (second edition), University of Chicago Press, Chicago.

Gillooly, W.B.: 1973, 'The influence of writing-system characteristics on learning to read', *Reading Research Quarterly* 8(2), 167–198.

Goody, J.: 1977, *The Domestication of the Savage Mind*, Cambridge University Press, Cambridge, New York, London, and Melbourne.

Goody, J. & Watt, I.: 1968, 'The consequences of literacy', in J. Goody (ed.), *Literacy in*

Traditional Societies, Cambridge University Press, Cambridge, London, New York, New Rochelle, Melbourne, and Sydney, 27–68.

Graff, H.J.; 1979, *The Literacy Myth: Literacy and Social Structure in the 19th Century City*, Academic Press, New York, London.

Gray, W.S.: 1956, *The Teaching of Reading and Writing: An International Survey*, Unesco, Paris and Evans Brothers, London.

Grimes, J.E. & Gordon, R.G. Jr.: 1980, 'Design of new orthographies', in J.F. Kavanagh & R.L. Venezky (eds.), *Orthography, Reading, and Dyslexia*, University Park Press, Baltimore, 93–104.

Halle, M.: 1969, 'Some thoughts on spelling', in K.S. Goodman & J.T. Fleming (eds.), *Psycholinguistics and the Teaching of Reading*, International Reading Association, Newark, New Jersey, 17–24.

Havelock, E.A.: 1976, *Origins of Western Literacy*, Ontario Institute for Studies in Education, Toronto.

Hornberger, N.H.: 1989, 'Continua of Biliteracy', *Review of Educational Research* 59(3), 271–296.

Kavanagh, J.F. & Venezky, R.L.: 1980, *Orthography, Reading, and Dyslexia*, University Park Press, Baltimore.

Kyöstiö, O.K.: 1980, 'Is learning to read easy in a language in which the grapheme-phoneme correspondences are regular?', in J.F. Kavanagh & R.L. Venezky (eds.), *Orthography, Reading, and Dyslexia*, University Park Press, Baltimore, 35–50.

Lado, R.: 1957, *Linguistics Across Cultures*, University of Michigan Press, Ann Arbor, Michigan.

Lévi-Strauss, C.: 1964, *Le cru et le cuit*, Librairie Plon, Paris.

Lukatela, G. & Turvey, M.T.: 1980, 'Some experiments on the Roman and Cyrillic alphabets of Serbo-Croatian', in J.F. Kavanagh & R.L. Venezky (eds.), *Orthography, Reading and Dyslexia*, University Park Press, Baltimore, 227–247.

Malmquist, E. & Grundin, H.U.: 1980, 'Cross-national studies on primary reading', in J.F. Kavanagh & R.L. Venezky (eds.), *Orthography, Reading, and Dyslexia*, University ParkPress, Baltimore, 121–133.

McLuhan, M.: 1962, *The Gutenberg Galaxy: The Making of Typographic Man*, University of Toronto, Press, Toronto.

Mountford, J.: 1996, 'A functional classification', in P.T. Daniels & W. Bright (eds.), *The World's Writing Systems*, Oxford University Press, New York, Oxford, 627–632.

O'Connor, M.: 1996, 'The alphabet as technology', in P.T. Daniels & W. Bright (eds.), *The World's Writing Systems*, Oxford University Press, New York, Oxford, pp. 787–794.

Olson, D.R.: 1977, 'From utterance to text: The bias of language in speech and writing', *Harvard Educational Review* 47(3), 257–281.

Sampson, G.: 1985, *Writing Systems: A Linguistic Approach*, Hutchinson, London.

Scribner, S. & Cole, M.: 1981, *The Psychology of Literacy*, Harvard University Press, Cambridge, Massachusetts and London, England.

Stevenson, H.W.: 1987, 'Children's problems in learning to read Chinese, Japanese and English', in D.A. Wagner (ed.), *The Future of Literacy in a Changing World*, Pergamon Press, Oxford, New York, Beijing, Frankfurt, Sao Paulo, Sydney, Tokyo, and Toronto.

Sirat, C.: 1994, 'Handwriting and the writing hand', in W.C. Watt (ed.), *Writing Systems and Cognition: Perspectives from Psychology, Physiology, Linguistics and Semiotics*, Kluwer Academic Publishers, Dordrecht, Boston, and London, 375–460.

Stevenson, H.W.: 1987, 'Children's problems in learning to read Chinese, Japanese and English', in D.A. Wagner (ed.), *The Future of Literacy in a Changing World*, Pergamon Press, Oxford, New York, Beijing. Frankfurt, Sao Paulo, Sydney, Tokyo and Toronto, 131–150.

Stubbs, M.: 1980, *Language and Literacy: The Sociolinguistics of Reading and Writing*, Routledge & Kegan Paul, London, Boston, and Henley.

Taylor, I. & Olson, D.: 1995, *Scripts and Literacy: Reading and Learning to Read Alphabets, Syllabaries and Characters*, Kluwer Academic Publishers, Dordrecht, Boston, and London.

Taylor, I. & Taylor, M.M.: 1983, *The Psychology of Reading*, Academic Press, New York and London.

Venezky, R.L.: (1977), 'Principles for the design of practical writing systems', in J.A. Fishman (ed.), *Advances in the Creation and Revision of Writing Systems*, Mouton, The Hague, Paris, 37–73.

Wang, W.S.-Y.: 1980, 'Review of Winnifred P. Lehman, ed. *Language in the People's Republic of China* (Austin: University of Texas Press, 1975)', *Language* 56(1), 197–202.

NIGEL HALL

THE DEVELOPMENT OF YOUNG CHILDREN AS AUTHORS

Writing is a very complex process; it involves the orchestration of a range of elements – the physical creation of the text, organisation of the sound/symbol correspondences, control over linguistic structure – all of which are directed to the ultimate purpose of writing, the composition of a meaningful and purposeful text for a communicative situation. People do not learn to write in order to spell, handwrite or punctuate; while important, these are tools for the effective construction and presentation of written language and as such are areas dealt with in other reviews in this volume. People write because they have messages to send, ideas to record, and thoughts to clarify. These texts need to be composed, and it is the process of composition that in this review is called authorship. This review concentrates on how young children learn, and are taught, to compose meaningful texts; in other words how young children become authors.

HISTORICAL PERSPECTIVES ON YOUNG CHILDREN'S AUTHORSHIP

The notion of children, especially young children, as 'authors' is a relatively recent phenomenon in the history of teaching writing. That what young children wrote could be granted the status of authorship would have seemed nonsensical to most Western teachers even one hundred years ago. Learning to write did not involve authorship; it meant many years practising some of the sub-skills of writing, handwriting and spelling, rather than creating one's own texts. There were major two assumptions at work.

The first, and obvious, one was that being fluent in these sub skills was a necessary precondition to being able to function as an author. Brinsley in *Ludus literarius*, written in 1612, said that pupils should:

> have first the most excellent patterns, and never to rest until they
> have the very patterns in their heads, and as it were ever before
> their eyes (p. 209).

The second assumption was that even if young children had been able to compose their own texts, they did not have the capacity to write anything worth reading. Brinsley also wrote that if children relied too much at first on their own 'invention in making Epistles, Theames, Verses, disputing' then

V. Edwards and D. Corson (eds), Encyclopedia of Language and Education, Volume 2: Literacy, 69–76.
© *1997 Kluwer Academic Publishers. Printed in the Netherlands.*

the resultant work will be 'nothing but froth, childishnesse and uncertaintie' (p. 210).

Both these assumptions had underpinned writing instruction since the times of the Ancient Greeks (Welch, 1990) and moves away from them have proceeded very slowly indeed. Within the Western world far fewer people ever learned to write than learned to read. Teaching methodologies stressed learning by rote, imitation, repetition, variation, paraphrasing, transposition, constant practice and complete accuracy (Michael, 1987).

When those few children who did learn to write finally started to explore how texts could be ordered and structured, they studied 'composition', which was primarily concerned with understanding a range of tightly defined rhetorical rules. The rhetorical rules were strict and demanded as much obedience, copying and imitation as did earlier experiences of writing. Young children were, therefore confined to lives of repetitious, skill-based exercises in which exactness was the primary aim.

Three hundred years after Brinsley, not much seems to have changed. The British Board of Education in 1900 published schedules for each age group which made it clear that it was not until children were in Standard 6 (twelve years old) that they would compose 'a short theme or letter on an easy subject'. At earlier ages they were expected to copy (age seven), write from dictation (age eight to ten) and write from memory (age eleven). Shayer (1972) comments that in 1920 it was still the case that the pupil was 'always expected to imitate, copy or reproduce' (p. 10). Even in the 1980s in the UK, a range of inspector's reports criticised schools for relying far too much narrow writing activities: 'Copying from workbooks and cards occupied too great a part of the time of some 5 and 6 year olds' (DES, 1982).

CHALLENGES TO CONVENTIONAL ASSUMPTIONS

The absolute faith in the two assumptions outlined earlier had been consistently challenged, albeit often by minority voices. A few authors had began to acknowledge that there were virtues in allowing younger writers to express themselves freely. John Rice 1765 wrote in *An introduction to the art of reading with energy and propriety*:

> No Matter: let the ill Construction of their Language and Impropriety of their Sentiments, be gradually corrected together: By which Means they may also acquire a Stile, or Method of expressing themselves on any Subject with Ease, and in their own way.

During the next one hundred and fifty years sentiments of this kind became more frequent. By the early twentieth century in the UK and USA, there was major opposition, from educationalists, teachers, and others to the restrictive notions of authorship that dominated the teaching of writing. These objections were partly fuelled by the failures of children to achieve competent authorship under this restrictive system, but it was also the case that the development of self-expression as a major force in young children's writing was influenced by recent psychological and philosophical ideas about childhood, learning and emotions.

As these criticisms grew, and as the arguments became more influential, so tensions arose which continue today to be a central features of discussion about teaching writing. Narrow, prescriptive approaches guaranteed an appearance of success in the early stages, while allowing children freedom of expression from the start was inevitably going to mean less accuracy. Equally, differences in notions of what counted as writing meant that measuring success was not simple. If writing was conceived solely as the acquisition of a set of narrow skills, then success could be measured relatively easily. If, on the other hand, writing was viewed as a range of complex textual skills, then measurement became more difficult.

For most of the twentieth century, prescriptivism has been in retreat, moving away from narrow curriculum practices and expectations, towards valuing children's voices in writing (see also the review by Owocki & Goodman, this volume). However, while older children gained more freedom, younger children were still seen as requiring some basics before they embarked on careers as authors. The age at which children were treated as capable of authorship steadily decreased through the century but, nevertheless, the beginning writer was still believed to need control over handwriting and spelling before authorship could be considered. Teachers became aware of the need to provide young writers with a better sense of involvement and purpose, and began to value their words, using what was generally known as a Language Experience Approach. In this, beginning writers dictated their texts to teachers who wrote them down, leaving the children to add illustrations (Goddard, 1974). Children's words could be now be related to their interests and concerns. For young children writing could at last be seen as a meaning-making activity.

THE DISCOVERY OF YOUNG CHILDREN'S AUTHORSHIP

Up until this point, notions about children's authorship, and beliefs about children's authorial capabilities had been dictated almost solely by the teaching methodologies. However, important psychological and philosophical shifts were taking place in the definition of writing, and in the conceptualisation of young children's literacy abilities. In the 1970s a range of studies were taking place which were leading to a reconceptualisation of the role which young children took in developing knowledge about literacy. Work by Ferreiro and Teberosky (1983), in particular, demonstrated that even the youngest children were not passive absorbers of school teaching, but were actively engaged in reading the world and building hypotheses about how it worked.

The most significant manifestation of this shift came with a study on spelling by Read (1963). Apart from the consequences for spelling, which were considerable (see Wilde's review in this volume), the pre-school children whom Read saw constructing theories about how the spelling system worked, were using their knowledge to write meaningful texts. When Bissex's young son Paul engaged her attention by writing R U DF (Are you deaf?) he was demonstrating that accurate control of handwriting and accurate knowledge of spelling were not preconditions for the generation of meaningful and relevant texts (Bissex, 1970). Probably for the first time ever, the development of authorship and the development of knowledge about the structural aspects of writing, could run side by side.

Just how significant were all these paradigm shifts for writing can be judged by briefly considering the extent of research into, and writing about, the development of children as composers of written text. From the 1970s onwards there has been an explosion of studies into young children's writing. At first these were mostly about spelling development but through 1980s the focus moved on from how young children constructed knowledge about spelling to what they could do with their writing.

THREE APPROACHES TO THE DEVELOPMENT OF AUTHORSHIP

A major set of contributors to this shift have been Donald Graves and his co-workers in New Hampshire, USA (Graves, 1983, 1994; Calkins, 1983, 1994). The approach of Graves, which has become known popularly as the 'process approach', became very influential in English-speaking countries. It was one in which children were from the start treated as authors. In doing so Graves was arguing that they had capabilities as meaning makers, and the task of the teacher was to help children learn how written texts could be bought under their control through processes of rehearsal, drafting, revision, editing and publishing; in other words, similar experiences to those that almost all writers go though in constructing a written text. The children learn to control these processes through participating in workshop sessions, often called writer's workshops, in which they wrote, shared with fellow authors, and refined their texts. The teacher's role was to listen to the children, learn from them, and create condition under which authorship could flourish. It is only relatively recently that Graves has acknowledged that less was said about teaching children: 'I think we now know better when to step in, when to teach, and when to expect more of our students' (Graves, 1994, p. xvi).

This movement has been incredibly successful, has undoubtedly been the dominant one of recent years, and has certainly contributed in a major way to the revaluation of young children's competence as authors; a revaluation which has led to many young children having very positive early experiences of becoming authors. However, the emphasis was certainly on the validity of personal experience and the nature of the general processes of authorship, and less attention was paid to the nature of texts, how instruction might facilitate learning about authorship and what, in specific ways, might count as development in authorship.

Authorship is a notoriously difficult concept to define. Kress rejects out of hand many qualities often referred to as part of authorship on the basis that they are qualities and are 'not about writing' (Kress, 1982). Thus according to Kress, 'novelty', 'individuality', 'emotion', 'imagination' and 'dynamism' describe qualities rather than writing, and, additionally, they are almost impossible to measure. Indeed, the original authors of the British National Curriculum wrote, 'The best writing is vigorous, committed, honest and interesting' (DES 1989, para 17.31) but then proceeded to exclude these qualities because they could not be fitted into a developmental programme. It seems that if it cannot be measured, then it cannot be used – even if such qualities represent the 'best' writing.

Resolving these issues has been a major focus of a group of writing researchers in Australia, often called the genre theorists (for an account of the development of this group, see Cope et al., 1993 and see the review by Freedman & Richardson in Volume 6). They have been severe critics of process writing and have argued that it is not sufficient that children enjoy writing and are encouraged to become reflective about their writing, but that the complexities of writing need to be taught to children. The genre theorists come from a linguistic tradition, and seeking to make explicit the ways in which language, both oral and written, works is a critical concern of their approach. Thus, they wanted to establish a sounder linguistic base for analysing both how texts work and what children do as they author texts.

There were a number of reasons for their criticism of process approaches. One was that there had been a concentration on narrative and autobiographical writing, rather than with the whole range of texts used in written communication. Although this has been denied by those behind the process movement, the evidence of their books would suggest that the criticism is certainly partially valid. Another criticism was that while children were engaging pleasurably with authoring texts, the teachers, by adopting what Halliday has termed 'benevolent inertia', were not providing the children with the tools which would enable them to explicitly analyse what they were doing when they wrote. Without this conscious perception of text, it was claimed that children could not develop as writers. For the genre theorists there was a clear role for intervention to give children the means to understand how text construction works. As a consequence, the tasks the genre theorists set themselves were to develop descriptions of different forms of text, and to develop a pedagogical model for teaching writing which would enable progress in authorship to occur and be identified.

It is this last ambition which has proved the most controversial. The claim has been made that the genre-based approach 'did not want simply to dismantle all the progressivists' language and educational theory, or all the teaching methodologies which had preceded it. Instead it sought to build on progressivism's insights, while learning from its mistakes' (Cope et al., 1993). Nevertheless, some members of the genre group have been concerned about the dangers of prescriptivism, when assessment monitors solely the ability to copy a fixed generic structure.

While it is uncertain whether the genre theorists have had much influence with their pedagogic model outside Australia, it is certainly the case that around the English speaking world the experiences of writing offered to even the youngest children have begun to encompass a far richer variety of written forms than ever before. It has also become clear that young children are interested in this wider range of forms, and can experience success in using them (Newkirk, 1989; Hall & Robinson, 1995).

PRESENT AND FUTURE DIRECTIONS

All the perspectives on authorship discussed so far have been driven by what has been termed system immanence, seeing children as part of movement to something else – 'better' authorship – rather than viewing young children's writing as something of interest in its own right. This does not mean that researchers and teachers had no concern for, or interest in, children's writing, but that it was seen essentially as a stage in development. Thus even when young children's writing development was studied more systematically through linguistic analyses (Harpin, 1976; Perera, 1984) the results tended to highlight limitations rather than reveal the successes with the complexity of what was being accomplished.

A more recent, and increasingly influential, perspective on young children's authorship examines more closely what young children actually do when they author texts. It starts from the belief that authorship is not a neutral process but is grounded in wider social ideologies and practices, and that in using print to mediate their lives, young children are strategic in using knowledge from a range of sources to orchestrate what seems an effective textual response to a social situation. This ability to be strategic is often destroyed by more conventional literacy practices, which tend to treat literacy as a fixed entity rather than something which is socially situated. This view claims that young children's authorship is a social semiotic process in which they draw on a range of meaning-making systems to represent their meanings. Thus oral language, art, music, writing, gesture, etc., are not treated as distinct and discrete systems, but as manifestations of an underlying semiotic unity. Harste, Burke and Woodward

(1984) were the first to explore young children's orchestration of systems as they wrote, and more recently evidence from studies by Dyson (1989 and 1993), Daiute (1989), Hubbard (1989) and Rowe (1994) has shown how the use of these different semiotic systems is intimately grounded in the child's life-worlds, and cultural positions. Thus, development as an author, 'involves learning to communicate using multimodal cue complexes and associated meanings of one's interpretive community' (Rowe, p. 22).

Thus, even at the very earliest stages of becoming an author children are involved in complex processes in which the construction of socially embedded meanings is the central focus. These processes may not be easily identifiable with more conventional writing beginnings, but they reveal very clearly that authorship is not a state that is achieved after the acquisition of knowledge about the writing system; it could, perhaps, more accurately be described as the driving force behind the development of technical competence.

The topic of young children's authorship has, during the last thirty years, emerged from obscurity to a position where it has a dynamic place in research and practice. There has been an astonishing growth of research and publication in the field, something which reflects increased interest in the subject of writing itself. It is an energetic area of enquiry which is having to address itself to a wider range of issues than ever before, in particular the potential impact on writing development of modern computer technologies. The consequence of this research for teachers is that they can better aid the development of young children's authorship through being informed by sounder linguistic, social and psychological knowledge about authorship. For children the consequence is that the experience of becoming an author has the potential to be enjoyable and to be personally and socially relevant; for, as Sperling (1996) put it,

> Students' theories about writers, texts, and readers are constructed in large part through the kinds of writing they are asked to do, the ways in which their writing tasks are structured, and the ways in which their writing function in the classrooms (p. 55).

The result of the last thirty years' study of young children's authorship is that the theories about the nature of authorship held by children today clearly have the potential to be radically different from those that could be held by children one hundred years ago.

Manchester Metropolitan University, England

REFERENCES

Bissex, G.: 1980, *Gnys At Wrk: A Child Learns to Read and Write*, Harvard University Press, Cambridge, Mass.

Calkins, L.: 1983, *Lessons from a Child: on the Teaching and Learning of Writing*, Heinemann Educational Books, Portsmouth, New Hampshire.

Calkins, L.: 1994, *The Art of Teaching Writing*, Heinemann Educational Books, Portsmouth, New Hampshire.

Cope, B., Kalantzis, M., Kress, G., Martin, P. & Murphy, L.: 1993, 'Bibliographical essay: Developing the theory and practice of genre-based literacy', in B. Cope & M. Kalantzis (eds.), *The Powers of Literacy: A Genre Approach to Teaching Writing*, Falmer Press, London, 1992, 231–247.

Daiute, C.: 1989, 'Play as thought: Thinking strategies of young writers', *Harvard Educational Review* 59, 1–23.

Department of Education and Science (DES): 1982, *Education 5–9: An Illustrative Survey of 80 First Schools in England*, HMSO, London.

Department of Education and Science (DES): 1989, *English 5–16*, HMSO, London.

Dyson, A.: 1989, *Multiple Worlds of Child Writers: Friends Learning to Write*, Teachers College Press, New York.

Dyson, A.: 1993, *Social Worlds of Children Learning to Write in an Urban Primary School*, Teachers College Press, New York.

Ferreiro, E. and Teberosky, A.: 1983, *Literacy Before Schooling*, Heinemann Educational Books, Portsmouth, New Hampshire.

Goddard, N.: 1974, *Literacy: Language Experience Approaches*, Macmillan, London.

Graves, D.: 1983, *Writing: Teachers and Children at Work*, Heinemann Educational Books, Portsmouth, New Hampshire.

Graves, D.: 1994, *A Fresh Look at Writing*, Heinemann Educational Books, Portsmouth, New Hampshire.

Hall, N. and Robinson, A.: 1995, *Exploring Writing and Play in the Early Years*, David Fulton, London.

Harpin, W.: 1976, *The Second 'R': Writing Development in the Junior School*, Unwin Educational Books, London.

Harste, J., Woodward, V. and Burke, C.: 1994, *Language Stories and Literacy Lessons*, Heinemann Educational Books, Portsmouth, New Hampshire.

Hubbard, R.: 1989, *Authors of Pictures: Draughtsmen of Words*, Heinemann Educational Books, Portsmouth, New Hampshire.

Kress, G.: 1982, *Learning to Write*, Routledge, London.

Michael, I.: 1987, *The Teaching of English from the Sixteenth Century to 1970*, Cambridge University Press, Cambridge.

Newkirk, T.: 1989, *More than Stories: The Range of Children's Writing*, Heinemann Educational Books, Portsmouth, New Hampshire.

Perera, K.: 1984, *Children's Writing and Reading: Analysing Classroom Language*, Blackwell, Oxford.

Read, C.: 1970, 'Pre-school children's knowledge of English phonology', *Harvard Educational Review* 41, 1–34.

Rowe, D.: 1984, *Preschoolers as Authors: Literacy Learning in the Social World of the Classroom*, Hampton Press, New Jersey.

Shayer, M.: 1972, *The Teaching of English in Schools 1900–1970*, Routledge and Kegan Paul, London.

Sperling, M.: 1996, 'Revisiting the writing-speaking connection: Challenges for research on writing and writing instruction', *Review of Educational Research* 66, 53–86.

Welch, K.: 1990, 'Writing instruction in ancient Athens after 450 BC.', in J. Murphy (ed.), *A Short History of Writing Instruction from Ancient Greece to Twentieth Century America*, Hemagoras Press, California, 1990, 1–17.

GRETCHEN M. OWOCKI & YETTA M. GOODMAN

THE TEACHING OF WRITING

Children develop written language as they internalize and make sense of the literate actions, routines, and values of the members of their socio-cultural communities. As they experience literacy in their social worlds, they develop personal concepts about written language, and personal commitments to the various forms and functions that written language takes. Because unique literacy histories are the result of different children experiencing different environments, teachers must respond to the varied knowledge and varied ways of knowing that are a part of every classroom literacy event.

EARLY DEVELOPMENTS

The literature on language arts instruction dates back 2,500 years (Squire, 1991), but the ways in which we teach writing today have been predominately shaped by events of the twentieth century. Historically, writing instruction focused on penmanship and spelling for young children, and grammar and usage for older children. Teachers were overseers and drill-masters (Shannon, 1990). Schools were organized so that children in a grade received the same instruction at the same time. This reflected the belief that children would learn to write in a formal school setting where they could be taught in a step-by-step manner. It also reflected the ways in which the needs of teachers were then perceived; because many had little or no teacher-training, educational leaders believed that a pre-formulated curriculum was necessary to guide their teaching.

Although Pestalozzi, Froebel, and Montessori had as early as the 1800s been advocating for less controlled, child-centered classrooms, it was not until the early part of the twentieth century that their ideas began to spread. In the early 1900s, John Dewey and colleagues at the University of Chicago began exploring how learning to read and write could 'be carried on with everyday experience and occupation as their background and ... in such a way that the child shall feel their necessity through their connection with subjects which appeal to him on their own account' (1899, p. 153). Throughout the early 1900s, Dewey called for a democratic, experience-based education in which teachers would learn about the physical, historical, economic, and occupational conditions of the local community and use them as educational resources.

V. Edwards and D. Corson (eds), Encyclopedia of Language and Education,
Volume 2: Literacy, 77–85.
© *1997 Kluwer Academic Publishers. Printed in the Netherlands.*

MAJOR CONTRIBUTIONS

Until the early 1900s, research on writing as composing was scarce. Phillip Hartog's publication of *The Writing of English* in 1907 is cited by Wilkinson (1985) as an early contribution of major significance. Hartog, influenced by his visits to French schools, emphasized the importance of writing as a means of recording one's own observations, exploring thoughts, and developing the ability to clearly convey ideas. Function and audience were viewed as essential considerations in classroom writing. This piece provided early support for holistic practices in writing instruction.

During the early 1900s, major educational committees began to recommend more holistic practices as well. In 1914, for example, the United Kingdom Board of Education recommended that composition be practiced both orally and in written form, and that children record their own ideas. This was an endeavor to escape from a test-dominated, teacher-dominated model of instruction in which students reproduced the ideas of teachers and texts, wrote without oral language, and worked with material chosen by the teacher (Dixon, 1991).

In 1935 in the United States, the National Council of Teachers of English (NCTE) published *An Experience Curriculum in English*, edited by W. Wilbur Hatfield. A most influential document (Squire, 1991), this work emphasized both creative and utilitarian experiences in and through literature and language. Professional leaders began to explore this notion of experience, integrating the language arts into classroom activities.

Around this time, Alvina Treut Burrows, who began studying children's writing in the United States in the 1930s, was finding that it is within the function of communication that writing provides 'a responsive, satisfying audience' and empowers children 'to manipulate their characters with authority instead of always being the recipients of authority' (Burrows 1952, p. 135). With three other teachers, Burrows (Ferebee, Jackson, Saunders, & Treut, 1939) argued that in personal writing, aspects such as spelling and penmanship were less important than getting ideas on paper. When purpose suggested a need for clarity and correctness, children could experiment with different means of expression and organization. Although these and other progressive ideas were not initially implemented on a widespread basis, they were leading to changes in thinking and practice.

In the 1950s in the United States, the notion of a curriculum which integrated reading, writing, speaking, and listening was made popular by an NCTE commission headed by Dora V. Smith. Elementary teachers picked up on the term language arts (as opposed to English) because it suggested an integration of skills with experiences rather than skills taught in isolation (Squire, 1991).

In New Zealand, country-school teacher Elwyn Richardson's book *In the Early World* was published in 1964. Richardson described the ways in which he learned about teaching from his students and reflected on the ways in which his teaching eventually evolved into allowing students to pursue and share a variety of their own topics of interest. Richardson's book is still referred to in innovative publications (such as Learning Media, 1992) today.

In describing British teaching practices of the 1960s, Featherstone wrote to an American audience that writing and talking were important parts of the reading program. "Writing is a good way to learn, because emphasis on written expression makes it more likely that children will build on the mastery of the language they already possess. . . . Writing can't be taught in isolation, as a separate subject. In order to write, there must be something to write about. There have to be books of all sorts . . . and talk" (1969, p. 20).

James Moffett published *Teaching the Universe of Discourse* in 1968, which characterized learning as developmental, corresponding with intellectual and emotional growth. Moffett argued that children naturally learn language, and naturally learn through language, and emphasized English as a discourse, whether thought, spoken, or written. Around this time, Britton (1972) was also arguing that composing processes should be integrated with reading and speaking. Children at school should have the opportunity to refine and use language through the integration of reading, writing, playing, and reflecting on ideas. Moffett's and Britton's works have led to a wide body of research focusing on writing as an integrated, developmental process: in 1971, Janet Emig conducted a study of high-schoolers' writing, notable for its emphasis on composing processes (rather than the products of these efforts). In 1975, Donald Graves conducted related research with elementary students. Shaughnessy (1977), Murray (1982), Calkins (1983), and Dyson (1989) are some of the scholars who have supported and elaborated on the research in this area.

Writing as composing continues to become a major emphasis in schools (see also the review by Hall, this volume). Contemporary researchers and educators focus on the ways in which writing develops over time and is naturally integrated with other symbol systems. Writing is no longer viewed as something to be taught through grammar, spelling, and penmanship drills. When children have the opportunity to write, they actively develop and test hypotheses about written language as they construct meaning in their social worlds.

WORK IN PROGRESS

Children learn to write by writing (Featherstone, 1968; Goodman, 1992). When they first experience writing in their homes and communities, it is embedded in contexts that provide clues to its meanings. Family members are doing homework, writing grocery lists, or preparing notes for the next day at work. They are writing notes to preschool teachers, applying for drivers' licenses, and balancing checkbooks. Young children write their names on their pictures, post signs on their doors, and write letters to grandparents or friends. This writing in context makes it natural for children to generate hypotheses about the ways in which written language works. As they move through early childhood, continually testing their hypotheses, they begin to extract from the complex system of written language, the fundamentals that are necessary for communication. Their experiences with written language in social contexts are what lead to their knowledge of the specific features and the nature of the English language. When children come to school, they write with new people, in new contexts. Teachers organize their classrooms so that writing experiences extend and build on home knowledge, but provide opportunities for children to transact with new people in new ways. Always, learning takes place within context. As children write, teachers encourage talking, drawing, reading, and sociodramatic play, knowing that multiple symbol systems grow together, and provide a context that makes written language make sense. For example, rereading a story while dramatizing helps children fill in gaps in their story line, or clarify their language by reorganizing words, sentences, spellings, or punctuation. Illustrating a story gives children further ideas for writing and helps them express their meaning. Writing evolves within and is shaped by children's transactions with a variety of people through a variety of symbol systems (Dyson, 1989). 'People learn to write correctly by writing, not by plowing through mountains of workbooks' (Featherstone, 1968, p. 125).

Learning to write involves experimentation, risk-taking, and inventing new forms of writing. Experimentation is playing with different genres and functions, trying out new styles of writing, inventing spellings, exploring new uses of punctuation (Hall, 1996), or different word choices. As children experiment with written language, they elaborate their hypotheses, overcome conflicts, search for regularities in the system, and continually attach meaning to their own and others' written texts (Ferreiro & Teberosky, 1982). Risk-taking is central to experimentation. It is a strategy which allows children to try out new ideas and work through their hypotheses. Children who are pushed too quickly to write conventionally, or whose inventions are not treated as real literacy events, often become afraid to take risks, and begin to depend on others to answer their literacy-related questions. (Harste, Burke, & Woodward, 1981). Concepts about written language develop as children encounter inconsistencies within their personal systems or find that their writing does not allow them to effectively communicate, and then use social experiences and their own linguistic knowledge to revise these inconsistencies. A fear of being wrong does not facilitate this process. Teachers effectively respond to children's writing by encouraging risk-taking so that they learn from the consequences of the decisions they make while writing. They help children reflect on their own ideas, and continuously find teachable moments to sensitively provide an adult perspective.

Effective teachers know that when writers focus their attention on ideas, their concern is with getting words on paper rather than getting words right. Because children need to feel the flow of producing text (Meek, 1982) and also need to develop conventions, teachers involve them in the composing process. In this process, children discuss ideas, arrange them on paper, then edit or proofread, seeking out their writing miscues. Over time, teachers and children identify the miscues that are most important, and focus on moving those toward convention. They conference throughout the year, and rather than discussing all miscues, or all questions of clarity, one or two issues are addressed at a time (Murray, 1982).

Learning to write involves using written language to meet needs in academic and non-academic areas. Writing in both of these areas helps children develop control over the variety of functions and genres that written language takes, and helps them recognize the writing they do as writing. Britain's Bullock (1975) Report, *A Language for Life*, recommended that schools have organized policies for the use of language across the curriculum. By writing what they have learned about specific content in social studies, science, or math, children expand not only their cultural knowledge, but also their knowledge about writing. Teachers develop a sensitivity to the possibilities for writing by identifying the areas of the curriculum and the peripheral occasions where writing is frequent and by legitimizing the kinds of non-school writing they do (Wille, 1980). They help children widen their range of writing by offering opportunities to write for real audiences, discussing the nature of different kinds of writing, and giving feedback on efficacy and purpose (Wray, Bloom, & Hall, 1989).

A sound writing curriculum reflects the unique linguistic and cultural experiences of students by providing them with opportunities to make decisions about what to write. Because children have unique backgrounds and areas of expertise, and are differently committed to genres, topics, and functions, teachers offer opportunities to develop writing in their areas of experience and interest. 'A child is apt to be interested in what he has to say even though primers and beginning books bore him; there is less class or racial bias in his own material, and the vocabulary will be suitable, because it's his own' (Featherstone, 1968, p. 23).

Biliterate children need authentic opportunities to write in their second language (see also, the review by Viv Edwards on 'Writing in multilingual classrooms, this volume). They should also continue to write in their first language. Proficiency in the first language influences the rate of development as well as the proficiency of the second language because both build upon a mutual underlying base (Padilla et al., 1991), and children

naturally transfer knowledge from language to language (Trueba, 1991).
Writing in any language should focus first on making meaning.

Children easily learn to write with teachers who understand the factors
that influence writing and organize rich literacy environments that support
their learning. A rich environment includes reading and writing materials
that are accessible and relevant to children. Teachers, children, and family
members contribute to a classroom full of all sorts of books, magazines,
newspapers, reference materials, and displays of children's writing. Lined
and plain paper, empty booklets, pencils, crayons, and markers are available. Instructions for games, science projects, listening centers, feeding
classroom pets and using the word-processor are on hand. Younger children have access to materials such as post-office forms, receipts, coupons,
and packages from household products. Opportunities for writing telephone messages, shopping lists, menus, and medical prescriptions are
embedded in play experiences. The teacher who understands the factors
that influence writing creates a rich environment for writing, and observes
children to understand how they can be supported in their development.

PROBLEMS AND DIFFICULTIES

From the beginning of the century, researchers and composition scholars
have demonstrated that with the opportunity to write in a supportive, holistic context, children use their linguistic and cultural knowledge to develop
complex systems of written language. A focus on spelling, penmanship
and grammar in many schools raises a number of issues. First, it suggests
that there is still confusion regarding how children learn to write. It is not
universally understood that children learn to write through authentic experiences with writing. Second, for some it feels risky to set children free
to write if they have not mastered correct form. As teachers explore the
use of teachable moments, relevant mini-lessons, and children constructing knowledge together, they realize that holistic instruction does promote
children's development of the conventions of written language.

It may also be that experiences that allow for critical writing are not
readily accessible in schools. Organizing a classroom writing curriculum
that focuses on authentic issues and involves children in writing in powerful genres requires creative thinking on the part of teachers. For many
teachers, this is accomplished with minimal difficulty by discovering with
children the social concerns that they find important and worth pursuing.
Writing instruction is built into inquiring into real-world issues. In some
classrooms children operate a publishing center or are responsible for the
publication of a school newspaper. Others run a schoolwide post-office
or develop a library that can be used by other classrooms. Some children
write letters to the editors of newspapers, petition government officials,
or participate in organizing community clean-up efforts. Others take an

interest in environmental issues, cruelty to animals, or child-labor laws. As children learn about the world through these activities, they also learn about writing in varied and powerful genres.

Another difficulty that schools are confronted with is the impact of simplistic views of language instruction that are promoted by politically motivated forces. Standardized writing tests, spelling workbooks, handwriting kits, and other commercial packages are multi-million dollar efforts, but often are not based on scientific understandings about the ways in which children develop written language (see also the review by Luke, this volume). To teach writing, teachers do not need prescriptions for writing topics, questions to ask, or things to say during lessons; they do not require a classroom full of writing textbooks, tests, and teaching packages. When school funds are spent on this kind of material, the underlying message is that they ought to be used.

FUTURE DIRECTIONS

Classroom research is a major trend for the future because it helps teachers and children expand their understandings about literacy and literacy development. It helps teachers expand their professional understandings about the ways in which writing develops and about the ways in which their instruction can be organized to meet the developmental needs of children. An important element of the teacher-research movement is that it has led to dialogue among teachers about the nature of educational reform, and about the ways in which environments can be changed to improve writing instruction. It has also led to a view of teachers as professionals who reflect upon their practices and upon children's learning. Teachers are reading more, attending and presenting at conferences, and writing about their growing insights into how writing develops. Questions pursued by teacher-researchers include: What do my students know about written language? How do they use this knowledge to construct new understandings? What questions do they ask themselves and other children as they write? What evidence do I have to show children's development over time? How are children's linguistic and cultural knowledge used as resources for the writing curriculum? What opportunities arise for children to talk about writing and to work collaboratively on projects? What functions and genres of written language are explored in my classroom? How do the children in my classroom explore the specific features of written language. How does my students' writing change over time?

Classroom research helps children develop understandings about their own processes of literacy development, and about the politics of literacy. With a teacher's help, children can ask: What do I know about written language? How do I make my own discoveries about written language? What do my peers and teachers do to facilitate this discovery? How is my writing (including features, functions and genre) the same and different from that of my peers? How does my writing develop over time? What can I learn from the miscues I make while writing? What kinds of writing are used by the people in my family and community? How do I use written language to meet my personal and social needs? My academic needs?

Together, teachers and students pursue authentic research questions that lead to understandings about the personal and social aspects of literacy development, about effective classroom organization, and about the political nature of literacy and schooling. Answering these questions is useful for expanding children's and teachers' understandings, and is a tool for contributing to educational and political reform.

Saginaw Valley State University, USA
University of Arizona, USA

REFERENCES

Bullock, A.: 1975, *A Language for Life*, Her Majesty's Stationery Office, London.
Britton, J.: 1972, *Language and Learning*, Penguin, Harmondsworth, Middlesex, England.
Burrows, A.T.: 1952, 'Writing as therapy', *Elementary English* xxix, 135–136, 149.
Calkins, L.: 1983, *Lessons from a Child: On the Teaching and Learning of Writing*, Heinemann, Portsmouth, NH.
Dewey, J.: 1899, 'Three years of the university elementary school', in K.M. Paciorek & J.H. Munro (eds), *Sources*, Dushkin Publishing Group/Brown &Benchmark Publishers, Guilford, CT, 1996, 150–155.
Dixon, J.: 1991, 'Historical considerations: An international perspective', in J. Flood, J.M. Jensen, D. Lapp, & J.R. Squire (eds.), *Handbook of Research on Teaching the English Language Arts*, Macmillan, New York, 1991, 18–23.
Dyson, A.: 1989, *Multiple Worlds of Child Writers*, Teachers College, New York.
Emig, J.: 1971, *The Composing Processes of 12th Graders*, NCTE Research Report 13, National Council for the Teaching of English, Urbana, Ill.
Featherstone, J.: 1968, 'Experiments in Learning', *The New Republic*, December 14, 23–25.
Featherstone, J.: 1969, 'Why so few good schools?', *The New Republic*, January 4, 18–21.
Ferebee, J., Jackson, D., Saunders, D. & Treut, A.: 1939, *They All Want to Write: Written English in the Elementary School*, Bobbs-Merrill, New York.
Ferreiro, E. & Teberosky, A.: *Literacy Before Schooling*, Heinemann, Portsmouth, NH.
Goodman, Y.: 1992, 'The end', in Y.M. Goodman & S. Wilde (eds.), *Literacy Events in a Community of Young Writers*, Teachers College Press, New York, 1992, 217–225.
Hall, N. & Robinson, A. (eds).: 1996, *Learning About Punctuation*, Heinemann, Portsmouth, NH and Multilingual Matters, Clevedon, Avon.
Harste, J., Burke, C., Woodward, V.: 1981, *Children, Their Language and World: Initial Encounters with Print*, Project NIE-G-79-0132, National Institute of Education, USA.
Hartog, P. (1907) *The Writing of English*, O.U.P., Oxford.
Learning Media: 1992, *Dancing with the Pen*, Ministry of Education, Wellington, New Zealand.
Meek, M.: 1982, *Learning to Read*, The Bodley Head, London.
Moffett, J.: 1968, *Teaching the Universe of Discourse*, Houghton Mifflin, Boston.
Murray, D.: 1982, *Learning by Teaching*, Boynton/Cook, Upper Montclair, NJ.
Padilla, A.M., Lindholm, K.J., Chen, A., Kuran, R., Hakuta, K., Lambert, W., & Tucker,

G.R.: 1991, 'The English-only movement: Myths, reality, and implications for psychology', *American Psychologist* 46(2), 120–130.

Richardson, E.: 1964, *In the Early World*, New Zealand Council for Educational Research, Wellington.

Shannon, P.: 1990, *The Struggle to Continue*, Heinemann, Portsmouth, NH.

Shaughnessy, M.: 1977, *Errors and Expectations: A Guide for Teachers of Writing*, Oxford Publishing Company, New York.

Squire, J.R.: 1991, 'The history of the profession', in J. Flood, J.M. Jensen, D. Lapp, & J.R. Squire (eds.), *Handbook of Research on Teaching the English Language Arts*, Macmillan, New York, 1991, 3–17.

Trueba, H.: 1991, 'The role of culture in bilingual instruction: Linking linguistic and cognitive development to cultural knowledge', In O. Garcia (ed.), *Bilingual Education*, John Benjamins Publishing Company, Philadelphia, PA, 1991, 43–55.

Wilkinson, A.: 1985, 'Writing,' in N. Bennet & C. Desforges (eds.), *Recent Advances in Classroom Research*, Scottish Academic Press, Edinburgh.

Wille, F.W.: 1980, 'Developing and accommodating children's writing in the intermediate grades,' in W.T. Petty & P.J. Finn (eds.), *From Childhood Through Adolescence: What is Basic in Language Arts*, Department of Elementary and Remedial Education, State University of New York, Buffalo, NY, 1980, 29–37.

Wray, D., Bloom, W. & Hall, N.: 1989, *Literacy in Action*, The Falmer Press, London.

SANDRA WILDE

THE DEVELOPMENT OF SPELLING AND PUNCTUATION

Our understanding of how children learn to spell and punctuate has under-gone a major transformation in the past twenty-five years, as theory and research have illuminated the ways in which such learning is an acquisition of complex linguistic and conceptual systems rather than a compilation of discrete words and rules. Work has focused on general developmental progressions in spelling and punctuation, children's growing understand-ing of the nature and components of the systems they are learning, and the processes by which that learning occurs, both consciously and tacitly. This review will first discuss those factors for spelling (including the learning that takes place before spelling as such can begin), and then offer a briefer overview of punctuation.

EARLY LEARNING ABOUT WRITTEN LANGUAGE

Early developmental research (see also the review by Raban, this volume) has taught us that children's knowledge begins globally, with understand-ings about how written language works and about their culture's specific writing system (such as the Roman alphabet). For instance, Ferreiro and Teberosky's work in Latin America, conducted from a Piagetian perspec-tive (1982), showed that children discover gradually that letters are unique from other marks, that all parts of an utterance are represented in writing (in contrast to pictures, where only nouns are visible) and that the individ-ual words of speech are represented by separate units of written language. Clay (1975) showed how young writers explore principles of written lan-guage such as directionality, generativity, repetition, and contrast, learning not only the shapes of symbols but eventually, after a good deal of ex-perimentation, the constraints within which they are used. (All of this learning, of course, reflects the interaction of the child's own inventions and her increasing knowledge of the conventions she sees in the written language in her world.)

Scribbling is the precursor to alphabetic writing, and Harste, Woodward, & Burke (1984) have shown that scribbled writing begins to distinguish itself from scribbled drawing in both intention and form, and that this early writing, despite its lack of conventional symbols, does nonetheless take on visual features of the particular written language form that children see in the world around them (so that an Israeli scribble looks different

V. Edwards and D. Corson (eds), Encyclopedia of Language and Education,
Volume 2: Literacy, 87–95.
© *1997 Kluwer Academic Publishers. Printed in the Netherlands.*

from a North American one). The authors, in fact, suggest that the word 'scribble' is inappropriate for children's early writing since it misleadingly suggests a lack of organization and intentionality. Heald-Taylor (1984) has documented the evolution of scribbling into the use of letters: scribbles gradually become less global and the child may, for instance, begin to assign scribble segments to individual words. The transition to using letters may be gradual or rapid. Baghban (1984), reflecting the new interest in and appreciation of very early literacy development, conducted a case study of her daughter from birth to age three in which she discovered that scribble gradually became more linear and began to include letter-like shapes and letters, and that role-playing based on the use of written language she saw in the world around her was an integral facet of this development. Baghban also asserted that the use of terms like 'mock writing' and the concept of readiness are inappropriate given the strong intentionality of what young children do.

INVENTED SPELLING AND ITS DEVELOPMENT

Read (1975), in his exploration of preschoolers' understanding of phonology, revealed that young children's attempts to represent words through relating sounds to letters are not random but rather reflect logical categorizations of speech sounds even though they may not correspond to those recognized by adults and expressed in standard spellings. His groundbreaking work explained phonetically a number of features that would otherwise seem unusual. For instance, the word *pill* was spelled PEL by a young child since the "short i" sound is phonetically close to the letter-name e; *dragon* was spelled JRAGIN because /d/ before /r/ is affricated, making it phonetically close to /j/; and *stamps* was spelled STAPS because nasal sounds before other consonants are not very salient and are often realized primarily as nasalized vowels, a phenomenon which children (and indeed written English) have no way of representing directly. Most subsequent work has built on Read's insight that spellings need to be seen from the children's point of view, as inventions reflecting their current state of knowledge about written language.

A number of researchers have looked at invented spelling at different age and developmental levels. Paul (1976), in a classroom study in kindergarten, found that early spellings often consisted of representations of initial sounds only, then came to include final phonemes and long vowels and eventually the more difficult short vowel sounds, although not as consistently as Read had seen. She also discovered that children appeared to re-invent spellings rather than repeat one they had already used, and that once they had picked up a standard spelling from their reading, they tended to use it in their writing.

Beers and Henderson (1977) studied a number of features (short and long vowels; *m* and *n*, vocalic *r* as in *sir* and *faster*, flapped *t* or *tt* as in *later*; -ed and -*ing* endings) in writing samples taken from first graders over a six-month period. They discovered that features that were initially spelled phonetically gradually became more conventional although not yet always at a very sophisticated level. For instance, children began to use two letters to represent long vowels, but often made choices that were not only incorrect but implausible (such as MAED for made).

Treiman (1993), in an extensive study of first-grade spelling, found that young children's spelling is highly phonological and pointed out that it must be understood and classified in light of children's predictable under-standings about phonological relationships. For instance, children often represent a sound with a letter that stands for a related sound, as in SGY for *sky*, and they may treat as units certain sequences of phonemes like a vowel followed by /l/, so that *bell* is spelled BL. Treiman also pointed out that although children's phonemic systems often differ from those of adults, experience with reading helps them to develop in the direction of greater conventionality.

Zutell (1979) dictated word lists to children in Grades 1 through 4 in order to examine several spelling features: lax and tense vowels, the past tense suffix, consonant doubling, and vowel extension (as in *explain* and *explanation*). He found that there was virtually no change from first to second grade but that growth occurred in all the features after that, and that these results correlated with the students' scores on Piagetian decentration tasks. Schlagal (1992) looked at a number of features across grades 1 through 6 and classified them as early features; those like preconsonantal nasals and long and short vowels that young children are still exploring but that are resolved by fourth grade; constant features like consonant doubling and vowel markers that appeared in invented spellings in all grades; and later features like -*tion* suffixes and the consonant alternation of /k/ and /s/ as in *music* and *musician* that don't appear at all in invented spellings until later on.

Other studies have focused on the development of specific spelling features among older children. Barnes (1992) found that children who had been exposed to written words containing silent letters were more likely to include those letters in their spellings as they got older, although not always in the correct place in the word. Beers and Beers (1992) found that the spelling of the consonant endings -*ed* and -*ing* stabilized during second grade, but that changes in root words before suffixes took longer to develop, particularly for consonant doubling.

Similarly, Wilde (1986/1987) looked at a number of features in six children's classroom writing in third and fourth grade and found that they varied considerably in how accurately they were spelled (for instance, high-frequency words were spelled accurately 97.6 per cent of the time and low-frequency words 56.4 per cent of the time, and short vowels were spelled accurately 94.4 per cent of the time and reduced vowels like the schwa only 79.8 per cent of the time). Almost all of these features, which also included spellings of consonant patterns like doubling and hard and soft *c* and *g*, as well as suffixes and homophones, showed growth from third to fourth grade.

Henderson and Templeton (1986) summarized the development of spelling in terms of a progression through 'alphabet, pattern, and meaning' over time. They defined five developmental milestones (which they called 'stages'): a pre-alphabetic but intentional use of letters to represent meaning; spelling that is primarily phonetic; the increasing use of features like two-letter spellings for long vowels; an exploration of syllable-juncture patterns like consonant doubling; and an increasing knowledge that words with similar meanings often have similar spellings. (In an interesting side-light to these patterns, Invernizzi, Abouzeid, and Gill, 1994, pointed out that children's developmental spellings echo historical stages of English spelling; Anglo-Saxon spellings like WIF for wife are like those of young children, while Renaissance spellings like DISSCORD are like those of older children.)

Finally, although most spelling research focuses on qualitative change, Krashen (1993) compiled findings from a large number of studies to answer the question 'How well do people spell?' Studies ranging from 1897 to 1992 showed consistently high levels of spelling accuracy, around 98 per cent for first-year college students and 90 per cent or higher in fourth grade.

COMPONENTS OF SPELLING KNOWLEDGE

As the previous discussion suggests, learning to spell is a complex business that involves far more than just memorizing words and rules. A number of researchers have attempted to define precisely what is entailed in learning to spell.

Since at least part of spelling, particularly for younger children, involves assigning letters to sounds, it stands to reason that phonemic awareness – an ability to abstract out speech sounds – would have a relationship to quality of invented spelling, and Griffith (1991) found that this was indeed true, at both first and third grades. The version of English one speaks, however, does not have a significant influence on spelling. Stever (1980) pointed out that all young writers, regardless of dialect, go through similar processes of representing speech sounds in invented spelling but they all need to rely less on phonology to become better spellers.

Ehri has written extensively about the complexity of knowledge involved in learning to spell words, particularly the role of visual information. For instance, when Ehri (1980) showed second graders the nonsense word *wheople*, six of eight children who failed to reproduce it exactly used invented spellings that started with *wh*. Similarly, four of eight invented spellings produced by children who had seen *weepel* for the same sound sequence started with we (and three of these with *wee*). Sound and visual interact, however. Ehri (1987) reports how children who were encouraged to segment longer words like *chocolate* into syllables (choc-o-late) were better able to remember how to spell features like schwa vowels and silent letters in the words (although not double consonants, which were not highlighted by these pronunciations). Another aspect of the visual component of spelling was discussed by Marsh, Friedman, Welch, and Desberg (1980), who found that by fifth grade students begin to make use of analogy to familiar words to spell new words.

Hughes and Searle (1996) pointed out, in a long-term case study of two children, that visual and phonetic strategies, although both important, may be used differentially by different children. Both of the children in question still had many invented spellings in sixth grade. One of them, Elly, produced good phonetic spellings that were, however, not very sophisticated on other dimensions. The other subject, Joe, could not even phonemically segment words effectively, although some of his invented spellings looked like the standard spelling in the shape of either the word as a whole or individual letters. As often happens in case studies, we are reminded that patterns seen in the aggregate do not necessarily apply to all learners as individuals.

LEARNING TO SPELL: SOME INFLUENCES ON DEVELOPMENT

Although a lengthy discussion of instructional issues is beyond the scope of this review, it is nonetheless important to consider some of the instructional practices that can support development. Researchers have, for instance, examined the role of wide reading and writing in learning to spell. Krashen (1993) has summarized a number of studies that suggest both that reading has a direct effect on spelling ability and that extensive learning to spell can take place without formal instruction. Clarke (1988) examined the role of invented spelling in a study of two first-grade classes, one in which children were encouraged to use invented spellings, the other where they were expected to use standard spelling. She found that children encouraged to use invented spelling not only wrote longer pieces but also scored better on tests of word analysis and spelling. These differences were especially strong for low achievers. Interestingly, although Clarke reported the invented spelling children as having more spelling errors, which appeared to be a weakness, they wrote so much more that the number of words they spelled correctly was actually higher. For instance, according to my calculations for March, the traditional spelling group spelled correctly 92 per cent of words in stories with an average length of 16 words (an average of 15 words per story), while the invented spelling group spelled correctly 60 per cent of words in 38-word stories (an average of 23 words).

Other researchers have considered the role of social context in learning to spell. Kamii and Randazzo (1985), in a description of how children help each other to figure out the spellings of words in a collaborative classroom atmosphere, point out that this approach avoids the pitfalls of imposing instruction entirely from the outside. Nor does it expect children to construct spelling entirely on their own, emphasizing instead the exchange of ideas and mutual development of concepts. Similarly, Reddy and Daiute (1993) found, in a study of a third- and fourth-grade classroom, that children who were encouraged to talk to each other as they wrote spent a good deal of time discussing spelling, using a variety of strategies. The authors in fact defined 34 categories of spelling talk, such as asking the spelling of a whole word and talking about double letters.

Interviews with children about spelling are another source of information about their development. Weiner's (1994) discussions about spelling with four first-graders revealed knowledge about sound/symbol relationships, letter and meaning patterns, and other more general aspects of learning to spell such as risk taking and automaticity. Radebaugh (1985), focusing on conscious strategies among good and poor spellers in third and fourth grade, found that they mentioned a variety of strategies but that the stronger spellers were less likely to use letter-by-letter phonetic spelling and also used visual imagery fairly often.

PUNCTUATION

Theory and research about the development of punctuation are far less extensive that that on spelling, but recent work reflects a similar emphasis on punctuation as a linguistic and conceptual system. A valuable synthesis of earlier work in this area is to be found in Hall and Robinson (1996) (particularly in Nigel Hall's introductory chapter).

Ferreiro and Teberosky (1982), focusing on preschoolers, demonstrate how the beginning of punctuation development lies in realizing that punctuation marks are different from numbers and letters. Martens and Goodman (1996) explore the variety of punctuation marks that children have invented on their own, including dots or plus signs to separate words and a 'sadlamation point' to put at the end of a sentence describing an unhappy event.

Looking at specific punctuation marks, Cordeiro, Giacobbe, and Cazden (1983) discovered that first-graders who were provided with instruction about apostrophes, quotation marks, and periods still used them appropriately only about half of the time, and that periods were especially difficult to teach about since rules for their use are so abstract. In a later study, Cordeiro (1988) discovered that first- and third-graders used periods inappropriately in consistent ways that reflected underlying hypotheses, such as separating adverbial phrases from a main clause. Edelsky (1983), working with Spanish/English bilingual students from first through third grade, found that word segmentation and the use of punctuation marks developed in logical yet quite varied ways (See also Reitsma, this volume for a discussion of spelling in Dutch). For instance, sometimes children put periods at the end of every line, while at other times a piece would begin with a capital and end with a period but have no internal punctuation. She found some but not steady consistency for any single child.

Wilde (1996; see also Wilde, 1986/1987) examined the punctuation of six third- and fourth-graders and found that their knowledge bases varied widely. Some children used punctuation more appropriately than others; one student only once used a punctuation mark other than a period, while others used marks such as quotation marks and exclamation points frequently. Calkins (1980), in interviewing third-graders, discovered that those in a writing-oriented class knew far more about a wide variety of punctuation marks and how to use them than those in a class where writing mechanics were taught through drills and workbooks.

FUTURE DIRECTIONS

This selective rather than exhaustive overview of our current understanding of spelling and punctuation development illustrates a large and varied knowledge base that is of mainly very recent origin. At this point, the general parameters of children's understanding of English spelling and how it grows and changes over time have been laid out. Curriculum and instruction have begun to feel the impact of this knowledge base. Of many possible future research directions, a few stand out as being of special interest or importance:

Longitudinal studies of individual children. Hughes and Searle (1996) have conducted a long-term study whose results will soon be published at length. Much of the developmental research in spelling consists of "snapshots" of children at various age levels, and there will be much to learn from looking at the same children over a period of time.

In-depth studies at particular developmental levels. Treiman's book-length study of first graders (1993) provided an extensive look at the spellings of children who are relative beginners as spellers; similar extensive studies at other ages and developmental levels (and perhaps particularly for children who are not succeeding at spelling) would make an important contribution.

More studies based on interviews, observations, and other direct data-collection with children. If learning to spell and punctuate involve the development of conceptual and linguistic systems, it is important that we continue to work at discovering how they are perceived from the child's perspective.

Naturalistic studies of development within various classroom contexts. There is a particular need to examine the role of instruction in development in ways that are not simple measurements of outcomes under various conditions, but which use qualititative methods to explore the lived experience of children's learning to spell and punctuate.

More research of all kinds on punctuation. Compared to the research on spelling, punctuation development is virtually untapped territory, with room for inquiry of many kinds.

Portland State University, USA

REFERENCES

Baghban, M.: 1984, *Our Daughter Learns to Read and Write: A Case Study from Birth to Three*, International Reading Association, Newark, De.

Barnes, W.G.W.: 1992, 'The developmental acquisition of silent letters in orthographic images', in S. Templeton & D.R. Bear (eds), *Development of Orthographic Knowledge and the Foundations of Literacy: A Memorial Festschrift for Edmund H. Henderson*, Lawrence, Hillsdale, NJ, pp. 191–212.

Erlbaum, B., Carol S., & Beers, J.W.: 1992, 'Children's spelling of English inflectional morphology', in S. Templeton & D.R. Bear (eds), *Development of Orthographic Knowledge and the Foundations of Literacy: A Memorial Festschrift for Edmund H. Henderson*, Lawrence, Hillsdale, NJ, pp. 231–252.

Beers, J.W., & Henderson, E.H.: 1977, 'A study of developing orthographic concepts among first graders', *Research in the Teaching of English* 11, 133–148.

Calkins, L.M.: 1980, 'When children want to punctuate: basic skills belong in context', *Language Arts* 57, 567–573.

Clarke, L.K.: 1988, 'Invented versus traditional spelling in first graders' writings: Effects on learning to spell and read', *Research in the Teaching of English* 22, 281–309.

Clay, M.M.: 1975, *What did I write?: Beginning writing behaviour*, Heinemann, Portsmouth, NH.

Cordeiro, P.: 1988, 'Children's punctuation: An analysis of errors in period placement', *Research in the Teaching of English* 22, 62–74.

Cordeiro, P., Giacobbe, M.E., & Cazden, C.: 1983, 'Apostrophes, quotation marks, and periods: Learning punctuation in the first grade', *Language Arts* 60, 323–332.

Edelsky, C.: 1983, 'Segmentation and punctuation: Developmental data from young writers in a bilingual program', *Research in the Teaching of English* 17, 135–156.

Ehri, L.: 1980, 'The development of orthographic images', in U. Frith (ed.), *Cognitive processes in spelling*, Academic Press, London, pp. 311–000.

Ehri, L.: 1987, 'Learning to read and spell words', *Journal of Reading Behavior* 19, 5–31.

Ferreiro, E. & Teberosky, A.: 1982, *Literacy before Schooling*, Heinemann, Exeter, NH.

Griffith, P.L.: 1991, 'Phonemic awareness helps first graders invent spellings and third graders remember correct spellings', *Journal of Reading Behavior* 23, 215–233.

Hall, N. & Robinson, A. (eds): 1996, *Learning about Punctuation*, Multilingual Matters, Clevedon, England and Heinemann, Portsmouth, NH.

Harste, J.C., Woodward, V.A., & Burke, C.L.: 1984, *Language Stories and Literacy Lessons*, Heinemann, Portsmouth, NH.

Heald-Taylor, B.G.: 1984, 'Scribble in first grade writing', *Reading Teacher* 38, 4–8.

Henderson, E.H. & Templeton, S.: 1986, 'A developmental perspective of formal spelling instruction through alphabet, pattern, and meaning', *The Elementary School Journal* 86, 305–316.

Hughes, M. & Searle, D.: 1996, 'Joe and Elly: Sight-based and sound-based approaches to literacy', *Talking Points* (The Whole Language Umbrella), Spring, 8–11.

Invernizzi, M., Abouzeid, M., & Gill, J.T.: 1994, 'Using students' invented spellings as a guide for spelling instruction that emphasizes word study', *The Elementary School Journal* 95, 155–167.

Kamii, C. & Randazzo, M.: 1985, 'Social interaction and invented spelling', *Language Arts* 62, 124–133.

Krashen, S.: 1993, 'How well do people spell?', *Reading improvement* 30, 9–20.

Krashen, S.: 1993, *The Power of Reading: Insights from the Research*, Libraries Unlimited, Englewood, Co.

Marsh, G., Friedman, M., Welch, V., & Desberg, P.: 1980, 'The development of strategies in spelling', in U. Frith (ed.), *Cognitive Processes in Spelling*, Academic Press, London, pp. 339–353

Martens, P. & Goodman, Y.: 1996, 'Invented punctuation', in N. Hall & A. Robinson (eds), *Learning About Punctuation*, Multilingual Matters, Clevedon, England & Heinemann, Portsmouth, NH, pp. 37–53.

Paul, R.: 1976, 'Invented spelling in kindergarten', *Young Children* 31, 195–200.

Radebaugh, M.R.: 1985, 'Children's perceptions of their spelling strategies', *Reading Teacher* 38, 532–536.

Read, C.: 1975, 'Children's categorizations of speech sounds in English' (Research Report No. 17), National Council of Teachers of English, Urbana, Il.

Reddy, M. & Daiute, C.: 1993, 'The social construction of spelling', *New Directions for Child Development* 61, 79–95.

Schlagal, R.C.: 1992, 'Patterns of orthographic development into the intermediate grades', in S. Templeton & D.R. Bear (eds), *Development of Orthographic Knowledge and the Foundations of Literacy: A Memorial Festschrift for Edmund H. Henderson*, Lawrence Erlbaum, Hillsdale, NJ, pp. 31–52.

Stever, E.F.: 1980, 'Dialect and spelling', in E.H. Henderson & J.W. Beers (eds), *Developmental and Cognitive Aspects of Learning to Spell*, International Reading Association, Newark, De, pp. 46–51.

Treiman, R.: 1993, *Beginning to Spell: A Study of First-Grade Children*, Oxford, New York.

Weiner, S.: 1994, 'Four first graders' descriptions of how they spell', *The Elementary School Journal* 94, 315–330.

Wilde, S.: 1987, 'An analysis of the development of spelling and punctuation in selected third and fourth grade children', Doctoral dissertation, University of Arizona, 1986, *Dissertation Abstracts International*, 47, 2452A.

Wilde, S.: 1996, 'Not just periods and exclamation points: The continued development of children's knowledge about punctuation', in N. Hall & A. Robinson (eds), *Learning About Punctuation*, Multilingual Matters, Clevedon, England & Heinemann, Portsmouth, NH, pp. 64–73.

Zutell, J.: 1979, 'Spelling strategies of primary school children and their relationship to Piaget's concept of decentration', *Research in the teaching of English* 13, 69–80.

SUE WALKER

HANDWRITING SKILLS

Handwriting research is multi-disciplinary. It is an area that has attracted interest from developmental and experimental psychologists; physiotherapists and occupational therapists; medics; computer scientists; calligraphers and typographers as well as educationists. (see, for example, Wing, 1979; Wann et al., 1991 and Kao et al., 1986).

The focus of this review, however, is the teaching of handwriting. As such, it is concerned with the questions and issues that teachers in the classroom face, such as when joined writing should be taught, whether beginning writers should be taught print script or cursive letters in the early stages, whether a particular model should be followed, the kind of writing instrument to use, helping left-handed children.

EARLY DEVELOPMENTS

The lack of research in relation to the teaching of handwriting has been noted by Twyman (1978) and Alston & Taylor (1987). In general, the literature in the field engages in debate about particular approaches to the subject rather than using research-based evidence to support particular views. Many authorities on handwriting are passionate about their approach to handwriting teaching and focus on a particular style of writing (see for example, Gourdie, 1955). There are, however, a number of useful surveys of approaches to teaching handwriting: many of these concentrate on particular countries.

Gray (1955) draws on papers from the 1940s and 1950s to support the view that the teaching of print script has some merit. Askov, Otto & Askov (1970) and Peck, Askov & Fairchild (1980), list research mainly in schools in the USA. Sassoon's work on joins in handwriting of children between seven and fifteen years old focuses on practices in UK schools, though her references are from a wide range of international and interdisciplinary sources (Sassoon, 1988). Suen's bibliography of mainly US sources (1975) is divided into a number of sections including 'handwriting instruction, systems and practices', 'left-handed writing' and 'diagnostic and remedial teaching'.

V. Edwards and D. Corson (eds), Encyclopedia of Language and Education,
Volume 2: Literacy, 97–105.
© *1997 Kluwer Academic Publishers. Printed in the Netherlands.*

MODELS OR METHOD?

A key issue of debate is whether children should be taught a particular model or style of handwriting. In a model-based handwriting scheme getting the shape, slant and proportion of the letters right is an essential part of handwriting teaching. Italic is one example: emphasis is placed on making oval shapes, and when children progress from pencil to pen, to using a broad nibbed pen to give the letters thick and thin strokes. Non-model based approaches are concerned less with shape and encourage children to focus on the movement between letters.

Models

Over the years, many models have been introduced to the educational system: for example, in the UK, copperplate, Marion Richardson, print script and Nelson handwriting; in France, the *ronde* or *anglaise*; in the US the Zaner-Bloser system or D'Nealian handwriting. The rationale behind the models is as varied as the models themselves: italic handwriting is founded on historical principles and dates back to the sixteenth century script used in the papal chancery in Rome; the Zaner-Bloser alphabet takes a 'building blocks' approach where six strokes form the basis of the model; the Marion Richardson approach encourages flow by incorporating writing patterns in handwriting learning; the Casteilla method in France is a cursive style adapted for use with ball point pen. A summary of widely used models in the UK is given in Myers (1983); Alston & Taylor (1987) summarise developments in the US and Australasia; Gray (1976) summarises models and educational policy in most European countries, the US and Canada; and Lehman (1976) discusses models used in the US.

One of the problems for children in learning a model-based system is that they are encouraged to copy lettershapes exactly. Many children find this very difficult and consistency of lettershape seems an unreasonable expectation for beginner writers. Children can be discouraged by not being able to produce perfect characters. Such an approach also neglects the fact that handwriting is used for many purposes and that different styles of handwriting are appropriate for different levels of formality. Research by Wing (1979) supports the view that teaching a particular model has limitations: in a study looking at the variability of handwritten characters, he concludes that 'Different shapes are often used to represent the same letter by different people, and this reflects educational and cultural influences as well as personal choice and context of letter ie position in the word', p. 296.

Accurate copying of a model can also be difficult for teachers. Sassoon (1988), for example, reports on studies that compare teacher's handwriting with the particular model that their school is following. This work showed that there was considerable variation in the teacher's representation of models and suggests that reliance on a strict model is inappropriate.

Non model-based approaches

Some authorities believe that teaching a particular style of handwriting interferes with encouraging the movements necessary for speed and flow. Sassoon (1990a) stresses the 'movement of writing' as crucial in learning to write. She argues that handwriting teaching should concentrate on starting and finishing letters in the correct place and on making letters ready for joining, and on making appropriate joins – ones that encourage flow. Another pioneer of this approach in the UK was Nicolete Gray whose 'running script' stressed that correct letter formation was essential for a fast, flowing adult hand (Gray, 1979).

TO JOIN OR NOT TO JOIN ...

One of the issues that teachers have to face is when to introduce joined writing. There are three approaches: cursive writing from the start; print script initially, followed by a cursive form; flowing individual letters in readiness for joining. Lurcat (1985) says that different teaching approaches emphasise different things, and that cursive writing helps the flow and print script the shape. She believes that if children learn cursive writing on entry to school, the 'trajectoire' or movement from one letter to another can be established first, and that later attention can focus on the shape of the letters.

Those in favour of joined writing on entry to school include Cripps & Cox (1989) who argue that: cursive writing follows on naturally from young children's flowing scribble movements; children don't have to change from print script to cursive writing as they move up the school; emphasis is on whole words rather than individual letters; children learn letter strings and this helps spelling, and correct letter formation is ensured from the beginning because joining strokes lead to the correct starting point.

In some countries, for example France, children are successfully taught a cursive style on entry to school. Cotton's observations in nursery schools in Paris (1991) show that very young children had no difficulty in reading and writing 'l'ecriture cursive'. She reports that teachers felt strongly that joined writing is easier than printing because it is a natural development from the continuous flow of early scribble and it lets children focus on words rather than letters as individual units.

Some researchers and teachers, however, argue against introducing joined writing on entry to school because they say many young children have insufficient motor control (see, for example, Laszlo, 1986).

In the second approach to teaching handwriting children are taught a form of print script on entry to school. In such schemes letters are often very geometric and end abruptly on the baseline. There is no attempt to produce a flowing letter in readiness for joining. In some cases the print script letters children learn initially bear no resemblance to the cursive form children learn later. This is well-illustrated by the Zaner-Bloser method: a geometric system leading on to a loopy cursive – there is no obvious relationship between the two sets of letters. Some systems, however, are less extreme, for example, the Nelson method widely used in the UK. Here there is a clear relationship between the initial print-script style letters used in the first stage and the later cursive form.

The third approach to teaching handwriting promotes the view that 'flowing separate letters' are what should be aimed at in the early stages (Sassoon, 1990a). In such a method emphasis is placed on the correct formation of letters (starting and finishing in the right place) and on 'exit strokes' or 'flicks' that make it easy for children to move on to joined writing when they are ready.

NON-LATIN SCRIPTS

Discussion so far has concentrated on the Latin alphabet, yet in many classrooms worldwide there are many languages – and scripts – in use (see also reviews by Burnaby and Wilde and Viv Edwards' review of Writing in multilingual classrooms, this volume). This presents many opportunities for monolingual and bilingual children alike to learn about the nature of different writing systems: direction of writing, position of letters in relation to a baseline, conventions of articulation and so on (see The Multilingual Resources for Children Project, 1995). Sassoon (1995) focuses on the particular issues people face when learning a second writing system. She compares the rules of different writing systems and identifies some of the problems children have in transferring from one writing system to another. Differences between kind of educational system and attitudes to writing and education in other countries can have important consequences for second script learning. Throughout the book, Sassoon emphasises the need to recognise cultural differences in education systems and attitudes to writing and education.

TOOLS OF THE TRADE

Writing instruments

The choice of the writing tool is a controversial issue (see Twyman, 1978). Many handwriting models were devised for pen and ink: italic, for example, is written with a broad-nibbed pen held at 45 degrees which results in letters having thick and thin strokes; copperplate is written with a flexible steel nib which produces thick strokes when pressed and fine strokes when not. The question for teachers is whether it is appropriate to teach models designed for pen and ink when the tools children use are likely to be ball point pens or felt and fibre tips.

Some authorities have responded to the newer writing instruments by producing more appropriate models. Nicolete Gray, for example, in her proposals for 'the running script' emphasises the fact that ball point pens can be used to produce strokes in all directions (Gray, 1979). The Casteilla series of writing books in France, dating from 1964, adapts the traditional ronde for ball point pen (Casteilla, 1964).

Penholds

How to hold a pen is covered in most handwriting manuals though often in a rather general way: the position of the fingers in relation to the barrel is sometimes illustrated and writers emphasise the need for a relaxed hold. Few writers acknowledge that different writing instruments may have to be held differently to write effectively. Penholds have been the focus of some research in recent years. Sassoon, Nimmo-Smith & Wing (1986), for example, report a study of changes in penhold as a function of age in English school children. They devised a classification system for describing penholds (drawing on work carried out in Australia by Ziviani, 1983) and used this to analyse the penholds used by 7–16 year old children. Their work suggests that the majority of children hold their pens too tightly and that a large number (65 per cent) of children have their thumb closest to the tip of the pen (contrary to recommendations usually given by teachers and in handwriting manuals). The most interesting finding of this work was that the writing of children using unconventional penholds did not suffer in terms of writing speed. In a similar vein, Ziviani (1987) looks at developmental stages in children's holding of pencils concentrating on the dynamic tripod grasp. Her paper refers to a number of studies on motor skills and posture in young children.

Lines on the paper?

Frameworks for the position of letterforms along a writing line are part of the apparatus for learning to write in any language. Children learning to write English, for example, have to learn about the relationship of letters to a baseline: some letters sit on it, some extend below. Devanagari script and those based on it (for example, those for writing Panjabi and Bengali) have letters hanging from a top line. Chinese characters sit within notional square and the position of the elements of the character in relation to the square is important for meaning. Handwriting copy books in all language display a range of conventions for representing letter shapes and writing lines (see, for example, The Multilingual Resources for Children Project, 1995 for some of these conventions in Gujarati, Nastaliq, Hindi and Chinese). Exercise books in France are often divided into squares and part of the process of learning to write is organising writing in terms of this baseline grid both horizontally and vertically.

Many teachers teach handwriting without using copybooks and their grids. In the UK, for example, teachers in primary schools choose between lined or unlined paper. Views are mixed as to which is best: those in favour of unlined paper argue that lines impose constraints on, for example, size of writing whereas those in favour of lines think that they help children organise their writing more effectively. Many writers of books about the teaching of handwriting are in favour of using unlined paper, particularly with young children (see, for example, Jarman, 1979).

Whether to use lined or unlined paper is also an area that has attracted the interest of researchers. Work by Burnhill & Hartley in the late 1970s supported the use of lined paper for facilitating more legible handwriting than unlined paper (1975 and 1980). This view is also supported by Pasternicki (1987) who reviews the case for and against lined paper and provides a useful reference list.

HANDWRITING AS A MEANS OF ORGANISING THINKING

Most handwriting authorities are interested in the letterforms used, the methods used to teach it and practical issues such as how to hold pens and how to sit. There has been very little work on the use of handwriting as a tool for organising information. In the 1970s, Baudin and Twyman expressed concern that people made only limited use of graphic possibilities in their writing (see Baudin, 1977; Twyman, 1978). They argued that teachers should pay more attention to non-linear methods of presenting information such as trees, lists and tables. Twyman (1978) argues that teachers of handwriting should encourage children to organise a piece of writing in such a way as to enhance its meaning. Recently, however, this theme has received more attention. Moline (1995), for instance, in a book written specifically for teachers looks at a range of ways of presenting information visually and provides many examples of children's handwriting in use. Lowe (1996) argues that the teaching of visual literacy is neglected by teachers and that by encouraging children to 'design' information they have a greater chance of understanding.

HANDWRITING PROBLEMS

Handwriting problems of a cognitive, psychological or visual kind are discussed from a number of perspectives in the literature. Sassoon (1990b) provides a useful summary of the nature of these problems and discusses how they might reveal themselves in children's handwriting. The UK journal *Handwriting Review* contains many short contributions which focus on handwriting problems. Left-handedness is an issue that often worries teachers. Sassoon (1990a) provides a policy for left handers that is adaptable to most classroom situations. This includes placing the writing paper to the writer's left side and allowing them to slant it according to their needs, encouraging children to hold their pens far enough from the point so that their writing is not obscured, and providing free-flowing pens that do not smudge. Teachers should also be aware of specific difficulties that some left-handers face such as directional problems, letter movement and slant. Sassoon suggests, for example, that providing children with a model that has a slight backwards slant will offer encouragement, rather than unrealistically expecting left-handers to copy accurately letters that slope forward. Earlier work on handedness by Clark (1974) includes a chapter on writing problems. Alston's review (1992) of Bishop (1990) is a useful summary of some key issues.

TERMINOLOGY

Sassoon (1990a) stresses the importance of the use of consistent terminology within a school to describe letters, the parts of letters and lines that mark the height of letters. This can present problems for teachers because there are no established terms. Many teachers develop their own terminologies appropriate to the children that they teach. Twyman & Walker (1991) present a series of tables that cover issues important in the teaching of handwriting: categories of letters, orientation, parts of letters, lines and heights and variant forms. In these tables, based on a small survey in the UK, they list the terms used by teachers, hand writing authorities, palaeographers and printers and recommend those that may be the most appropriate to use in schools.

FUTURE DIRECTIONS

One area that could well be the focus of attention in future years is the exploration of handwriting as a tool for organising thought. As well as emphasising links between writing, reading and drawing, such an approach brings with it the study of the use of styles of handwriting for different purposes and for different audiences. Encouraging children to write quickly and legibly will continue to be a key issue for teachers and researchers, particularly in relation to modern writing tools. And, finally, because handwriting has such an interesting history, it may be that analysis and evaluation of past educational methods could provide interesting ways forward.

University of Reading, England

REFERENCES

Alston, J. & Taylor, J.: 1987, *Handwriting: Theory, Research and Practice*, Croom Helm Ltd, Beckenham, Kent.
Alston, J.: 1992, 'Review of "Handedness and developmental disorder"', *Handwriting Review*, 161–163.
Askov, E., Otto, W. & Askov, W.: 1970, 'A decade of research in handwriting: Progress and prospect', *Journal of Educational Research* 64, 99–111.
Baudin, F.: 1977, 'Reflections on the theme: At the edge of meaning', *Visible Language* 11(2), 81–92.
Bishop, D.V.M.: 1990, *Handedness and Developmental Disorder*, Blackwell Scientific Publications: Oxford.
Burnhill, P., Hartley, J., Fraser, J. & Young, M.: 1975, 'Writing lines: An exploratory study', *Programmed Learning and Educational Technology* 12(2), 82–87.
Casteilla, A.: 1964, *Methode d'Ecriture Moderne Cursive au Crayon a Bille*, Les Nouveautes de l'Enseignement: Paris.
Clark. M.M.: 1974, *Teaching Left-handed Children*, Hodder & Stoughton: London.
Cotton, P.: 1991, 'The importance of good models: Should children be exposed to joined writing on school entry in France and many European countries', *Reading* April, 27–32.
Cripps, C. & Cox, R.: 1989, *Joining the ABC: How and Why Handwriting and Spelling should be Taught Together*, LDA, Wisbech, Cambs.
Gourdie, T.: 1955, *Italic Handwriting*, The Studio Publications, London.
Gray, W.S.: 1955, *The Teaching of Reading and Writing: an International Survey*, Unesco, Paris.
Gray, N.: 1976, 'The teaching of writing in schools', *Summary Report of the Second Working Seminar on the Teaching of Letterforms*, 4–10 July 1976, Association Typographique Internationale, Reading.
Gray, N.: 1979, 'Towards a new handwriting adapted to the ball point pen', *Visible Language* XIII(1), 63–69.
Jarman, C.: 1979, *The Development of Handwriting Skills: A Resource Book for Teachers*, Simon & Schuster Education, Hemel Hempstead.
Kao, H.S.R., van Galen, G.P. & Hoosain, R.: 1986, *Graphonomics: Contemporary Research in Handwriting*, Elsevier Science Publishers, Amsterdam.
Laszlo, J.: 1986 'Development of perceptual motor abilities in children 5 years to adults' in C. Pratt, A Garton, W. Tunmer & A. Nesdale (eds.), *Research Issues in Child Development*, Allen & Unwin, Sydney, 137–144.
Lehman, C.: 1976, *Handwriting Models for Schools*, The Alcuin Press, Portland, Oregon.
Lowe. R.K.: 1996, 'Pictorial information design for schools', *Information Design Journal* 8(3), 41–51.
Lurcat, L.: 1985, *L'Ecriture Graphique a L'Ecole Maternelle*, Les editions: ESF, Paris.
Moline, S.: 1995, *I See What You Mean*, Longman, Melbourne.
Myers, P.W.: 1983, 'Handwriting in English education', *Visible Language* 27(4), 333–356.
Pasternicki, J.: 1987, 'Paper for writing: Research and recommendations' in J. Alston & J. Taylor (eds), *Handwriting, Theory, Research and Practice*, Croom Helm: Beckenham, 68–80.

Peck, M., Askov, E.N. & Fairchild, S.H.: 1980, 'Another decade of research in handwriting', *The Journal of Educational Research* 73, 283–298.

Sassoon R.: 1988, Joins in Children's Handwriting, and the Effects of Different Models and Teaching Methods, unpublished PhD thesis, Department of Typography & Graphic Communication, The University of Reading.

Sassoon, R.: 1990a, *Handwriting: The Way to Teach it*, Stanley Thornes (Publishers) Ltd, Cheltenham.

Sassoon, R.: 1990b, *Handwriting: A New Perspective*, Stanley Thornes (Publishers) Ltd, Cheltenham.

Sassoon, R.: 1995, *The Acquisition of a Second Writing System*, Intellect, Oxford.

Sassoon, R., Wing, A.M. & Nimmo-Smith, I.: 1986, 'An analysis of children's penholds' in H.S.R Kao, G.P. van Galen, & R. Hoosain (eds), *Graphonomics: Contemporary Research in Handwriting*, Elsevier Science Publishers, Amsterdam, 93–106.

Suen, C.Y.: 1975, 'Handwriting education: A bibliography of contemporary publications', *Visible Language* IX(2), 325–344.

The Multilingual Resources for Children Project: 1995, *Building Bridges: Multilingual Resources for Children*, Multilingual Matters: Clevedon, Philadelphia, Adelaide.

Twyman, M.: 1978, 'Teaching handwriting: An education digest', *Education*, 10 November.

Twyman & Walker: 1990, 'Preliminary thoughts on nomenclature for teachers of handwriting', *Visible Language* XXIV(2), 176–194.

Wann, J., Wing, A.M. & Sovik, N.: 1991, *Development of Graphic Skills: Research Perspectives and Implications*, Academic Press, London.

Wing, A.M. (ed): 1979, *Behavioural Studies of the Handwriting Skill*, special issue of *Visible Language* XIII(3).

Ziviani, J.: 1983 'Qualitative changes in dynamic tripod grip between seven and fourteen years of age', *Developmental Medicine and Child Neurology* 25, 778–782.

Ziviani, J.: 1987. 'Pencil grasp and manipulation', in J. Alston & J. Taylor (eds), *Handwriting, Theory, Research and Practice*, Croom Helm: Beckenham 24–26.

VIV EDWARDS

WRITING IN MULTILINGUAL CLASSROOMS

Gentle probing of even those societies which are officially monolingual invariably exposes a surprising level of linguistic diversity. The increasing interdependence of nations which has marked the second half of the twentieth century, however, has ensured that unprecedented numbers of city schools in Europe and the English speaking world are serving multicultural, multilingual populations. Historic and demographic trends determine the educational response to diversity. For instance, in North America, large concentrations of speakers of French, Spanish and Chinese have led to the development of programs whose aim is to produce children bilingual and biliterate in both English and the language of the home (see volume 5). In contrast, where school populations are more diverse, the sole medium of instruction is likely to be the (official or unofficial) national language.

This review explores the teaching of writing in multilingual classrooms of this kind. Following Smith (1982), a distinction is made between composition and transcription. The emphasis for present purposes is on composition, but for a discussion of the development of transcription skills, see Walker's review (this volume) on handwriting, and Wilde's review (also this volume) of spelling.

EARLY DEVELOPMENTS

For many years, the focus of research in multilingual classrooms was on the acquisition of spoken language (see volume 3). Gradually, this focus has broadened to include first the development of reading skills in a second language (see the review by Edwards, this volume), and later the development of writing skills. The various early influences which helped to fuel an interest in writing in multilingual classrooms include the new understandings of the writing process; the realisation that writing is influenced by social context; and the development of more positive attitudes towards bilingualism.

The traditional view of writing was that children needed to be taught a complex set of skills in strict sequence (see reviews by Hall and Owocki and Goodman, this volume). Children were expected to spend a great deal of time practising their writing skills: copying handwriting patterns, forming letters, writing words, then sentences and paragraphs with the

V. Edwards and D. Corson (eds), Encyclopedia of Language and Education,
Volume 2: Literacy, 107–115.
© *1997 Kluwer Academic Publishers. Printed in the Netherlands.*

appropriate punctuation. Decontextualized exercises were used to drill children in the requisite skills.

The research findings of recent years suggest that children are active rather than passive participants in the writing process, interacting with and using language to construct meaning for themselves and others. Investigations of children's writing at home (e.g. Bissex, 1980) and at school (e.g. Graves, 1983; Calkins, 1983) have focussed on what precisely happens when children write; the many functions of writing; and the development of children's control over the written word. The findings of this research have resulted in important changes in the teaching of writing to native speakers (see the review by Goodman & Owocki, this volume) which have also had wide ranging implications for second language learners.

The realisation of the role of culture on children's development as writers also proved to be a highly significant early development. Answers to the question of who writes what, when and to whom can differ greatly from one community to another. Shirley Brice Heath (1983), for instance, describes how writing in Trackton, an African-American community in the south east USA, is usually a female activity: most men write only for financial reasons: signatures on cheques; figures and notes for income tax returns. Women, on the other hand, use writing to remember important dates, phone numbers and addresses, and on greetings cards and absence notes for children. More extended writing, such as church bulletins and orders of service, is negotiated cooperatively at meetings: no one individual takes responsibility.

Another early development which served as a catalyst for reasearch on writing in multilingual classrooms was the dramatic change in attitudes towards bilingualism which began in the 1960s. Until that time, it had been widely assumed that children who spoke more than one language would find themselves at an intellectual and social disadvantge over their monolingual peers. Growing awareness of the methodological flaws underlying much earlier research, however, prepared the ground for alternative hypotheses concerning the workings of the bilingual brain. Particularly important was the notion of a common underlying proficency (Cummins, 1979): various cognitive and intellectual skills – including literacy related skills – are not relearned with exposure to each new language; instead they are transferred from one language to another.

MAJOR CONTRIBUTIONS

Research findings tend to cluster around three main themes: ways in which the writing behaviours of second language writers are grounded in the home culture; the significance of different oral discourse patterns on literacy development; support for children's writing development in English; and the development of biliteracy.

Writing and culture

Building on the work of Shirley Brice Heath (1983), various writers (e.g. Street, 1995; Bhatt et al., 1994; Gregory, 1998) have attempted to describe and analyze writing in different social and cultural contexts. In doing so, they often make it possible to challenge myths concerning the literacy experiences of second language learners. Many monolingual teachers assume that the educational underachievement of language minority students can be explained in terms of minimal exposure to the written word. Such assumptions have been shown to bear little relationship to reality.

Urzúa (1986), for instance, discussed the literacy experiences of three Cambodian refugee families. In Vuong's home, there was no shortage of reading materials. In contrast, Cham and Sonkla lived with their widowed mothers in apartments where there was very little evidence of reading material. Those who stress the value of children's early literacy experiences might expect Vuong to have made much more rapid progress than Cham and Sonkla. However, this was not the case. Vuong was struggling with literacy in a class where the teacher emphasized discrete skills, full-group instruction, copying and filling blanks. Cham and Sonkla, in contrast, were in a class where the teacher placed emphasis on writing as a developmental process and on reading with meaning rather than on sub-skills. Both children were reading and writing enthusiastically.

Other writers such as Goodman & Wilde (1992) relate the experiences of children at home and in the community specifically to their development as writers in school. In a study of a Native American community in Arizona, various contributors show clearly how the social history which children bring to school – their language, beliefs and knowledge of their community – affects both their writing and their view of themselves as writers. Goodman (1992: 218) comments:

> Through this study we ... began to understand the many forces, including many that are not even overtly present at the moment writing occurs, that influence writers and their compositions. These include parental, cultural, and community values about writing; attitudes of the larger society toward the young author as learner; personal relationships in the classroom (both teacher-learner and learner-learner); and the personal life history of the learner.

Kenner (1997) explores this issue in relation to the writing development of three to four year olds in a multilingual nursery in London. It emerged that these young children had already formulated notions of genre. Bilingual children also showed an understanding of specific patterns of language and literacy use in their families and produced their own texts paying attention to script and genre.

Oracy and literacy

A number of writers (eg Michaels & Cazden, 1986) describe the differential treatment of children whose discourse style differs from the middle class white norms which dominate most classrooms and the consequences for children's literacy development (see also, the review by Edwards in volume 3). Take, for instance, 'sharing time' or 'show and tell', a classroom routine where children report something that has happened to them or talk about something they have brought from home. Children are encouraged to be explicit and not to assume that other members of the class will know what they are talking about. This provides a valuable oral preparation for literacy: it promotes skills important in both reading and writing such as finding the most important idea, ordering events, and summarising the main point of a story. However, Black and White children appear to behave in different ways in these sessions.

White children tend to have a marked beginning, middle and end to their stories, with no shifts in time and place. They use the same 'topic-centred style' as the teacher, who picks up on their topic and expands it with comments and questions. In contrast, many Black children have a 'topic-associating' style. They tend to tell stories made up of a series of personal anecdotes which shift in time and place and have no explicit point.

White teachers sometimes feel that Black children 'ramble on' and interrupt them with inappropriate questions. Yet closer analysis shows that Black children do produce well-structured stories; the problem lies rather in the teachers' ability to recognise what they are doing. By cutting Black children short, they may well be depriving them of valuable opportunities for rehearsing written language.

More recent writers such as Hyon & Sulzby (1994) and Champion et al. (1995) have questioned whether the topic-associating style is, in fact, the dominant pattern for African-Americans. None the less, the findings of the earlier research underline the importance of teacher sensitivity to culturally-based discourse patterns.

Supporting children's writing development in English

A range of writers consider practical classroom issues in relation to writing, including Edwards (1995) and MRC (1995) in the UK; Gibbons (1991) in Australia; and Rigg & Enright (1986) and Williams & Snipper (1990) in the USA. These issues will be considered under the headings of confidence building and taking risks, rehearsal for writing dialogue journals and promoting writing in other languages.

Confidence building and taking risks

The consensus view is that writing is best seen as a process involving several different stages, including drafting, revision and editing (see Goodman & Owocki's review, this volume). This approach to writing is particularly helpful in the case of second language learners for two main reasons. First, the opportunity to rehearse ideas, vocabulary and structures provides a valuable boost to children's confidence. Second, this approach has the potential to reduce children's anxiety and to encourage risk-taking. Because children are not expected to produce perfect copy at the first attempt, process writing can help alleviate the sense of failure which they often feel when their writing is 'corrected'.

Rehearsal

Various writers have focussed on the importance of rehearsal for writing in multilingual classrooms. Mauro & Forty (1994), for instance, describe a range of group writing possibilities in work on poetry. Role play also offers valuable opportunities for writing both in English and in community languages. Wheatley (in Minns 1991) describes work around role play with six and seven year in a classroom where a special area had been set aside for role play as a police station. Wheatley (1991) and Savva (1990) describe role play writing around food. In addition, the opportunity to retell familiar stories is a valuable preparation for writing. Henry & Hill (1991), for instance, describe how children in a class of 10–12 year olds became interested in retelling stories they remembered from their own early childhood as a prelude to recording them in writing.

Dialogue journals

The use of dialogue journals is one of the better documented areas of writing in multilingual classrooms. Students write regularly about whatever they choose and for as long as they want. Teachers respond to the content rather than correcting the writing or making evaluative comments. Student and teacher make equal contributions, offering observations and opinions, asking and answering questions. When students write in dialogue journals they are obviously working on fluency not accuracy. By removing the fear of making mistakes, dialogue journals encourage risk-taking behaviours which help students develop as writers.

The considerable potential of dialogue journal writing with second language learners has been highlighted by Peyton & Reed (1990) who offer examples of this approach with children of all ages and at all levels of competence in English. For children with no English and little experience of literacy, journals can start as interactive picture books. When children are literate in another language and bilingual support teachers are available, there is no reason why the dialogue journal should not be written in the community language.

Dialogue journals allow the teacher to tailor responses to the language needs of the child in question and to offer very useful models in the target language. They give teachers and children the opportunity to get to know each other better. They can also accommodate personality differences.

Promoting writing in other languages

Teachers often assume that their sole responsibility is for teaching children literacy skills in English and that other languages have no part to play in this process (Edwards & Redfern, 1992). However, our understanding of the ways we learn has greatly expanded in recent years. It is much clearer now that the cognitive skills associated with literacy are not acquired separately in different languages (Cummins, 1977). Learning which has taken place in one language is readily transferred to English or other language learning situations. This changed perception is leading many teachers to seek out opportunities for writing in other languages in order to consolidate and extend children's competencies (MRC, 1995; Edwards, 1995).

Various writers discuss the potential of information technology as a bridge to literacy in both English and community languages. The concept keyboard, for instance, can be very useful with both very young children who have limited experience of the written word and with older beginners in English already literate in the community language. Foster (1992) describes how she used overlays in English, Bengali and Panjabi with a mixed language group of recently arrived secondary school children. Park (1992) describes the use of Spanish overlays with a recently arrived Spanish child.

Multilingual word-processing has also received attention; initiatives include 'The Multilingual Word-processing Project' (NCET, 1992) and Parents, Allwrite and Languages (PAL) (Abbott, 1994) and the Multilingual Wordprocessing in the Primary School Project (Chana et al., 1997a; 1997b). There is widespread agreement that wordprocessing helps to raise the status of community languages in the eyes of both monolingual and bilingual speakers. It also has considerable potential for more actively involving parents from other language communities in the life of the school (see also the review by Abbott, this volume).

Multilingual wordprocessing can be used to produce signs and labels, and translated letters to parents. Its most common use, however, would seem to be in producing books in other languages. These books are written in many different ways by children, parents and teachers – alone or in collaboration. The presence of the wordprocessor is a very powerful catalyst for children's writing. However, wordprocessing is by no means the only option. Many handwritten books are equally effective.

Writers such as MRC (1995) and Chana et al. (1997b) also discuss the technical aspects of multilingual wordprocessing. Some programs are dedicated to the other language script; others allow for the use of both English and the other script in the same document. In languages like Urdu and Arabic, the precise form of a grapheme depends on its position in the word and programs make use of contextual analysis to ensure that the correct variant. As part of an ongoing research project on the introduction of wordprocessing in Urdu into a primary school in southern England, Chana et al (1997b) also discuss the training needs of teachers and parents in the new technology.

FUTURE DEVELOPMENTS

No doubt because writing has emerged as a focus for research more recently than either the development of spoken language or of reading, we are still very much in a pre-theoretical phase: most publications on writing in multilingual classrooms are descriptive; a large proportion are teacher accounts of their own classroom experience. Exceptions to this general trend are study of various aspects of writing in a Native American school community documented by Goodman & Wilde (1992) and their colleagues, and Kenner's equally meticulous analysis of the bilingual writing development of children in a multilingual nursery. All these give valuable indications as to the directions which future research is likely to take.

A range of problems raised in Edwards' review of reading in multilingual classrooms in this volume apply equally to discussions of writing. These include teacher ignorance of other cultural practices, attitudes towards parents, and the broader political agenda which seeks to marginalise children's literacy development in minority languages (see the review by Baugh in Volume 1). Questions of this nature will also form a profitable focus for future research.

University of Reading, England

REFERENCES

Abbott, C.: 1994, 'Supporting writing in community languages through the eevelopment and use of a multilingual wordprocessor, and the involvement of parents and community groups in its use', Paper given at the sixth conference on 'Computers and Writing', University of Wales, Aberystwyth.

Bhatt, A., Barton, D., & Martin-Jones, M.: 1994, *Gujarati Literacies in East Africa and Leicester*, Working Paper 56, Centre for Language in Social Life, University of Lancaster.

Bissex, G.: 1980, *GNYS at Work: A Child Learns to Write and Read*, Harvard University Press, Harvard, Mass.

Calkins, L.: 1983, *Lessons From a Child*, Heinemann, London.

Champion, T., Seymour, H. & Camarata, S.: 1995, 'Narrative discourse of African American children', *Journal of Narrative and Life History* 5(4), 333–352.

Chana, U., Edwards, V. & Walker, S.: 1997a, 'Multilingual wordprocessing in the primary school', in A. Shreeve (ed.), *IT in English: Case Studies and Materials*, National Council for Educational Technology, Coventry.

Chana, U., Edwards, V. & Walker, S.: in press, 'Hidden resources: multilingual wordprocessing in the primary school', *Race, Ethnicity and Education* 1.

Cummins, J.: 1979, 'Linguistic interdependence and the educational development of bilingual children', *Review of Educational Research* 49, 222–251.

Edwards, V.: 1995, *Writing in Multilingual Classrooms*, Reading: Reading and Language Information Centre, University of Reading.

Edwards, V.: 1997, 'Unexpected benefits of multilingual technology', *Times Educational Supplement* 27 June: 35.

Edwards, V. & Redfern, A.: 1992, *The World in a Classroom: Language and Education in Britain and Canada*, Multilingual Matters, Clevedon, Avon.

Gibbons, P.: 1991, *Learning to Learn in a Second Language*, Primary English Teaching Association, Newtown, New South Wales.

Goodman, Y. & Wilde, S. (eds.): 1992, *Literacy Events in a Community of Young Writers*, Teachers College Press, New York & London.

Graves, D.: 1983, *Writing: Teachers and Children at Work*, Heinemann, London.

Gregory, E.: 1998, 'Siblings as mediators of literacy in linguistic minority communities', *Language and Education* 12, 33–54.

Heath, S.B.: 1983, *Ways with words*, Cambridge: Cambridge University Press.

Henry, A. & Hill, M.: 1991, 'Powerful stories', in Open University (1991) Open University, Milton Keynes.

Hyon, S. & Sulzby, E.: 1994, 'African American kindergartners' spoken narratives: Topic associating and topic centre styles', *Linguistics and Education* 6: 121–152.

Kenner, C.: 1997, *Social Scripts: Children's Writing in a Multilingual Nursery*, Unpublished PhD thesis, University of Southampton.

Mauro, E. & Forty, M.: 1994, 'Season of mists and Club biscuits', *Language and learning* March/April, 9–13.

Michaels, S. & Cazden, C.: 1986, 'Teacher/child collaboration as oral preparation for literacy', in B. Schieffelin (ed.), *The Acquisition of Literacy: Ethnographic Perspectives*, Ablex, Norwood, NJ, 132–154.

Minns, H.: 1991, *Primary Language: Extending the Curriculum with Computers*, National Council for Educational Technology, Coventry.

Multilingual Resources for Children Project (MRC): 1995, *Building Bridges: Multilingual Resources for Children*, Multilingual Matters, Clevedon.

National Council for Educational Technology (NCET): 1992, *Look – My Language is on the Computer: Information Technology in the Multilingual Classroom*, Unpublished ms, NCET, Coventry.

Peyton, J. & Reed, L.: 1990, *Dialogue Journal Writing with Nonnative English Speakers: A Handbook for Teachers*, Teachers of English to Speakers of Other Languages, Alexandria, Va.

Rigg, P. & Enright, D. (eds.): *Children and ESL: Integrating Perspectives*, Teachers of English to Speakers of Other Languages, Washington DC.

Savva, H.: 1990, 'The rights of bilingual children', in R. Carter (ed.), *Knowledge About Language and the Curriculum*, Hodder & Stoughton, Sevenoaks, Kent.

Smith, F.: 1982, *Writing and the Writer*, Heinemann, London.

Street, B.V.: 1995, *Social Literacies: Critical Approaches to Literacy in Development, Ethnography and Education*, Longman, London.

Urzúa, C.: 1986, 'A children's story', in P. Rigg & D. Enright (eds.), *Children and ESL: Integrating Perspectives*, TESOL, Washington DC, pp. 93–112.

Wheatley, V.: 1991, 'Wordprocessing in a nursery school', in G. Keith (ed.), *Knowledge About Language: Reflecting About Learning with Computers*, National Council for Educational Technology, Coventry.

Williams, J. & Snipper, G.: 1990, *Literacy and Bilingualism*, Longman, New York and London.

Section 3

Focus on the Social Context of Literacy

JOHN EDWARDS

THE SOCIAL PSYCHOLOGY OF READING

Reading has a vast literature, the bulk of which is concerned with methods and processes of skills acquisition and development. There has been a great neglect of what might be termed the social psychology (or, sociology) of reading – which, for present purposes, can be understood as the influence of the social environment upon reading. It is clear that this influence is considerable. Teachers do not want merely to produce people who can read – they want to produce people who are readers. Thus, a social psychology of reading must not only include a consideration of factors relevant to the acquisition of skills and strategies, but should also seek to illuminate all features of the uses to which basic knowledge is applied. The topic, then, is principally about such matters as *what* people read, the *amount* of reading that is done, the *purposes* and *effects* of reading, and so on. These socially-influenced issues intertwine, of course, with skill levels – someone who is barely literate is obviously unlikely to become a voracious reader – but reading *practices* are not always predictable from ability. This, in some sense, is the heart of the matter, especially in societies where basic literacy levels are high: how can we describe and account for variation in reading practices, habits and attitudes?

These questions are not new: they have been asked in virtually all literate societies (see, for instance, the discussion of Dutch reading practices in the review by Reitsma, this volume). More specifically, complaints about generally poor reading practices seem as perennial as grumblings over the inadequacies of the younger generation. Such complaints are essentially founded on the belief that reading is the key to knowledge and, more particularly, to a knowledge critical to cultural maintenance and transmission (see also the review by Luke, this volume). Steiner (1975, p. 31) notes: 'it is no overstatement to say that we possess civilization because we have learnt to translate out of time.' This cross-generational 'translation' naturally involves an educated, *reading* public.

The social psychology of reading is, indeed, a particularly important and timely topic. On the one hand, as Nell (1988) points out, new schools of literary criticism have been affected by a relativism which suggests that the book is, in fact, created by the reader (Tinker, 1965), that 'the reader of a novel is himself a novelist' (Lubbock, 1957, p. 17), that a book is 'a relationship, an axis of innumerable relationships' (Borges, 1964, p. 13),

V. Edwards and D. Corson (eds), Encyclopedia of Language and Education,
Volume 2: Literacy, 119–126.
© *1997 Kluwer Academic Publishers. Printed in the Netherlands.*

that 'the reader makes literature' (Fish, 1980, p. 11). All of this argues even more strongly for closer attention to all those matters germane to the act of reading. On the other hand, the past few years have seen – with the electronic revolution – an accelerating debate about the very future of the book in a computer age. Negroponte's *Being Digital* (1995) depicts a glorious and increasingly book-less future, while Birkerts' *The Gutenberg Elegies* (1994) defends the more traditional pleasures and values of the text. Of course, words on computer screens, like words in books, are *read* – but it is surely no exaggeration to say that the act of reading, constant for many centuries, is undergoing considerable change; many writers would claim that the essence of the change is social and psychological.

Although the proportion of illiterate people has been in steady decline for some time, an increase in absolute numbers means that one-third of the world's population can still neither read nor write. The problem is not, of course, spread equally around the globe – the proportion drops to only three or four per cent in industrialised societies. However, even here, there are important regional disparities. More importantly, illiteracy *per se* is not the major issue of interest. So-called *functional literacy* (see reviews by Rogers and Verhoeven, this volume) refers to a socially meaningful ability, one that goes beyond elementary skills. The UN, for example, considers that a person with less than nine years education is functionally illiterate; UNESCO has defined a literate person as one having the ability to fully participate in group culture, whose skills permit further individual and social development (see Oxenham, 1980). Definitions here are varied, and far from crystal-clear – but it is clear that illiteracy in this broader sense constitutes a major problem, even in 'developed' nations. Kozol (1985), in his assessment of the American scene, notes that about one-third of all adults are functionally illiterate (the proportion varies along class and racial lines); he also points out that functional *literacy* does not imply highly-developed capacities – it means only mundane skills, like being able to understand road signs, or read product warning labels, or look up telephone numbers. A Canadian survey found virtually the same proportion cited by Kozol (8% illiterate, and another 25% functionally, or 'marginally' illiterate: Creative Research Group, 1987; see Edwards, 1991, for further details).

Beyond elementary literacy, and beyond functional literacy, there is yet another factor – most central for present purposes – to be reckoned with. Maeroff (1982) and Neuman (1986) have referred to aliteracy. Aliterate persons are functionally literate – but they don't read. The term may be new but the phenomenon (as implied above) is old; concern over lack of reading, the allegedly poor quality of what is read and the evil influences of distractors (television, of course, is the primary modern villain here) have been discussed for some time (Edwards, 1981). For example, in her well-known work, *Fiction and the Reading Public*, Leavis (1965 [1932], p. 231) observed that 'the reading capacity of the general public . . . has never been so low as at the present time.' More recent research shows a continuingly low value placed upon reading (see, for example, Bettelheim & Zelan, 1981, on children's reading habits and attitudes). It would be tedious and repetitive to discuss here the available studies and statistics, which derive from many quarters (see, for brief overviews, Edwards, 1981 and Nell, 1988). However, whether the information comes from polls and surveys, from experimental studies, or from the remarks and insights of writers and social commentators, it would seem that general levels of reading (both quality and quantity) are low in most societies. This is the essential framework within which a modern social psychology of reading must exist. And, to repeat, the latter is a theoretical thrust which remains woefully underdeveloped – despite being of longstanding historical importance, and despite being of the utmost contemporary concern. We are in a pre-theoretical phase now, and have been for some considerable time. That is, although some writers – Nell (1988) would be a modern example here – have attempted in a desultory way to construct explanatory models, the bulk of the work consists of purely descriptive and often very localised efforts: who reads, how much is read, what is read, and so on. This descriptive work is often of great interest but there is, however, a need to think about tentatively moving onwards; if we do so, we will likely design more fully-fleshed data-gathering instruments, surveys which pay closer attention (in the interests of generalisability) to previous work, questionnaires and interviews whose relevance extends beyond the specific context under study.

MAJOR CONTRIBUTIONS

Several important studies have had a bearing upon the social psychology of reading, as defined here. One or two of these have been unjustifiably neglected – perhaps because the whole area has yet to achieve much theoretical coherence. Waples and Tyler (1931), for example – in their *What People Want to Read About* – provide an intensive study of topics of reading interest. A further publication (Waples, Berelson & Bradshaw, 1940) discusses the complexity of adult reading responses; it also advocates the use of the case-study method to probe more deeply into reading practices, habits and attitudes, and this was taken up by Strang (1942) in her investigations with more than one hundred respondents. Leavis's very personal study (1932) has already been referred to; when it first appeared, it evoked a large critical response. Interested in the question of 'what has happened to fiction and the reading public since the eighteenth century', Leavis proceeded with what she termed an 'anthropological' method. Few would describe it that way today, but Leavis does include a survey of sorts, based upon a questionnaire sent to popular novelists. A more systematic, if drier, approach is that of Link and Hopf (1946). In a study commissioned by the American Book Manufacturers' Institute, the authors considered who reads, what kinds of books are read, what competitors for readers' attention exist, and how (and why) people go about choosing their books.

In the late 1970s, Greaney and his associates began to pay rather more systematic attention to the social aspects of reading. Greaney (1980), for example, found that the amount and type of leisure reading were related to such variables as basic ability, sex, socioeconomic status, family size and primary-school type (see also Greaney & Hegarty, 1987). Greaney and Neuman (1990) also investigated the functions of reading, in a study of children in more than a dozen countries. Utility, enjoyment and escape were the three recurring motivations, and it was found that girls rated the second factor more positively than did boys (sex differences, particularly in the early years, are a consistent finding in the literature). Anderson and colleagues have also done useful work, including an influential report, *Becoming a Nation of Readers* (Anderson, Hiebert, Scott & Wilkinson, 1985) and a study which relates children's reading to other leisure-time activities (Anderson, Wilson & Fielding, 1988). The authors term this latter work 'the most intensive study that has yet been done' of out-of-school activities (p. 286), linking their work explicitly with that of Greaney; the study demonstrates generally low levels of leisure reading.

Ravitch and Finn's (1987) large-scale survey (of some 8,000 17-year-old American children) focusses on knowledge of history and literature; part of it assessed amount and type of reading, an evaluation well-embedded in a network of other variables.

Nell (1988) provides a model of 'ludic' (i.e., pleasure) reading as part of a work which comprises both a set of empirical studies and a (rather limited) literature survey. His work has been reasonably criticised for its psychoanalytic bent and its methodological difficulties while, at the same time, praised as establishing a base from which further study of 'ludic' reading can proceed (see Venezky, 1990). Of greatest interest in Nell's work is its documentation of voracious readers: one family studied comprised a father who claimed to read 30 books a month, a mother who read 25, and two daughters who read 18 and 28 books monthly. This massive 'escapist' reading, this reading 'fever' (as one respondent put it) will surely prove to be one of the most interesting aspects of a thoroughgoing social psychology of reading.

WORK IN PROGRESS

In 1993, the Roehampton Institute in London launched the pilot phase of a survey of 8,000 British children's reading habits. A report on the pilot project (involving 320 children) was published in 1994 (Children's Literature Research Centre), and the full report appeared in 1996. The sort of information elicited from respondents here would seem to be of the greatest relevance: what children read, how they come into contact with reading material, what reading preferences exist, how satisfying reading proves to be, how reading relates to other leisure activities, and so on. The size of the main sample will also allow meaningful discussion of the influence of such variables as sex, age, parental occupation, ethnic and class group, etc.

Another recent and germane investigation is that of McKenna, Kear and Ellsworth (1995). They have investigated the reading attitudes of a stratified sample of over 18,000 American primary-school children, through the administration of a 20-item scale. The results relate attitudes to reading ability, sex and ethnicity.

This brief overview of a selection of the more relevant publications on (or possibly contributing to) the social psychology of reading has only touched upon important results found. As may be imagined, these vary considerably, but there are some emerging generalities, and these can be summarised most efficiently here by turning, finally, to some work at St Francis Xavier University in Nova Scotia.

In 1990, Walker surveyed the reading habits and attitudes of about 250 students and 75 faculty members, as well as those of some 40 local secondary-school teachers. The main findings: (a) there was a very small group of 'core' readers; (b) material read was largely of a 'light' or ephemeral nature; (c) reading for pleasure was not a generally favoured leisure activity; (d) television viewing was not the primary reason for low reading levels; (e) amount of reading material in the home, being read to as a child, and parental value placed upon reading per se were important determinants of reading habits; (f) important sex differences emerged with regard to the quantity and type of reading done; (g) reading habits correlated to some extent with school marks and achievement. When Walker asked teachers to comment upon their students' reading, it was found that they generally held very negative views of both amount and type. Interestingly (though perhaps not surprisingly), university teachers tended to blame secondary schools for inadequately preparing students, and high-school teachers blamed primary-school practices (we might reasonably guess, then, that primary teachers would point the finger at poor home environments and attitudes).

The data generated by Walker's work were of sufficient interest to suggest further and more comprehensive study. Work now in the final stages of completion investigates reading practices and attitudes across a wide range of the population of Nova Scotia (which, earlier government figures suggest, is a good representation of the larger Canadian picture. Preliminary findings, including those of Walker – when mapped against the existing literature – suggest further that results from Nova Scotia will have extra-Canadian generalisability as well). Province-wide, there are 22 school boards: of these, two are francophone and were excluded for present purposes; all but one of the others agreed to participate in the work. For each of 19 districts, then, we selected (with local assistance) one Grade 6 and one Grade 12 class (the former being the highest primary-school grade, the latter the highest secondary-school one). All children in each class were given questionnaires to fill out themselves, and all were given forms for both parents. Questionnaires were also distributed to all teachers in each of the 38 participating schools. Allowing for some non-returns, our total sample comprised about 3,000 people.

The actual questionnaires cannot be described here in any detail, but several general points can be made. First, forms for children, teachers and parents, while not exactly the same, were designed to produce complementary and interlocking information. Second, teachers and parents were asked for information about their own reading habits and attitudes and to provide their perceptions of children's reading practices. Third, the questions asked reflect both a close reading of the previous literature and the desire to advance the general and theoretical state of the social psychology of reading. The actual items, then, elicit information dealing with: age, sex, family size and income level, parental occupations, overall school achievement patterns, school subject preferences, reading ability and attitude, amount of time spent reading, quantity and type of material read, factors influencing choice of reading, past and present enjoyment and interest levels, home and school encouragement of reading, home reading practices, reading as related to other leisure-time pursuits, and so on. Beyond categorical and scaled responses, qualitative data were also elicited: lists of favourite books, magazines and authors, for example. All in all, allowing for multiple-section questions, each subject has responded to well over 100 queries.

We believe that, taking both overall sample size and level of questionnaire detail into account, this survey is (with the Roehampton effort) among the most comprehensive of its kind.

FUTURE DEVELOPMENTS

What is wanted, overall, is a theoretical picture which will draw upon the sorts of data-items noted, and which will treat basic issues such as: who reads, how do people become readers, what are the motivations for amount and type of reading, what are the essential descriptions of reading habits and attitudes, what are the outcomes of reading, and so on. Can we, in fact, hope to assemble a coherent theory of the social psychology of reading out of the many and varied relevant elements? It is certainly a large order, but (as with other important matters) we can at least hope to make real progress in that direction.

A more fully-fleshed social psychology of reading would be an important entity in itself, incorporating what are currently many disparate findings. In addition, more formalised knowledge here would have practical significance in a world where reading habits are under particular scrutiny. There is at the moment (to cite just one example) considerable concern about the amount of horror-story reading by teenagers. Often described as the fastest-growing genre, this material and its consumption predictably attract a variety of opinion. In some schools, for example, teachers use these adolescent shockers on the grounds that, after all, they *are* of obvious interest and (it is hoped) will lead to 'better' things. The view is, in other words, that virtually any reading is better than nothing. Others disagree vehemently: the reading of books produced to a formula, where plots are endlessly recycled and where characters are wooden stereotypes, is seen to induce the sort of non-progressive escapism that Nell (1988) has discussed at length. Clearly, a fuller picture of reading habits and practices *per se* – particularly one stressing developmental trends – would be of value here.

An evolving social psychology of reading would complement the broad picture we already have of basic skills development and teaching methods. Ideally, it would fold together the results of empirical research and the insights – both contemporary and historical – of the many commentators on reading. It would not be, then, the sterile and decontextualised exercise which is, regrettably, characteristic of much modern social scientific work. We are dealing here with a topic which obviously requires systematic research, but it is also one which can make a real contribution to – and therefore ought, where appropriate, to draw upon – cultural and literary studies.

St Francis Xavier University, Canada

REFERENCES

Anderson, R., Hiebert, E., Scott, J. & Wilkinson, I.: 1985, *Becoming a Nation of Readers*, National Institute of Education, Washington.

Anderson, R., Wilson, P. & Fielding, L.: 1988, 'Growth in reading and how children spend their time outside of school', *Reading Research Quarterly* 23, 285–303.

Bettelheim, B. & Zelan, K.: 1981, 'Why children don't like to read', *Atlantic Monthly* 248(5), 25–31.

Birkerts, S.: 1994, *The Gutenberg Elegies: The Fate of Reading in an Electronic Age*, Ballantine, New York.

Borges, J.L.: 1964, *Labyrinths*, New Directions, New York.

Children's Literature Research Centre (Roehampton Institute): 1994, *Contemporary Juvenile Reading Habits*, British Library, London.

Children's Literature Research Centre (Roehampton Institute): 1996, *Young People's Reading at the End of the Century*, Roehampton Institute, London.

Creative Research Group: 1987, *Literacy in Canada*, CRG, Toronto.

Edwards, J. (ed.): 1981, *The Social Psychology of Reading*, Institute of Modern Languages, Silver Spring MD.

Edwards, J.: 1991, 'Literacy and education in contexts of cultural and linguistic heterogeneity', *Canadian Modern Language Review* 47, 933–949.

Fish, S.: 1980, *Is There a Text in This Class?*, Harvard University Press, Cambridge.

Gibson, E. & Levin, H.: 1975, *The Psychology of Reading*, MIT Press, Cambridge.

Greaney, V.: 1980, 'Factors related to amount and type of leisure time reading', *Reading
Research Quarterly* 15, 337–357.

Greaney, V. & Hegarty, M.: 1987, 'Correlates of leisure-time reading', *Journal of Research
in Reading* 10, 3–20.

Greaney, V. & Neuman, S.: 1990, 'The functions of reading: A cross-cultural perspective',
Reading Research Quarterly 25, 172–195.

Kozol, J.: 1985, *Illiterate America*, Doubleday, New York.

Leavis, Q.D.: 1965 [1932], *Fiction and the Reading Public*, Chatto & Windus, London.

Link, H. & Hopf, H.: 1946, *People and Books: A Study of Reading and Book-Buying
Habits*, Book Manufacturers' Institute, New York.

Lubbock, P.: 1957, *The Craft of Fiction*, Compass, New York.

Maeroff, G.: 1982, 'Dismay over those who shun reading', *New York Times*, 28 September.

McKenna, M., Kear, D. & Ellsworth, R.: 1995, 'Children's attitudes toward reading: A
national survey', *Reading Research Quarterly* 30, 934–956.

Negroponte, N.: 1995, *Being Digital*, Knopf, New York.

Nell, V.: 1988, *Lost in a Book: The Psychology of Reading for Pleasure*, Yale University
Press, New Haven.

Neuman, S.: 1986, 'The home environment and fifth-grade students' leisure reading',
Elementary School Journal 3, 335–343.

Oxenham, J.: 1980, *Literacy: Writing, Reading and Social Organisation*, Routledge &
Kegan Paul, London.

Ravitch, D. & Finn, C.: 1987, *What Do Our 17-Year-Olds Know?*, Harper & Row, New
York.

Steiner, G.: 1975, *After Babel*, Oxford University Press, Oxford.

Strang, R.: 1942, *Exploration in Reading Patterns*, University of Chicago Press, Chicago.

Tinker, M.: 1965, *Bases for Effective Reading*, University of Minnesota Press, Minneapolis.

Venezky, R.: 1990, 'Review of lost in a book (Nell)', *American Journal of Psychology*
103, 136–141.

Walker, S.: 1990, 'A survey of reading habits and attitudes in a university population'
(unpublished report), Psychology Department, St Francis Xavier University.

Waples, D. & Tyler, R.: 1931, *What People Want to Read About*, University of Chicago
Press, Chicago.

Waples, D., Berelson, B. & Bradshaw, F.: 1940, *What Reading Does to People*, University
of Chicago Press, Chicago.

LUDO VERHOEVEN

FUNCTIONAL LITERACY

Concern about levels of literacy has been growing in many parts of the world in recent decades and is reflected in the greater general awareness of the numbers of illiterates and the consequences of illiteracy for the individual. Increased interest in this area has served as a catalyst for research from which 'functional literacy' has emerged as an important theme. This model of literacy recognizes personal and social needs and has played a key role in furthering our understanding of the distribution, consequences and causes of illiteracy.

EARLY DEVELOPMENTS

Early developments crucial to any discussion of functional literacy include attempts to explain the differences between speech and writing and successive definitions of literacy itself.

Differences between spoken and written communication have attracted the attention of writers for some time. As Olson (1977) points out, in oral communication the listener uses a wide range of contextual cues to understand the intentions of the speaker whereas, in written communication, such cues are almost completely absent. In a similar vein, Cummins (1984) distinguishes between context-embedded and context-reduced communication. However, as Tannen (1982) has made clear, oral and literate modes of expression do not fully coincide with speech and writing. For example, a personal letter focuses on interpersonal relationships and shared knowledge, while a lecture may be used to present written material orally.

This discussion is ongoing. More recent contributions include Harris (1986) who presents a diachronic analysis of the nexus between script and speech, with special emphasis on writing as representation; Scinto (1986) and Coulmas (1991) who discuss the psychology and the nature of written language; and Olson & Torrance (1991) who bring together a series of papers on (dis)continuities between oracy and literacy.

Clarity about the relationship between speech and writing has obvious implications for attempts to define literacy. UNESCO (1953), for instance, proposes that:

> A person can be called (il)literate if he/she can(not) read and write with understanding a short simple statement on his/her everyday life.

V. Edwards and D. Corson (eds), Encyclopedia of Language and Education,
Volume 2: Literacy, 127–132.
© *1997 Kluwer Academic Publishers. Printed in the Netherlands.*

The vagueness of terms such as 'understanding', 'simple' or 'statement on everyday life' makes this definition problematic and underlines the importance of searching for greater precision. Over a period of time, the emphasis has shifted from structural aspects of reading and writing to broader definitions which take account of the functions of written language in a range of social contexts (cf. Stubbs, 1980; Guthrie & Kirsch, 1983).

The term 'functional literacy' was introduced in order to emphasise the demands of literacy in a complex world, especially in the context of employment and economic development. Gray (1956) talks of literacy as

> ... the process and content of learning to read and write to the
> preparation for work and vocational training, as well as a means
> of increasing the productivity of the individual.

– a definition in wide use by the 1960s in UNESCO publications. In this view, literacy is a complex set of skills defined in terms of the print demands of occupational, civic, community and personal needs. More recent assessment measures have tended to stress the vocational and economic implications of literacy skills. For instance, in national assessment profiles for young adults in the United States, a distinction was made between reading, writing, numeracy and document processing skills (cf. Kirsch & Jungebluth, 1986; Venezky, 1990). Another recent trend concerns self-assessment in which people are asked to report reading and writing difficulties and the practical problems which they cause in everyday life (Hamilton, 1987). This approach clearly acknowledges the values of literacy for the individual.

The information revolution is another related issue. According to Levine (1986, 1994), the bureaucratisation of work, the permeation of social life by written materials and the greater complexity of these materials has had a considerable impact on the kinds of skills which are required for reading. The enormous range of potential applications for computers has also led inevitably to a redefinition of what is understood by basic literacy (see also Abbott, this volume).

MAJOR CONTRIBUTIONS

Sociocultural perspectives provide an interesting alternative to the economic or technological perspectives which dominated discussions of literacy for a considerable period of time. Street (1984, 1994) speaks of transition from an 'autonomous' to an 'ideological' view of literacy. The autonomous view refers to mainly Western theories which define literacy in terms of universal cognitive or technical skills that can be learned independently of specific contexts or cultural frameworks. The ideological view, on the other hand, defines literacy practices from the perspective of cultural and power structures in society (see also the reviews by Street and Luke, this volume).

Auerbach (1992) distinguishes four distinct pedagogical concomitants of the ideological view: variability and context-specificity in literacy practices; literacy acquisition as a learner-centred process; the politicisation of content in literacy instruction; and the integration of the voices and experiences of learners within a critical framwork. Various ethnographic studies undertaken from an ideological perspective pay attention to the role of literacy practices in reproducing or changing power structures (Fingeret, 1983; Rockhill, 1987; Luke, 1988; Lind, 1990). However, Stuckey (1991) puts these challenges to the autonomous model into perspective, arguing that literacy cannot be seen as the ultimate mediator or arbiter of social problems.

Recent studies attempt to articulate what is actually involved when people engage in cultural activities (see, for instance, Barton & Ivanič, 1991) and make it clear that it is no longer feasible to see literacy/illiteracy as a simple dichotomy. Literacy is a lifelong, context-bound set of practices in which individual needs vary with time and place (see also, Rogers, this volume). Other important themes include the notion of multiple literacies and language policies which promote cultural diversity.

Modelling functional literacy

The sociolinguistic concept of communicative competence (cf. Hymes, 1971) has considerable potential for developing our understanding of functional literacy at the level of the individual. In the context of language teaching, Canale and Swain (1980) suggest that communicative competence comprises four different competencies: grammatical competence, discourse competence, strategic competence and sociolinguistic competence. Bachman (1990) proposes a similar definition, but also includes psycho-physiological mechanisms, such as prosody and processing speed.

Most discussions of communicative competence have focused on oral language. However, Verhoeven (1994a) extends the existing framework to writing by adding a fifth level – (de)coding competence – and extending the other competences to include attributes which apply specifically to written communication. He presents functional literacy as encompassing both grammatical competence (which is taken to include phonology, lexis and morpho-syntax) and discourse competence (in which cohesion and coherence are fundamental). Strategic competence involves the planning, execution and evaluation of writing; while sociolinguistic competence entails both an understanding of the literacy conventions appropriate to a given society and cultural knowlege. However, in the context of writing, writers also require (de)coding skills: they need to be familiar with the conventions such as the directionality of scripts and the relationship between grapheme and sound in the case of alphabetic and syllabic writing and between logograph and meaning in the case of writing systems such as Chinese; and, in order to focus on meaning rather than form, this knowledge must be automatised.

PROBLEMS AND DIFFICULTIES

The main area of difficulty in any discussion of functional literacy is the notion of how literacy levels are to be assessed, both in more general terms and in relation to members of ethnic and other minority groups.

For various reasons, reliable demographic information on functional literacy patterns in different societies is difficult to obtain. This raises a whole range of questions in relation to assessment. A competence-based approach, such as the one outlined above, has much to recommend it. Not only can reading and writing be separately assessed but a distinction can be made between decoding skills and comprehension skills in reading, and between transcription and composition skills in writing. Various writing genres could be analysed with a view to developing assessment tasks for different target populations populations which could serve as the basis for more principled assessments of literacy levels. This approach would make it possible to identify a range of uses for reading and writing within a given community (see also reviews by Edwards, this volume). It would also permit placement at appropriate points on a continuum of achievement, one end of which is marked by no literacy skills, the other the ability to perform complex literacy skills. Between these two poles, lies the ability to code or decode words and to perform simple literacy tasks.

Sampling poses problems for assessing literacy levels. In many surveys, minority groups are either overlooked or underrepresented. Yet there are strong arguments for paying particular attention to high risk groups such as ethnic minorities, dialect speakers, school leavers, the long-term unemployed, unskilled workers and prisoners in any discussion of functional literacy levels.

It is clear that particular attention needs to be paid to the situation of ethnic minority communities (cf. Fishman, 1980; Verhoeven, 1994b). In a multi-ethnic society, different groups use a wide range of written codes in different situations. One written code will be used in wider communication in society, a second for intragroup communication and yet another for religious purposes. In exploring functional literacy, we need to take account of the multilingual and multicultural realities of ethnic minority communities. It is essential that literacy skills in all languages are recognised as important human resources.

The choice of language in literacy tasks for second language speakers is clearly crucial (see Agnihotri's review of 'Sustaining local literacies', this volume). In a multilingual society, different ethnic groups often use a range of written codes for different functions and at different levels of competence. The extent to which members of an ethnic minority group will use their own language, in addition to the majority language, in written communication will depend on factors such as the written tradition of the minority language and the status of the ethnic group in question.

FUTURE DIRECTIONS

Current information on the demographics of literacy is far from satisfactory. Even when population censuses include data on literacy, this information is usually based on self-evaluations, the reliability of which are open to question. In addition, most statistical data assume a simple dichotomy between literate and illiterate, ignoring intermediate levels of competence. This is an area which clearly requires a great deal more attention than it has received to present.

The notion of literacy as a single unified construct is another concern. As Street (1994) points out, we should not talk of 'literacy as such' but rather of 'literacy practices'. A multiplicity of literacies can be related to specific cultural contexts, power relations and ideology. It is clear that the great divide between literacy and illiteracy rests uneasily with this notion of literacy. In order to achieve a clearer picture of the nature and distribution of literacy, there is an urgent need to study reading and writing practices in diverse cultural and ideological contexts.

University of Nijmegen, the Netherlands

REFERENCES

Auerbach, E.: 1992, 'Literacy and ideology', *Annual Review of Applied Linguistics* 20(12), 71–85.

Bachman, L.F.: 1990, *Fundamental Considerations in Language Testing*, Oxford University Press, New York NY.

Barton, D. & Ivanič, R. (eds.): 1991, *Writing in the Community*, Sage, London.

Canale, M. & Swain, M.: 1980, 'Theoretical bases of communicative approaches to second language testing and teaching', *Applied Linguistics* 1, 1–47.

Coulmas, F.: 1991, *The Writing Systems of the World*, Blackwell, Oxford.

Cummins, J.: 1984, 'Wanted: A theoretical framework for relating language proficiency to academic achievement among bilingual students', in C. Rivera (ed.), *Language Proficiency and Academic Achievement*, Multilingual Matters, Clevedon, 1984, 2–19.

Fingeret, A.: 1983, 'Social network: A new perspective of independence and illiterate adults', *Adult Education Quarterly* 33, 133–146.

Fishman, J.A.: 1980, 'Ethnocultural dimensions in the acquisition and retention of biliteracy', *Journal of Basic Writing* 3, 48–61.

Gray, W.S.: 1956, *The Teaching of Reading and Writing*, Scott Foreman, Chicago.

Guthrie, J. & Kirsch, I.: 1983, 'What is literacy in the United States? Reading competencies and practices', Technical Report 5, International Reading Association, Newark.

Hamilton, M.: 1987, *Literacy, Numeracy and Adults: Evidence from the National Child Development Study*, ALBSU, London.

Harris, R.: 1986, *The Origin of Writing*, Duckworth, London.

Hymes, D.: 1971, *On Communicative Competence*, Philadelphia University Press, Philadelphia.

Kirsch, I.S. & Jungebluth, A.: 1986, *Literacy: Profiles of America's Young Adults*, NAEP, Princeton, NJ.

Levine, K.: 1986, *The Social Context of Literacy*, Routledge & Kegan Paul, London.

Levine, K.: 1994, 'Functional literacy in a changing world', in L. Verhoeven (ed.), *Functional Literacy. Theoretical issues and educational implications*, John Benjamins, Amsterdam/Philadelphia, 1994, 113–132.

Lind, A.: 1990, *Mobilizing Women for Literacy*, Unesco Bureau of Education, Paris.

Luke, A.: 1988, *Literacy Textbooks and Ideology*, Falmer Press, London.

Olson, D.R.: 1977, 'Oral and written language and the cognitive processes of children', *Journal of Communication*, 10–26.

Olson, D.R. & Torrance, N.: 1991, *Orality and Literacy*, Cambridge University Press, Cambridge.

Rockhill, K.: 1987, 'Gender, language and the politics of literacy', *British Journal of Sociology of Education* 2, 153–167.

Scinto, L.F.M.: 1986, *Written Language and Psychological Development*, Academic Press, London.

Street, B.V. (ed.): 1984, *Literacy in Theory and Practice*, Cambridge University Press, Cambridge.

Street, B.V.: 1994, 'Cross-cultural approaches to literacy', in L. Verhoeven (ed.), *Functional Literacy. Theoretical Issues and Educational Implications*, John Benjamins, Amsterdam/Philadelphia, 1994, 95–112.

Stubbs, M.: 1980, *Language and Literacy: The Sociolinguistics of Reading and Writing*, Routledge & Kegan Paul, London.

Stuckey, E.:1991, *The Violence of Literacy*, Portsmouth, NH: Boynton/Cook, Heinemann.

Tannen, D.: 1982, 'Oral and written strategies in spoken and written narratives', *Language* 58, 1–21.

Unesco: 1953, *World Illiteracy at Mid-Century*, Unesco, Paris.

Venezky, R.L.: 1990, 'Definitions of literacy', in R.L. Venezky, D.A. Wagner & B.S. Ciliberti (eds.), *Toward Defining Literacy*, International Reading Association, Newark De, 1990, 2–16.

Verhoeven, L.: 1994a, 'Modeling and promoting functional literacy', in L. Verhoeven (ed.), *Functional Literacy. Theoretical Issues and Educational Implications*, John Benjamins, Amsterdam/Philadelphia, 1994, 3–34.

Verhoeven, L.: 1994b, 'Linguistic diversity and the acquisition of literacy', in L. Verhoeven (ed.), *Functional Literacy. Theoretical Issues and Educational Implications*, John Benjamins, Amsterdam/Philadelphia, 1994, 199–220.

BRIAN V. STREET

SOCIAL LITERACIES

This review focuses on current approaches to literacy under three main headings: the 'autonomous' model of literacy; 'new literacy studies'; and critical literacy. A brief description of the major contributions in each area is followed by a critical review of the strengths and weaknesses of each. The review concludes with a consideration of future developments.

EARLY DEVELOPMENTS

Until recently the dominant view of literacy amongst researchers, practitioners and policy makers was what has been characterised as the 'autonomous' model of literacy (Street, 1984). According to this view, literacy is a neutral technique which can be applied across all social and cultural contexts with generally uniform effects. The model is rooted in earlier psychological theories of individual cognitive development and social theories of progress and development, from simple to complex society, and from 'traditional' to 'modern'. The major tenet of this perspective is that there is a 'great divide' between oral and written forms of communication (Finnegan, 1988). In societies characterised by mainly oral modes of communication, it is assumed that certain features of 'modern' society are lacking, notably the ability to detach oneself from immediate meanings and contexts, formal logic and a 'modernising' perspective on life (Lerner, 1958; Goody, 1977, 1986, 1987).

The acquisition of literacy, then, has major implications for both individuals and for societies. As individuals acquire literacy, so their world views expand: they are able to juxtapose different sets of ideas critically and so develop scientific and logical thinking. Economic and political institutions are believed to change with the spread of literacy, so that rational economic planning and capitalist entrepreneurship replace barter and exchange. In world terms, such a change leads to a new world order in which the model offered by western 'developed' societies is imitated by 'under developed' societies.

According to Anderson and Bowman (1965) and to earlier UNESCO (1976) approaches to education, the spread of literacy is associated with most features of 'modernisation', notably economic take off, rational health planning, female emancipation etc. In political terms, patrimonial social orders give way to bureaucratic and democratic systems, where promotion

V. Edwards and D. Corson (eds), Encyclopedia of Language and Education,
Volume 2: Literacy, 133–141.
© *1997 Kluwer Academic Publishers. Printed in the Netherlands.*

is on merit not kinship or social position. Decision making is democrat-
ically ordered through such institutions as political parties, voting and a
division of political and judicial institutions. At a macro level, development economists and policy makers tended to take it for granted that these
outcomes follow from the spread of literacy. However, among researchers,
how and in what conditions literacy leads to such effects provides the basic
focus for enquiry.

Similar changes in the social order are claimed also to follow the acquisition and spread of literacy if the dominant philosophical mode is religious.
According to the autonomous model of literacy, those with literacy are able
to develop 'Religions of the Book' in which local, parochial beliefs are
substituted for a broader, world viewpoint. Instead of Yoruba religion, for
instance, which may change as local priests and elders change, a religion
of the Book, such as Christianity or Islam can fix theological ideas and
fundamental premises more permanently over time by writing down its
major narratives and tenets (Goody, 1986). There is also a tendency to
proselytise and develop missionary zeal for spreading these ideas to other
societies so that the religion extends across time and space. Local religions, on the other hand, remain rooted in local cultures and change with
them. In all cases, communication through literacy becomes less rooted
in the immediate and personal, ideas and beliefs can be detached from
parochial pressures and placed in broader perspective and the society can
reflect more critically on its own character and plan to change.

At the individual level, similar changes are believed to follow from the
acquisition of literacy. As with the social level, the major feature of literacy
is seen to be the ability to lay different ideas side by side and to evaluate
them critically. Logic, critical thought and scientific perspectives then
follow. Individuals who might be rooted in restricted modes of thought are
able to develop elaborated and critical thinking and to better make rational
choices. A great deal of psychological research is devoted to the cognitive
implications of the acquisition of literacy (Oakhill, Beard & Vincent, 1995;
Olson, 1977, 1994; see also the review by Olson in volume 3).

Much of this appears 'natural' in the everyday discourse of many contemporary western societies. Media representations of literacy and its
significance, pathologise those with difficulties in reading and writing,
whether adults or 'failed' school children. Schools are berated for failing
the society if literacy levels are seen to fall – by various measures rooted
in the autonomous model. The issue of 'falling standards' has dominated
public debate about literacy in a number of societies in recent years (Hirsch,
1987). Adult literacy campaigns have been created, in both the developed
and developing world contexts, to overcome this 'disadvantage' and their
publicity tends to reinforce the popular conception of literacy.

The theoretical roots of these ideas are in technological determinism
– a belief that social progress follows from specific technical develop-

ments such as the printing press, or television, or currently computing and
Information Technology; from theories of cognitive development at individual level tested through experimental methods, though often apparently
validated through more speculative methods (cf. Ong, 1982); and from
modernisation theory and the concept of progress derived from eighteenth
century European Enlightenment thinking (Oxenham, 1980).

The strengths of the autonomous model of literacy are claimed to be
the focus on individual and technical skills and the ability to 'deliver', in
pedagogic terms, mastery of reading and writing. This is achieved through
an ability to screen out the social and cultural 'interference' of traditional
beliefs and mindsets.

Problems and Difficulties

The major criticisms of the autonomous model are that it is insensitive to
cultural variation, narrowly economistic, and ethnocentric in its focus upon
western forms of literacy at the expense of local traditions and meanings.
Because of these weaknesses, new models of literacy have been developed
in recent years that attempt to take a more critical and a more culturally
relative perspective (Street, 1984, 1993; Finnegan, 1988; Gee, 1991).

MAJOR CONTRIBUTIONS

This review examines briefly two such perspectives – the 'new literacy
studies' and 'critical' literacy – which put the emphasis on the 'social'
character of literacy rather than on individual cognitive skills. Although
there are significant differences between these views of literacy, they agree
in rejecting the autonomous model and conceptualising reading and writing
as social practices – hence the overall label of 'social' literacies (Street,
1995).

'New Literacy Studies'

In contrast with the early developments in literacy theory outlined above,
an alternative view of reading and writing more 'social' in its orientation has developed in recent years amongst researchers and practitioners –
especially those teaching adult literacy or working on Third World development programmes in literacy. Both the teachers and researchers have
been forced by their exposure to the situation on the ground to recognise
that literacy varies from one context to another, that readers and writers
have different conceptions of the meanings of what they are doing and
that these meanings are not just 'individual' or 'cognitive' but derived
from cultural processes. The academic and schooled literacy of dominant

western elites represents only one form of literacy amongst many, just as the language variety used by such elites is only one dialect amongst many. What it means to engage in reading and writing varies considerably in everyday life, in communities and neighbourhoods, in workplaces in urban and rural environments (Barton & Ivanič, 1991; Hamilton et al., 1994). The focus on spelling correctly or on punctuation that characterises schooled literacy, for instance, is less important in such contexts than a focus on communication and social relations.

Ethnographic research on the actual uses and meanings of literacy practices in specific social contexts has revealed a multiplicity of literacies that by the very weight of evidence throw into doubt the certainties and simplicities of the autonomous model with its single (western based) literacy (Street, 1993b). Amongst high school children in Philadelphia, for instance, writing may be used out of school to develop rap songs or poems about personal identity: what matters here is that the vocabulary is recognisable to peers and that the 'right' to write at all has been established (Shuman, 1993; Camitta, 1993). In a Pacific atoll on the other hand, it may be sermons that represent the major use of writing and the 'voice' of the pastor evokes hierarchy and shared religious meanings in which the congregation are relatively passive (Besnier, 1995); alternatively, personal letter-writing may be the major literacy event, with the culture-specific discourse conventions of Polynesian languages transfered across the vernacular and into English usage (Vetter, 1991). Again amongst villagers in Iran, the uses of literacy may be associated with, on the one hand, Islamic learning and reading the Qur'ān and, on the other, with the practicalities of selling fruit to the city. This activity requires literacy for writing labels on boxes, keeping lists and invoices, writing cheques and reading inventories (Street, 1984). In a Zafimaniry village in Madagascar literacy is highly valued ideologically, and children are encouraged to attend the local French-based school where they learn to incant texts and to scribe by rote. Yet in everyday life, literacy plays no real part, has little bearing on work activities or on the epistemological bases for classification or inquiry (Bloch, 1993): in that sense it remains a sign of something else rather than a material practice of real importance. Again, in contemporary South Africa, researchers have identified multiple forms of literacy practices, that vary between urban and rural areas, amongst political activists in settlement sites and agricultural workers in traditional farms, for taxi drivers in Cape Town or election campaigners taking messages about the 'New South Africa' to non-literate voters (Prinsloo & Breier, 1996).

In all of these cases, the close ethnographic study of literacy in social context based upon a broader conception of literacy as a social practice, forces us to suspend our own conceptions of what 'literacy' means and to be open to variation. The theoretical roots of this approach are in the ethnography of communication, and in the disciplines of anthropology and sociolinguistics. Its strengths are that it is grounded in accounts of real social practice, whereas the autonomous model derives its evidence from either experiments on individual skills or from general inferences and speculations about social change. Its implications for pedagogy, as will be explained below, are for the use of 'real' materials in teaching and for an emphasis on meanings rather than the formalist precisions of the autonomous model.

Problems and Difficulties

The weaknesses of the 'New Literacy Studies' are that they complicate the design of programmes and curricula in ways that might prevent further action; that it is hugely demanding on designers and organisers but, most especially, on teachers. In a sense, teachers are required to become ethnographers, sensitive to the cultural variations amongst their learners and able to address present and future literacy needs of their students (Heath, 1983). The anthropological perspective has been variously charged with being relativist, romantic, and irrelevant to the practical needs of the 'modern' world (Prinsloo & Breier, 1996).

Critical Literacy

It is particularly to these latter charges that the 'critical' view of literacy is addressed. Those who espouse this perspective argue that the nature of the world is changing radically and that the ethnographic approach simply privileges 'lost' or 'disappearing' world views and ways with words. In a world where power will lie with those who can command the genres of power, adherence to this approach will disadvantage users (Lankshear & McLaren, 1993). These claims are rooted more broadly in recent critical revision of the Enlightenment claims for rationality, science and objectivity (see also Luke, this volume). A number of researchers, often working under the label 'post-modernism', have argued that the nature of the contemporary world has radically changed and that this change is as significant as those characterised in such dramatic terms as 'traditional to modern', or 'pre-literate to literate'. The major features of this change are to be found in the workplace and in the nature of labour markets, work processes, the relations of worker and 'boss', the production of goods and their distribution across the world. These are 'New Times' in which 'Fast Capitalism' supplants the simple economic imperatives of early capitalist development (O'Connor, 1994; Gee et al., 1996).

These changes can be observed at a material level in the 'global' nature of markets, the interrelation of economic processes in different parts of the world, the 'democratisation' of workplaces with 'flat' rather than hierarchical relations and the immediate targeting of production to consumer choices. They are also evident, though not always so visibly, in intellectual and ideological shifts in the modern world order. The dominant view of the 'modern' world was of rational, linear thinking based on belief in science and objective truth: the new world order turns out to be less predictable, less logical, more vicarious and disordered and more multi-faceted in both cultural and linguistic (and literacy) terms. This 'post-modern' world has different communication systems and needs, is more sensitive to and dependent on variation rather than standardisation and, in some senses, is less optimistic in that it denies a simple unilinear 'progress' from simpler to complex or from traditional to modern. The 'post' in 'post-modern' is not a sequential term but a shift of plane.

The meanings of literacy, then, have shifted radically in this new world order. The kinds of 'reading' and writing required of workers are quite different than in the 'modern' era (O'Connor, 1994; Gee et al., 1996). The major quality required of new labour forces is flexibility, an ability to move between different orders of communication – spoken, written, visual, computer-based. Some researchers have argued that this shift involves in some sense the 'end of language' in that analysis must focus far more on semiotic systems – on systems of signs such as icons, visual representations, computer display – rather than on language based writing systems (Kress & van Leeuwen, 1995). It is a world of international road signs, standardised labels on clothing, recognisable televisual images, commercial logos, bank by phone or by computerised display in multiple languages. In this sense literacy takes on a much broader meaning: there are 'multi literacies' – computer literacy, visual literacy, technological literacy – as well as the extended metaphors of political literacy and cultural literacy (Hirsch, 1987; see also Abbott, this volume). Academic literacy and the narrow modernist view of 'schooled' literacy (Cook-Gumperz, 1986) are not necessarily well suited to this new world order and certainly do not train new members of society to handle the complexity of the world they are entering.

The implications for pedagogy, and for education generally, are immense and scarcely realised. Indeed, it could be argued that the current emphasis in a number of western societies on 'back to basics' and the scare stories about 'illiteracy' and 'falling standards' (see, for instance, reviews by Clay, Goodman, Raban and Sprenger-Charolles & Béchennec's, this volume) represent a resistance to these changes and a harking back to a safer and more certain world order in which a single 'literacy' characterised a single dominant world view that was more stable and persistent. Literacy, then, remains a sign by which we know the world we live in. It refers not simply to the skills of reading and writing but to the way we think about ourselves as working and thinking beings: the literacy of the modern era is, then, a very different literacy than that of the post-modern era. The theoretical roots of this view are in sociology and critical theory. Its strengths lie in its ability to locate literacy in the larger world context and to address the workplace needs of the contemporary world.

Problems and Difficulties

The major critiques of critical literacy are that it is often presented in inaccessible language, ungrounded in actual descriptions of social or even individual practice, and dependent on large and often vague generalisation. It has also been suggested that, beneath an apparently radical exterior, Critical Literacy remains rooted in an 'autonomous' model of literacy which assumes that acquiring forms of literacy will provide access to forms of power (Prinsloo & Breier, 1996; Street 1995).

FUTURE DIRECTIONS

Whatever the criticisms, the 'social' approaches to literacy detailed here are beginning to influence practical work in literacy in both schools and adult programmes, in both development programmes and in the North. The impact of theory on practice will be one of the major directions for research in the coming decade, as the ideas associated with different positions are applied to specific programmes and contexts. The different positions – or mixes of positions – have implications for the design of literacy programmes, for curriculum and for the nature of teaching and learning, and for assessment.

The development of collaborative research between academics and practitioners, researchers and teachers, which is well advanced in a number of areas (Cochrane-Smith & Lytle, 1993) is also likely to influence the new directions in literacy theory, so that ethnographies of literacy and critical literacy will become areas for 'research with' rather than 'research on' (Cameron et al., 1992). The autonomous model of literacy, with its emphasis on individual skills and cognition, has tended to support a technical pedagogy focused on rote learning, skill manipulation and lack of critical enquiry or interaction. It is less likely, then, that researchers in this particular area will adopt Cameron's position; indeed, there are already calls by psychologists of reading to return to a research agenda based on a more individualistic, experimental and 'technical' view of literacy skills (Oakhill et al., 1995).

In terms of pedagogy, the 'new literacy studies' has often been associated with a liberal, whole language view of learning (Willinsky, 1990; Goodman, 1996; see also the review by Goodman in volume 6) though this does not necessarily follow from the theory. There is a sense in which a social view of literacy entails a social view of learning and a sensitivity to context and the social relations of context, including those between the facilitator and the learner. In development programmes that recognise this view, the emphasis is beginning to shift towards exposing learners to 'real' materials rather than artificial text books or primers (Archer & Cottingham, 1996; Rogers, 1994). In many contexts, the recognition that literacy is not neutral but associated with power relations entails a critical learning style of the kind espoused by Freire and his followers (Freire & Macedo, 1987). The critical perspective has been particularly wedded to a Freirean view and some of its exponents have adopted Freire's approach – conscientization, bottom up, learner-focused, using 'key words' from the local culture – and adapted it to the perceived needs of the 'post-modern' world (Lankshear, 1987; Lankshear & McLaren, 1993). The pedagogy here is of critical inquiry and facilitating adaptability and variation amongst learners.

Many workplace programmes display some tension between the immediate 'needs' of the company for more efficient workers and the recognition that adaptability and efficiency entail some degree of autonomy and critical perspective of the kind espoused by critical literacy theorists (O'Connor, 1994). Indeed, recent accounts of the implications of the post-modern condition for literacy suggest a convergence of capitalist, commercial imperatives and those of the critical approach: in both frames, the worker is 'emancipated' from previous unnecessary constraints and literacy is seen as a key to freedom and progress (Gee et al., 1996). From one perspective, this means that the new 'social' literacies are being re-incorporated into the traditional autonomous model and the need for alternative critical research and practice remains salient. From another perspective, this might provide evidence that critical and ethnographic approaches have now infiltrated mainstream domains of education and work and there is a need for return to more traditional perspectives (Oakhill et al., 1995). The positions outlined here seem likely to provide the basis for future research in these areas as well as the terms in which debates about practice and applications are conducted.

King's College, London, England

REFERENCES

Anderson, C.A. & Bowman, M. (ed.): 1965, *Education and Economic Development*, Frank Cass: London.
Archer, D. & Cottingham, S.: 1996, Regenerated Freireian literacy through empowering community techniques (reflect), Action Aid, London.
Barton, D. & Ivanič, R. (eds): 1991, *Writing In The Community*, Sage, London.
Besnier, N.: 1995, *Literacy, Emotion and Authority: Reading and Writing on a Pacific Atoll*, Cambridge: CUP.
Bloch, M.: 1993, 'The uses of schooling and literacy in a Zafimaniry village', in B. Street (ed.), 87–109.
Cameron, D. Frazer, E., Rampton, B & Richardson, K.: 1992, *Researching Language: Issues of Power and Method*, Routledge, London.
Cook-Gumperz, J.: 1986, *The Social Construction of Literacy*, CUP: Cambridge.

Finnegan, R.: 1988, *Literacy and Orality*, Blackwell, Oxford.
Freire, P. & Macedo, D.: 1987, *Literacy: Reading the Word and the World*, Bergin & Garvey: Mass, USA.
Gee, J.: 1991, *Social Linguistics: Ideology in Discourses*, Falmer Press, London.
Gee, J., Hull, G. & Lankshear, C.: 1996, *The New Work Order: Behind the Language of the New Capitalism*, Allen & Unwin: London.
Goodman, K.: 1996, *On Reading*, Scholastic Canada Ltd., Ontario.
Goody, J.: 1986, *The Logic of Writing and the Organisation of Society*, Cambridge University Press, Cambridge.
Goody, J.: 1987, *The Interface between the Written and the Oral*, Cambridge University Press, Cambridge.
Goody, J.: 1977, *The Domestication of the Savage Mind*, Cambridge University Press, Cambridge.
Hamilton, M., Barton, D. & Ivanič, R. (eds): 1994, *Worlds of Literacy*, Multilingual Matters, Clevedon.
Heath, S.B.: 1983, *Ways with Words*, Cambridge University Press, Cambridge.
Hirsch, E.D.: 1987, *Cultural Literacy: What Every American Needs to Know*, Houghton Mifflin Co: Boston.
Kress, G. & Van Leeuwen, T.: 1991, *Reading Images: the Grammar of Visual Design*, London: Routledge.
Lankshear, C. & McLaren, P. (eds): 1993, *Critical Literacy: Politics, Praxis and the Postmodern*, SUNY Press, Albany, NY.
Lankshear, C.: 1987, *Literacy, Schooling and Revolution*, Falmer Press, London.
Lerner, D.: 1958, *The Passing of Traditional Society*, NY: Glencoe Free Press.
O'Connor, P.: 1994, *Thinking Work: Theoretical Perspectives on Workers' Literacies*, Deakin UP: Victoria.
Oakhill, J., Beard, R. & Vincent, D.: 1995, 'The contribution of psychological research' *Special Issue of Journal of Research in Reading* 18(2).
Olson, D.: 1977, 'From utterance to text: The bias of language in speech and writing', *Harvard Educational Review*, 47(3), 257–281.
Olson, D.: 1994, *The World on Paper*, Cambridge University Press, Cambridge.
Ong, W.: 1982, *Orality and Literacy: The Technologising of the Word*, Methuen: London.
Oxenham, J.: 1980, Literacy: *Writing, Reading and Social Organisation*, Routledge & Kegan Paul, London.
Prinsloo, M. & Breier, M. (eds): 1996, *The Social Uses of Literacy: Case Studies from South Africa*, John Benjamins, Amsterdam.
Rogers, A., Holland, D., Millican, J., Eade, F. & Street, B.: 1994, *Using Literacy: A New Approach to Post-Literacy Materials*, ODA occasional papers on education, no. 10.
Street, B.: 1984, *Literacy in Theory and Practice*, Cambridge University Press, Cambridge.
Street, B. (ed): 1993a, *The New Literacy Studies*, Special edition of *Journal of Research in Reading*, vol. 16 (2), Blackwell, Oxford.
Street, B. (ed.): 1993b: *Cross-Cultural Approaches to Literacy*, Cambridge University Press, Cambridge.
Street, B.: 1995, *Social Literacies: Critical perspectives on Literacy in Development, Ethnography and Education*, Longman: London.
Unesco: 1976, *The Experimental World Literacy Programme: A Critical Assessment*, Unesco, Paris.
Vetter, R.: 1991, 'Discourses across literacies: personal letter writing in a Tuvaluan context', *Language and Education* 5(2), 125–145.
Willinsky, J.: 1990, *The New Literacy*, Routledge, London.

ALLAN LUKE

CRITICAL APPROACHES TO LITERACY

The development of critical approaches to literacy in the last two decades marks a significant and ongoing reorientation of literacy education. This has involved a shift away from psychological and individualist models of reading and writing towards those approaches that use sociological, cultural and discourse theory to reconceputalise the literate subject, textual practices, and classroom pedagogy. Such a change in foundational perspective has been linked to sociological analyses of the role of schooling in the intergenerational reproduction of power, knowledge and access to material resources. Critical approaches are characterised by a commitment to reshape literacy education in the interests of marginalised groups of learners, who on the basis of gender, cultural and socioeconomic background have been excluded from access to the discourses and texts of dominant economies and cultures.

The prevailing view among inter and post-war educational planners and curriculum developers was that literacy involved the acquisition and development of psychological skills and linguistic competences. The problem of functional literacy and illiteracy accordingly was seen in terms of individual differences and skills deficits that could be addressed through systematic instructional materials and models (see the review by Verhoeven, this volume). These psychological approaches were complemented by the emergence of human capital models of education in the 1960s that considered increased levels of literacy as a key strategy for economic and geopolitical competitiveness among developing, postcolonial countries and advanced industrial capitalist economies (Freebody & Welch, 1993). The postwar imperative for incrementally more 'technocratic', scientific approaches to literacy education came to be viewed as a calculated investment in the development of a skilled workforce.

Historical, ethnographic and sociolinguistic studies of literacy have reframed literacy as a social practice that is shaped, distributed and acquired in relation to community contexts and larger social institutions, discourse formations and ideological interests (Gee, 1996). In Australia, Canada, Britain and the US, these studies have been productively allied with other social theoretic approaches – including poststructuralist discourse theory, neomarxian cultural studies, and postcolonial and feminist studies – to develop new educational approaches to the teaching of textual representation

V. Edwards and D. Corson (eds), Encyclopedia of Language and Education,
Volume 2: Literacy, 143–151.
© 1997 Kluwer Academic Publishers. Printed in the Netherlands.

and practice, agency and action. The challenge for such critical approaches is posed by the new social conditions for literate practices brought about by rapidly changing demographies and cultures, technologies and economies.

FROM INDIVIDUAL TO SOCIAL VIEWS OF LITERACY

The study and development of literacy in schools has been dominated by reading psychology and, increasingly in the last two decades, by progressive and humanist approaches to the teaching of literature and writing. Since the 1920s, American educational psychologists have worked closely with professional teaching organisations, publishers, teacher education programs and universities to develop mass marketed textbooks, instructional approaches and standardised testing (Shannon, 1989; see also the review by Owocki & Goodman, this volume). From psychological perspectives, literacy has been construed variously in terms of the acquisition of behaviours, skills, cognitive and metacognitive strategies, information and linguistic processing skills. By such accounts, 'critical' reading is seen to entail higher order cognitive strategies which enable generic 'problem solving', 'critical thinking' and, perhaps, the identification of bias in texts.

Further major postwar influences on literacy teaching were reader response criticism and personal growth approaches to English teaching. These emphasised reading as a vehicle for the development of personal expression and critical response to literary texts (Willinsky, 1990). At the same time, developments in writing pedagogy have been strongly influenced by models of writing as a rhetorical, social and developmental 'process' which focused on issues of audience and context (Freedman & Medway, 1995).

In many English-speaking countries, these innovations in the teaching of reading, literature and writing have been historically connected with a larger project of progressive, student-centred education (Green, 1993). As such, they have been readily incorporated into those critical approaches to literacy education that set out to humanise and democratise the classroom environments encountered by students from cultural minorities and second language backgrounds (Edelsky, 1996; see also the reviews by Viv Edwards, this volume). Yet they begin from the individual as a key teleological principle, with individual growth conceived of in terms of cognitive development, aesthetic interpretation and personal expression. Within student-centred approaches to literacy, the development of 'voice' and participation in a community of readers and writers are viewed as key moments in individual 'empowerment', with social analysis and transformation typically taking a secondary role.

The lesson from recent ethnographic, historical and sociolinguistic research has been that literacy is not first and foremost an individuated and individual competence or skill but consists of socially constructed and locally negotiated practices (e.g., see the review by Street, this volume). Such a perspective requires that analysis begin from the examination of the ideological assumptions, structures and interests of institutions charged with the official transmission and control of literacy – schools, churches, state agencies, aid and development organisations, multinational publishers and corporations (Kapitzke, 1995). The social construction of literacy, then, can be investigated in relation to the hegemonic practices, knowledge and power relationships at work in identifiable local, and globalised historical, economic and political contexts (Besnier, 1995).

What will count as literacy thus is necessarily a point of political contestation, as evidenced by the near continual discourse of 'crises' over standards of literacy (see the reviews by Béchennec & Sprenger-Charolles, Clay, Kenneth Goodman and Raban, this volume). The central educational questions posed by critical approaches to literacy turn not on particular scientific truths about instructional methods or cognitive processes, but instead on normative debates about how literacy can and should be used in relation to the construction of social formations and institutions, social identities and everyday lives (Muspratt, Luke & Freebody, 1997). The debate over critical literacy, then, is nothing less than a debate over the shape of a literate society, its normative relations of textual and discourse exchange, and the relative agency and power of the literate in its complex and diverse cultures and communities.

CRITICAL PEDAGOGY APPROACHES

The concept of critical literacy emerged in the 1970s from radical educational theory to describe a pedagogy that focussed on the analysis and critique of social institutions and structures. Paulo Freire (1970) used the term to refer to the critical capacity to use language as a means for articulation of a transformative political analysis and agenda. Freire's work was committed to the political and economic emancipation of peasant and working classes in colonialist and neocolonialist contexts (Lankshear & Lawler, 1987). There traditional schooling had formed systematic barriers to social and economic participation by creating the pedagogic conditions for educational failure and by transmitting ruling class ideologies.

Freire proposed an alternative approach to education that was at once humanist and revolutionary, viewing literacy as a means for the reinstatement of 'voice' and agency for the 'oppressed'. For Freire, no curriculum could be neutral and 'reading the word' necessarily entailed 'reading the world', developing a critical analysis of an economic, social and political order. This could be achieved, he argued, through a 'dialogic' pedagogical approach that reinstated learners as teachers of marginalised experience and culture, and focussed on the writing of key words and themes based on that experience.

Critical pedagogy is based on a dialectical view of individual development and social history as the evolution of class consciousness and struggle. Becoming literate is the practice of attaining 'critical consciousness', both understanding one's social relations to the means of production and conceptualising actions that might change those relations and material conditions. Literacy education thus can be reconceptualised as a site for dialogue, ideology critique and productive cultural action.

In the 1980s and 1990s, there have been numerous international applications of Freire's work. In the US, it has become part of a broader project of 'critical pedagogy' that incorporates elements of minority education, progressive education, and revisionist approaches to literature, history and social studies curriculum (e.g., Lankshear & McLaren, 1995). There are documented applications to large-scale national literacy campaigns, to university and college writing programs for women and minorities, adult basic and community education programs, and community writing and publishing programs (e.g., Shor, 1987; Horsman, 1990). These innovations all begin from a belief that the practice of literacy has an intrinsic critical potential that can be focussed on renaming and reappropriating the phenomenal and material worlds.

For Freire, critical literacy is a means to understand one's relationship to the means of production, and to realise control over one's work, knowledge, political rights and freedom. Yet it is not simply based on a revolutionary premise. It is also based on an epistemological premise that there is a knowable material and political reality available to dialectical analysis and dialogic education.

FEMINIST AND POSTSTRUCTURALIST APPROACHES

French discourse theory in the 1970s and 1980s raised two key questions for literacy education. The work of Michel Foucault asked whether the natural or social world was indeed knowable, accessible or analysable without recourse to the constitutive filters of language and discourse. Further, the work of Jacques Derrida questioned whether any texts could have intrinsic authoritative or canonical status, and indeed whether definitive or authoritative readings and interpretations were at all possible. Both questions potentially destabilise the assumptions of traditional, progressive and radical approaches to literacy education. They suggest strongly that classroom environments can be remodelled to encourage a more open play of textual analyses and reconstruction and a critical understanding of the ways in which discourse constructs identities and cultures, life worlds and trajectories.

Poststructuralist and feminist educational theories have refocussed critical literacy programs on the study of how dominant texts and discourses position and define human subjects in relations of knowledge and power. From this perspective, languages, texts and discourses are the normative technologies for constructing social categories, organisations, and identities (Baker & Luke, 1991). Consequently, the significant task for critical literacy becomes the destablisation of taken for granted categories and constructions of, for example, gender and cultural identity, social action, disciplinary codes and knowledge, or history (e.g., Lee, 1996). The result is a classroom focus on the critical deconstruction of the texts of literary and popular culture, with an eye for understanding how power relations work through discourse. In England and Australia, poststructuralist and feminist classroom practices have encouraged the critical analysis of how gender identities and roles were constructed through textbooks, media and other everyday texts, including student writings (e.g., Gilbert & Taylor, 1991; Luke, 1994; Buckingham & Sefton-Green, 1995).

Poststructuralist and feminist educational work sets as its goal a critical deconstruction of master narratives, of patriarchal discourses and 'regimes of power' at work in everyday life. Its normative goal, then, is neither utopian nor revolutionary, but entails the provision of a pedagogy conducive to the critique of fixed meanings, and the generation of new and different kinds of texts, identities, and voices. Intellectual, academic and literate practice is thus refocussed on the politics of representation.

Substantial recent work has focused on teaching primary and secondary school students the deconstruction and critique of the representation of gender and culture in literary and popular culture (e.g., Comber, 1993; Kamler, 1994). Poststructuralist text analysis has provided a futher means for developing indigenous and postcolonial perspectives on the texts of mainstream educational culture (Walton, 1996). These approaches attempt to provide students with critical perspectives on identity in contemporary society, an understanding of how modes of discourse position and construct readers and viewers. Within this focus deconstructive analyses become a means for exploring ways of constructing texts, 'readings', and selves in contestation with dominant categories and classifications of literary, popular and functional texts.

TEXT ANALYTIC APPROACHES

One salient critique of Freirean and poststructuralist approaches to critical literacy is that their emphasis on ideological analysis and text deconstruction may fail to provide lower socioeconomic and minority students, those most likely to be disenfranchised by conventional instructional methods, with extensive knowledge about how texts work. Advocates of 'genre approaches' to writing have argued that any critical approach to literacy teaching that aims to shift achievement patterns of lower socioeconomic and minority students must deploy explicit instruction in the linguistic and semiotic codes of text, and must provide sufficient engagement with canonical text forms that are linked to institutional access and power in capitalist economies (Cope & Kalantzis, 1993).

North American approaches to genre tend to broadly appeal to the need for social power, with less direct reference to either questions of ideology critique or the teaching of literacy as a means for the redistribution of capital (see the review by Freedman & Richardson in volume 6). In Australia, curriculum interventions based on the teaching of systemic functional grammar (Halliday & Martin, 1993) have been implemented in many states. These models have defined critical literacy as the demystification of how specialised academic texts and scientific discourses work, and the provision of a flexible repertoire of functional linguistic tools that will enable broader and expanded access to dominant social institutions.

There has been substantial debate over whether and how a mastery of linguistic knowledge can and should be combined with the broader forms of social and discourse analysis advocated by other approaches to critical literacy (Hasan & Williams, 1996). In the model of 'critical language awareness' developed by Fairclough (1993), students are taught how to use elements of functional grammatical analysis as part of discourse analysis that encourages them to critically evaluate, contest and reconstruct a range of literary, bureaucratic and popular texts (see the review by Janks in Vol. 1). This approach has been applied in the contexts of postcolonial education, adult basic education, English as a Second Language teaching, early childhood reading and writing programs, and literature study (e.g., Janks, 1993; Hamilton, Barton & Ivanič, 1994). It sets out to provide explicit knowledge about how to manipulate modes of information by showing how the texts of dominant disciplines, discourses and institutions work in relation to particular linguistic markets and contexts. At the same time, these approaches encourage students to develop strategies for identifying and contesting the pragmatic devices that texts use to try to position and manipulate readers (Kress, 1989).

CRITICAL LITERACY AND THE CHALLENGES OF NEW TECHNOLOGIES

Literacy education itself is a social and cultural practice. As a curriculum practice, it requires historically situated, interest-bound decisions about which canonical texts and genres, which values, voices and ideologies, which social practices and relations, which literate tastes and habituses will become the official knowledge of schools (Luke, 1988). These are not arbitrary, neutral or scientific decisions.

The approaches to the teaching of critical literacy described here are deliberately normative historical responses to the emergent cultural, economic and social conditions of the postwar period. The impetus for the development of these critical approaches can be traced to, inter alia, the economic and social consequences of traditional and neo-colonialist educational systems, the emergent discourses and knowledge claims of women, cultural minorities, migrants, and indigenous peoples, and new patterns of work, consumption and leisure in consumer, media-based cultures and economies. What distinguishes these critical approaches from their historical predecessors is that they stand on claims of social relevance and efficacy, rather than professing to capture scientific truths about the nature of the acquisition, use and value of literacy for individuals.

Educational institutions now face an unprecedented set of cultural, economic and technological challenges, many of which call into question longstanding assumptions about the value and utility of traditional print literacy (see also the review by Abbott, this volume). The texts and practices of everyday life are changing at a disorienting pace, requiring complex 'multiliteracies' (New London Group, 1996) for dealing with the dynamic modes of symbolic and visual representation developing in 'first wave' (e.g., television, cinema) and 'second wave' technologies (e.g., the internet, multimedia software) (Kellner, 1996). Teachers and schools must contend with increasingly multicultural and multilingual student cohorts, who are developing social identities in relation to the texts of popular multimediated cultures. Curriculum and instruction must respond to the challenge of preparing these students for globalised economies, new workplaces based on the exchange of text and discourse, and new forms of work, leisure and consumption (Gee, Hull & Lankshear, 1996). Educational systems thus are being asked to prepare students for textual and pedagogical environments, at once local and global, virtual and face-to-face, public and private, some of which have yet to be fully realised or even invented.

The historical lesson is that new technologies do not simply replace or erase older systems of communication, but rather they combine and generate new and hybrid forms, media and criteria for expression. What this means is that any approaches to critical literacy must begin to deal with hybrid, multimediated texts, social practices and relations around texts, and shifting fields of power and knowledge. This will require a broad range of public pedagogies that engage with computer-based forms of representation and communication, and move towards the constructive development of critical criteria for analysing these new media and popular texts. Further, governments and communities worldwide must attend to rudimentary issues of equity of access to communications technologies and dominant modes of representation.

At the same, time, longstanding issues and problems of print literacy will persist. While advanced capitalist countries and media corporations develop the parameters and exclusions of a new information order, the questions raised by the various approaches to critical literacy described here remain. The selective curricular traditions and exclusionary transmission of print literacy practices on the basis of class, culture, gender and geography continue internationally, as do the need for dynamic and locally sustainable approaches to critical literacy.

Shared across contemporary approaches to critical literacy is an emphasis on the need for literates to take an interventionist approach to texts and discourses of all media, and a commitment to the capacity to critique, transform and reconstruct dominant modes of information. In their present form, they converge on the key question of representation and are increasingly being used to reexamine questions of identity and power in the textual cultures of new media and institutions. The focus of Freire's initial project remains central to the teaching of critical literacy in new social conditions: an emphasis on the capacity of literates and literacies to transform the construction and distribution of material and symbolic resources by communities and social institutions. What remains ever problematic is which directions those transformations might take, and how any new literacy can figure in relation to the emergent institutional cultures and identities, texts and technologies of postmodern economies and societies.

University of Queensland, Australia

REFERENCES

Baker, C.D. and Luke, A. (eds): 1991, *Towards a Critical Sociology of Reading Pedagogy*, John Benjamins, Amsterdam.
Besnier, N.: 1995, *Literacy, Emotion, and Authority*, Cambridge University Press, Cambridge.
Buckingham, D. and Sefton-Green, J.: 1994, *Cultural Studies Goes to School*, Taylor and Francis, London.
Comber, B.: 1993, 'Classroom explorations in critical literacy', *Australian Journal of Language and Literacy*, 16, 73–83.
Cope, B. and Kalantzis, M. (eds): 1993, *The Powers of Literacy*, Falmer, London.
Edelsky, C.: 1996, *With Literacy and Justice for All*, Taylor & Francis, London.
Fairclough, N. (ed): 1993, *Critical Language Awareness*, Longman, London.
Freebody, P. & Welch, A.R. (eds): 1993, *Knowledge, Culture and Power*, Falmer, London.
Freedman, A. & Medway, P. (eds): 1994. *Genre and the New Rhetoric*, Taylor & Francis, London.
Freire, P.: 1970, *Pedagogy of the Oppressed*, Seabury, New York.
Gee, J.P.: 1996, *Social Linguistics and Literacies*, Taylor & Francis, London.
Gee, J.P., Hull, G., & Lankshear, C.: 1996, *The New Work Order*, Allen & Unwin, Sydney.
Gilbert, P. & Taylor, S.: 1991, *Fashioning the Feminine*, Allen & Unwin, Sydney.
Green, B. (ed.): 1993, *The Insistence of the Letter*, Falmer, London.
Halliday, M.A.K. & Martin, J.R.: 1993, *Writing Science: Literacy and Discursive Power*, Falmer, London.
Hamilton, M, Barton, D., & Ivanič, R. (eds): 1994, *Worlds of Literacy*, Multilingual Matters, Clevedon, UK.
Hasan, R. & Williams, G. (eds): 1996, *Literacy in Society*, Longman, London.

Horsman, J.: 1990, *Something in My Mind Besides the Everyday*, Women's Press, Toronto.

Janks, H.: 1993, *Language, Identity and Power*, Hodder & Stoughton, Johannesburg.

Kamler, B.: 1994, 'Lessons about language and gender', *Australian Journal of Language and Literacy* 17, 129–138.

Kapitzke, C.: 1995, *Literacy and Religion*, John Benjamins, Amsterdam.

Kellner, D.: 1996, *Media Culture*, Routledge, New York.

Kress, G.: 1989, *Linguistic Processes in Sociocultural Practice*, Oxford University Press, Oxford.

Lankshear, C. & Lawler, M.: 1987, *Literacy, Schooling and Revolution*, Falmer, London.

Lankshear, C. & Mclaren, P.L. (eds): 1993, *Critical Literacy*, State University of New York Press, Albany.

Lee, A.: 1996, *Gender, Literacy, Curriculum*, Taylor & Francis, London.

Luke, A.: 1988, *Literacy, Textbooks and Ideology*, Falmer, London.

Luke, C.: 1994, 'Feminist pedagogy and critical media literacy', *Journal of Communication Inquiry* 18(2), 30–47.

Muspratt, S., Luke, A., & Freebody, P. (eds): 1997, *Constructing Critical Literacies*, Hampton Press, Creskill, NJ.

New London Group: 1996, 'A pedagogy of multiliteracies', *Harvard Educational Review* 66, 60–92.

Shannon, P.: 1989, *Broken Promises*, Bergin and Garvey, Granby, Mass, USA.

Shor, I. (ed): 1987, *Freire for the Classroom*, Heinemann, Portsmouth, NH, USA.

Walton, C.: 1996, *Critical Social Literacies*, Northern Territory University Press, Darwin.

Willinsky, J.: 1990, *The New Literacy*, Routledge, New York.

ELSA ROBERTS AUERBACH

FAMILY LITERACY

During the past twenty-five years, educators have increasingly recognized the importance of parental roles in children's literacy acquisition and academic achievement. With this recognition has come a proliferation of ethnographic research on family interactions around literacy in various cultural and socio-economic contexts, as well as a shift in educational policy toward programming to support family literacy interactions. There is considerable debate about the meaning of the ethnographic research and its implications: some educators and policy makers claim that inadequate family literacy practices are the cause of educational problems and see family literacy programming as the solution to educational reform while others see cultural differences between home and school literacies and structural socioeconomic factors as shaping literacy acquisition. This review will examine family literacy research and programming, with a focus on the various paradigms related to this debate.

EARLY DEVELOPMENTS

Denny Taylor's seminal work, *Family Literacy: Young Children Learning to Read and Write* (1983) set the stage for subsequent research and practice in family literacy. Her ethnography of the families of six middle-class children who were successfully learning to read was the first to examine family literacy practices in depth. She found a wide range of literacy experiences and interactional patterns in the homes she studied. Parents often intentionally avoided doing school-like reading and writing activities. Instead, Taylor found that literacy was integrated in socially meaningful ways into the fabric of everyday life in the families.

A second study of family literacy contexts, Heath (1983), compared the discourse and literacy practices of three communities in the Piedmont Carolinas – a Black working class community, a white working class community, and white middle class community. She found significant patterns of difference in ways of using and perceiving literacy between the communities; most importantly, though, she found that there was a match between the home and school literacy practices of the white middle class children, whereas there was disparity between home and school literacies for children of the other two communities. The fact that their home literacy and discourse practices differed from the expectations of the teachers put

V. Edwards and D. Corson (eds), Encyclopedia of Language and Education,
Volume 2: Literacy, 153–161.
© *1997 Kluwer Academic Publishers. Printed in the Netherlands.*

these children at an educational disadvantage (see the review by A.D. Edwards in Volume 3).

Numerous other ethnographies of the relationship between literacy-related home interactions and children's academic achievement indicated that when children were socialized in the home for mainstream literacy, they were more successful in school, and, conversely, where the children's home literacies did not conform to teachers expectations, achievement according to school norms was impeded (e.g., Michaels, 1981; Wells, 1986). In some cases, educators and policy makers interpreted these findings to mean that non-mainstream families lacked the "necessary" literacy skills, attitudes, practices, or home environments for fostering children's literacy development. The discourse of an intergenerational cycle of illiteracy became common; parents underachievement was blamed for children's problems in school.

Based on these assumptions, family literacy programs in the early to mid 1980's were often designed to transmit mainstream, school-like literacy practices into the homes of poor and language minority families; often, educators based programs on the assumption that non-mainstream children came from literacy impoverished home environments where parents neither valued nor supported children's literacy acquisition. In some cases, parents were given specific guidelines, materials, and training to carry out school-like practices in the home. Other programs focused on encouraging children and parents to read together (e.g., Tizard, Schofield & Hewison, 1982).

MAJOR CONTRIBUTIONS

In the mid-eighties, two developments changed the way in which family literacy came to be seen. On the one hand, there was new research about the family literacy contexts of a broad range of cultural and linguistic groups; on the other, there was a critique and reconceptualization of program models largely based on the findings from this research.

Much of the ethnographic research about family literacy challenged the notion that the homes of poor and language minority families are literacy impoverished. Instead, these studies (reviewed in Auerbach, 1989) showed that there is enormous diversity in home literacy practices among and within cultural groups; rather than being literacy impoverished, the home environments of poor, undereducated and language minority children often are rich with literacy practices and artifacts; although beliefs about literacy and its pay-offs vary, marginalized families generally not only value literacy, but see it as the single most powerful hope for their children; even parents who themselves have limited literacy proficiency support their children's literacy acquisition in many ways.

Taylor & Dorsey-Gaines (1988) examined the literacy contexts of U.S. inner city black families living below the poverty level in conditions where daily life was a struggle for survival. They found multiple uses of literacy, literacy practices, and print rich home environments. Even though the social conditions facing these families presented enormous challenges, literacy was integrally intertwined with daily life. Reviewing the literature about home environments conducive to literacy acquisition, Fitzgerald, Spiegel & Cunningham (1991) found that although both low and high literacy level parents viewed literacy artifacts and events, in particular, interacting with books, as important in the pre-school years, the lower literacy level parents valued early literacy experiences even more than parents with higher literacy levels.

Additional research suggested that even parents who are themselves not literate in English actively support their children's literacy acquisition. For example, a study of literacy among Mexican-American families (Delgado-Gaitan, 1987) found that a wide range of text types were an integral part of daily life in families where the parents had little prior schooling and minimal English proficiency. Other studies of immigrants in the U.S. found that parents were not only very concerned with their children's academic achievement, but supported it in numerous ways (Goldenberg & Gallimore, 1991; Ortiz, 1992).

Given the force of this research evidence, Auerbach (1989) argued that programs based on assumptions of inadequate family literacy practices were grounded in a deficit perspective on family literacy. Subsequently, a second generation of family literacy programs has emerged, one in which virtually all of the proponents of family literacy claim to oppose deficit perspectives and to embrace family strengths. However, despite this apparent agreement, there continue to be significant differences in assumptions, goals, and practices among family literacy programs. Auerbach (1995) proposed that these differences can be grouped into three paradigms informed by different ideological and theoretical perspectives: the *intervention prevention* approach, the *multiple literacies* approach, and the social change approach.

The intervention prevention model for family literacy posits that literacy problems are rooted in undereducated parents' inability to promote positive literacy attitudes and interactions in the home. Since parents are seen as children's first teachers, they are said to bear primary responsibility for children's literacy development. As such, proponents of this view support intervention programs aimed at changing parents' beliefs about literacy and literacy interactions with their children (Nickse, Speicher & Buchek, 1988; Darling, 1992). Such programs are seen as the best means to ensure that patterns of undereducation and illiteracy will be prevented from passing from generation to generation. Intervention programs take various forms: in the U.S., the National Center for Family Literacy advocates comprehensive programs which include four components: parent literacy; preschool literacy; parent-child interactions around literacy; and parenting skills. Other programs offer single practice solutions like training parents to read stories or sending books home in backpacks. Still others focus primarily on the parenting practices in which literacy is embedded. Despite their anti-deficit discourse, many of these programs bear similarities to the deficit model of the mid-eighties (see Auerbach, 1995).

While the intervention model defines the problem as flawed home literacy practices and the solution as changing patterns of family interaction, the multiple literacies perspective defines the problem as a mismatch between culturally variable home literacy practices and school literacies; it sees the solution as investigating and validating students' multiple literacies and cultural resources in order to inform schooling. The starting point of the multiple literacies perspective is that, whatever their literacy proficiency, participants bring with them culture-specific literacy practices and ways of knowing. Regardless of educational background, the households of poor and language minority families are rich with "funds of knowledge" which often are unrecognized and untapped by educators (Moll, 1992).

In this paradigm, instruction is based on a stance of inquiry in which educators listen to students, find out about their lives and cultural contexts, and make room for their literacy practices in teaching (Weinstein-Shr, 1995). Teachers are urged to learn about the educational resources that children bring with them as well as the sociolinguistic rules and parenting practices of their cultures (Moll, 1992). Community resources may be brought directly into the classroom (Madigan, 1995); learners may be involved in the research process as co-investigators of literacy practices, values and beliefs (Gadsden, 1995). Curriculum materials often include genres (eg. folktales, fables) and stories from the home culture (Ada, 1988). The emphasis in this approach is on cultural maintenance and negotiation rather than cultural assimilation. In some cases, this may mean maintaining the first language by learning to read and write in it, teaching it to children, and preserving oral histories in writing. Many programs emphasize critically examining cross-cultural parenting issues rather than training parents in parenting practices identified by experts (Weinstein-Shr, 1995). A number of programs focus on the investigation of home and school literacies, with bridges being built between the two domains through teacher-parent dialogue, home-school journals, etc. (Shockley, Michalove & Allen, 1995; Voss, 1996).

The social change paradigm encompasses all of the principles of the multiple-literacies tendency, but goes beyond them, emphasizing issues of power as well as culture. The central assumption of this perspective is that educational problems originate in a complex interaction of political, social, and economic factors in the broader society rather than in family inadequacies or differences between home and school cultures. Goals in a social change view focus more on challenging institutions and social problems than on changing families.

A key aspect of social change programs is participant involvement in program design. In some cases, programs are initiated by parents themselves in response to needs that they have determined (Delgado-Gaitan, 1991). Dialogue among peers is stressed in place of skills training or transferring information from experts to learners; participants share their experiences in order to gain a critical understanding of their social nature as well as to strategize for action. In some cases, this dialogue takes the form of sharing experiences through storytelling (Arrastía, 1995). In others, it takes the form of reading about and discussing social issues. McCaleb (1994) describes a project in which critical themes in community life were identified through dialogue among parents and then used as the basis for books which were co-authored by parents and children. Once participants have an increased understanding of the social nature of problems they are confronting (e.g., that their children's problems in schools may be the result of institutional practices), they may work together to challenge institutions, for example, engaging in advocacy related to children s schooling (Delgado-Gaitan, 1991).

WORK IN PROGRESS

Because of the intensity of interest in family literacy as a frontier of educational reform, there has been a virtual explosion of research and programming in the past several years. The National Center for Family Literacy for example, estimates that there are now over 1000 family literacy programs in the U.S. alone. One of the most significant recent developments is the attempt to theorize and articulate differences between the paradigms discussed above. Key in this endeavor was an International Forum on Family Literacy convened in October 1994, bringing together educators from around the world to draft a Declaration of Principles which critiques deficit-driven approaches to family literacy and proposes alternatives. Participants included practitioners and scholars from the U.S., the U.K., Canada, Australia, and Latin America representing a spectrum of linguistic and cultural groups. A forthcoming volume, *Many Families, Many Literacies* (Taylor, ed.) will include not only the principles developed at this forum, but reports on work in progress, perspectives of practitioners, community members, parents, and researchers in support of multiple, context-specific, and community-determined definitions of family literacy, of parent and community control in programming, and of non-intrusive, culturally-sensitive instructional content.

Although much of the early work in family literacy originated in the U.S., there has been an increasing number of initiatives in the U.K., Australia, Latin America, and South Africa recently as well. On the research front, ongoing work focuses on home literacy in a range of contexts and its implications for schooling. For example, researchers at Edith Cowan University are studying reading and writing in six different communities across Western Australia and discovering a rich diversity of literacy practices (Breen, 1996). Barton (1994) reports on a study in Lancaster, England which is researching people's everyday reading and writing done in the home and community.

Another direction in current research focuses on the impact of family literacy practices and programs on children's academic achievement. A study by Purcell-Gates based at Harvard University's Graduate School of Education is investigating uses of print in 20 homes of poor white families in the U.S. Preliminary findings suggest that the more literacy-related events the children experienced in their homes, the more they knew about print and print uses. Paratore of Boston University (Boston, Massachusetts), studying the impact of a family literacy program on children's school success, suggests that even when parents are active in their children's literacy development and participate in family literacy training, children may not be doing significantly better in school. Thus, despite claims of those who see family literacy as a direct solution to educational problems, these studies suggest that causal relations between home literacy practices and school success need to be problematized; a complexity of factors that go beyond direct parent-child literacy interactions must be taken into account.

In terms of programming, new initiatives are emerging in Australia (Toomey, 1994), England (*RaPAL Bulletin* 1994), and Scotland (Keen 1996). *Many Families, Many Literacies* (Taylor, forthcoming) also includes accounts of new programs being developed in South Africa, Mexico, Canada, and Brazil, as well as Hispanic and Native American communities in the U.S.

PROBLEMS AND DIFFICULTIES

One of the greatest problems in family literacy work is the gap between research and practice. Despite evidence of multiple family literacies, programming often continues to focus on mainstream practices. Further attention needs to focus on assessing and interpreting the impact of family literacy programming. On the one hand, there is strong evidence of the importance of familial contributions to children's literacy acquisition. Some educators interpret this research evidence to mean that family literacy programs are the key to educational reform. On the other hand, preliminary evidence from work in progress (Paratore and Purcell-Gates) suggests that there is no direct cause-effect relationship between programming and children's educational success, which, in turn, suggests that the premise that family literacy, in itself, determines school success may be flawed. Increasing evidence points to the view that a complex array of socio-economic factors must be taken into account and their interrelationship must be problematized.

Compounding this dilemma is the fact that there is no consensus on how to assess the impact of family literacy programs. For some, the key indicator is children's academic achievement. Others argue that indicators must include changes in parental ability to advocate on behalf of their children as well as their ability to challenge socio-economic inequities. Still others argue that success must be measured in terms of the ways schools become more responsive to home and community literacies. A growing consensus (as evidenced at the International Forum) is that single measures of the impact of family literacy programs are reductionist.

Some argue further that there is an insidious subtext to massive policy efforts claiming that family literacy is the solution to educational problems; they argue that the promise that family literacy will cure the disease of illiteracy is a new way to blame undereducated people for their own problems and to deflect attention from school reform by locating the source of educational problems in families. However, if one agrees that claims for the effects of family literacy are overblown, and that it cannot deliver on its promises, one must ask whether it nevertheless has merits. Those who reject family literacy as a single solution to literacy problems face the question of how not to throw the baby out with the bath water, of clearly articulating what family literacy can and cannot do.

Finally, ethical questions pose an additional challenge in terms of programming. Any initiatives designed to intervene in the internal workings of family life must be approached with extreme caution. This issue is explored at length in *Many Families, Many Literacies*.

FUTURE DIRECTIONS

Tasks facing family literacy researchers include continuing to theorize about the meaning of ethnographic findings by extending cross-cultural research on family literacy contexts, as well as pursuing basic research around the question of how we know what's important in the home for literacy acquisition. Beyond this, further research about the interface between home and school literacies is necessary: to what extent and in what ways can home and school literacies inform each other?

A key direction will be to try to reduce the gap between research and policy or programming: too often policy makers adopt reductionist or ethnocentric interpretations of research in program design. A major direction for researchers will be to make the implications of their findings for programming explicit and participate in program design. Another critical area for future research is in developing both criteria and tools for assessment which can reflect the complexity of factors which contribute to literacy development. Once the notion of assessment has been more extensively theorized, it may be possible to research the long term impacts of family literacy programs.

A key direction for practitioners will be to document their own practice in order to inform theory and research. As the base of practice expands, it will be particularly important to acknowledge and incorporate the extensive experience of educators on the ground in the development of both research and policy priorities. Teacher research opportunities have the potential to enormously enrich the knowledge base about how home and school literacies can support each other.

University of Massachusetts at Boston, USA

REFERENCES

Ada, A.: 1988, 'The Pajaro valley experience', in T. Skutnabb-Kangas & J. Cummins (eds.), *Minority Education: From Shame to Struggle*, Multilingual Matters, Philadelphia, PA, 223–238.

Arrastía, M.: 1995, 'Our stories to transform them: A source of authentic literacy', in G. Weinstein-Shr & E. Quintero (eds.), *Immigrant Learners and Their Families: Literacy to Connect Generations*, Center for Applied Linguistics & Delta Systems, Inc., McHenry, Il, 101–109.

Auerbach, E.: 1989, 'Toward a social-contextual approach to Family Literacy', *Harvard Educational Review* 59, 165–181.

Auerbach, E.: 1995, 'Deconstructing the discourse of strengths in family literacy', *Journal of Reading Behavior* 27, 643–661.

Barton, D.: 1994, 'Exploring Family Literacy', *RaPAL Bulletin* 24, 2–5.

Breen, M.: 1996, 'Families reveal a richness of literacy in the home', *ARIS Bulletin* 7, 3.

Delgado-Gaitan, C.: 1987, 'Mexican adult literacy: New directions for immigrants', in S.R. Goldman & K. Trueba (eds.), *Becoming Literate in English as a Second Language*, Ablex, Norwood, NJ, 9–32.

Delgado-Gaitan, C.: 1991, 'Involving parents in the schools: A process of empowerment', *American Journal of Education* 100, 20–46.

Fitzgerald, J., Spiegel, D. & Cunningham, J.: 1991, 'The relationship between parental literacy level and perceptions of emergent literacy', *Journal of Reading Behavior* 23, 191–213.

Gadsden, V.: 1995, 'Representations of literacy: Parents' images in two cultural communities', in L. Morrow (ed.), *Family Literacy Connections in Schools and Communities*, International Reading Association, Newark, NJ, 287–303.

Goldenberg, C. & Gallimore, R.: 1991, 'Local knowledge, research knowledge, and educational change: A case study of early Spanish reading improvement', *Educational Researcher* 20, 2–14.

Heath, S.B.: 1983, *Ways with Words*, Cambridge University Press, Cambridge, England.

Keen, J.: 1996, 'Family literacy in Lothian: connect – community learning programme with and for parents', *RaPAL Bulletin* 28/29, 22–30.

Madigan, D.: 1995, 'Shared lives and shared stories: Exploring critical literacy connections among family members', in L. Morrow (ed.), *Family Literacy Connections in Schools and Communities*, International Reading Association, Newark, NJ, 269–286.

McCaleb, S.: 1994, *Building Communities of Learners: A Collaboration among Teachers, Students, Families and the Community*, St. Martin's Press, New York.

Michaels, S.: 1981, ' "Sharing Time": Children's narrative styles and differential access to literacy', *Language in Society* 10, 423–442.

Moll, L.: 1992, 'Bilingual classroom studies and community analysis: Some recent trends', *Educational Researcher*, 20–24.

Nickse, R., Speicher, A. & Buchek P.: 1988, 'An intergenerational adult literacy project: A family intervention/prevention model', *Journal of Reading* 31, 634–642.

Ortiz, R.: 1992, 'The unpackaging of generation and social class factors: A study on literacy activities and education values of Mexican American fathers', Unpublished doctoral dissertation, University of California at Los Angeles, Los Angeles, CA.

Purcell-Gates, V.: 1994, 'Relationships between parental literacy skills and functional uses of print and children's ability to learn literacy skills. Final report to the National Institute for Literacy. Grant No. X257A20223.

RaPAL Bulletin 24: 1994, *Special Issue on Family Literacy*, Lancaster, England.

Shockley, B., Michalove, B. & Allen, J.: 1995, *Engaging Families, Connecting Home and School Literacy Communities*, Heinemann, Portsmouth, NH.

Taylor, D.: 1983, *Family Literacy: Young Children Learning to Read and Write*, Heinemann, Portsmouth, NH.

Taylor, D. (ed.): forthcoming, *Many Families, Many Literacies*, Heinemann, Portsmouth, NH.

Taylor, D. & Dorsey-Gaines, C.: 1988, *Growing Up Literate: Learning from Inner City Families*, Heinemann, Portsmouth, NH.

Tizard, J., Schofield, W., & Hewison, J.: 1982, 'Symposium: Reading collaboration between teachers and parents in assisting children's reading', *British Journal of Educational Psychology* 52, 1–15.

Toomey, D.: 1994, 'A young plant in Australia: Intergenerational literacy programs', *Fine Print Special Issue on Family Literacy* 16, 7–10.

Voss, M.: 1996, *Hidden Literacies: Children Learning at Home and at School*, Heinemann, Portsmouth, NH.

Weinstein-Shr, G.: 1995, 'Learning from uprooted families', in G. Weinstein-Shr & E. Quintero (eds.), *Immigrant Learners and their Families: Literacy to Connect Generations*, Center for Applied Linguistics & Delta Systems, Inc., McHenry, IL, 113–133.

Wells, G.: 1986, *The Meaning Makers: Children Learning Language and Using Language to Learn*, Heinemann, Portsmouth, NH.

ALAN ROGERS

ADULT LITERACY

The term 'literacy' has always been ambiguous, and recent studies have emphasised this ambiguity. The dominant view is that becoming literate is a one-off programme of 'learning to read and write' (Lind & Johnston, 1990). Others, however, see literacy as 'reading and writing in practice', a continuous and lifelong process (Street, 1984). This review looks on adult literacy as 'the promotion of reading and writing skills among adults' (however adults may be defined).

EARLY HISTORY

Universal literacy is a very recent idea. Even the Swedish campaigns inspired by religious enthusiasm in the seventeenth century (see also Hagtvet & Lyster, this volume) hardly envisaged that every adult (especially adult women) needed to learn to read (the Bible), let alone write (Arnove and Graff, 1987). Indeed there was a good deal of opposition to universalising literacy. It was thought that such education would teach the labouring classes to despise their lot in life and enable them to read seditious pamphlets. Literacy was simply necessary for those few who made their living by using these skills. It is only from the late nineteenth century that universal literacy came to be the norm of educational and economic debates. The concept of primary education as a universal and compulsory 'good' for all children was extended to adults.

Two fundamental pillars upheld this assumption: first, that widespread literacy is essential for a nation's economic and, to a lesser extent, its social development (Goody, 1975); and secondly, that literacy is a universal human right, the denial of which reflects badly on the state (Oxenham, 1980). Such attitudes led to strenuous government and non-government efforts to spread literacy skills more widely.

MAJOR CONTRIBUTIONS

Four main tributaries have fed the river of adult literacy learning campaigns. Early workers like Frank Laubach (1947) used child-tested methods of teaching reading and writing skills, and many of these still continue

V. Edwards and D. Corson (eds), Encyclopedia of Language and Education,
Volume 2: Literacy, 163–171.
© 1997 Kluwer Academic Publishers. Printed in the Netherlands.

to be used. Special primers (textbooks) are written starting with simple words and moving to more complex ones, often illustrated by pictures. Such primers are prepared in different ways, but in essence they are very similar. This approach sees literacy as a set of universal 'technical skills' which, once learned, can be used in all contexts (Street, 1993: 1–17).

The second major contribution to adult literacy was the notion of functional literacy, developed largely by UNESCO in the 1960s in an attempt to make adult literacy learning programmes more relevant to adults, and especially to their economic activities (see also Verhoeven, this volume). The emphasis in the early days on existing uses of literacy (Gray, 1969) soon gave way to new uses of literacy for communicating messages relating to production, health, social factors and, more recently, environmental issues.

The many new programmes which developed in the wake of functional literacy are generally regarded as a failure (UNESCO, 1976). They called for learning new farming or craft skills and knowledge while at the same time learning to read and, to a less extent, write. Functional literacy continues, although most programmes now teach in compartments – literacy skills at one time and production skills at another (Verhoeven, 1994).

A third major development in adult literacy can be traced to Paulo Freire (Freire and Macedo, 1987) who saw literacy as grounded in social conditions, a tool to overcome oppression. Learning to read and write could never (he argued) be neutral: it would always either 'domesticate' or 'liberate' the student-learner. The real use of literacy learning programmes was to help the participants to 'read the world' as well as to 'read the word'. Critical literacy (see also the reviews by Luke and Street, this volume) challenges the power assumptions on which each world is built, promoting dialogue which leads to 'conscientization' and to action designed to bring about social change. Modern approaches to Freirean literacy include the use of PRA (Participatory Rural Appraisal) methods to encourage the learning group to help create the special teaching-learning materials e.g. Archer & Cottingham, 1996 (see also Viv Edwards' review of 'Reading in multilingual classrooms', this volume).

Finally, since the mid-1980s, 'New Literacy Studies' (Willinsky, 1990), have promoted literacy as a life-long activity. Just as farmers learn farming skills by farming, so people learn literacy skills by engaging in literacy events (see Street, this volume). The Real Literacies Movement has grown out of the New Literacy Studies and seeks to promote the use of 'real materials' – everyday pieces of writing and print – in literacy learning programmes with adults (Barton 1994; ODA, 1994; Rogers 1994).

Just as there are different kinds of farming, so there are different literacies, not one 'literacy' (Street 1984). Literacy activities are culturally bound and can be analysed as 'literacy practices'. All written and printed materials reflect the power structure of given societies. These understandings call for local programmes. Universal literacy learning programmes and primers cannot meet the many different literacy needs, for example, of taxi drivers and hospital porters (Street, 1995, also this volume).

This 'cultural' model of literacy is contrasted with the 'technical' or 'autonomous' model of literacy (Street, 1993). The cultural model has influenced literacy programmes more in industrialised countries than in the developing world (Barton & Ivanič, 1991). The use of the 'language experience approach' for literacy learning (see Thompson, this volume) is one example of this influence.

WORK IN PROGRESS

The declining formal education system in many countries, both developing and industrialised, has led in some places to an increased emphasis on adult literacy programmes; but in other contexts, it has led to the search for newer and more effective forms of non-formal primary schools for children.

National campaigns are still launched in some developing countries, though with less frequency, because many international donors see such campaigns as expensive and fruitless (see also Agnihotri's review of literacy teaching in India, this volume). It was hoped that 1990 which marked both International Literacy Year and the Education for All programme would result in greater attention to adult literacy. In the event, most resources have been devoted to children's education. The main effect of national campaigns is to create a climate in which local adult literacy learning programmes can become more effective.

In industrialised countries, there is a growing awareness of the low level of literacy skills among large sections of the population (especially immigrant and displaced families). In the USA, for instance, some 25 per cent of adults are thought to be 'functionally illiterate' (Hunter and Harman, 1979). The current reconstruction of the workforce in these countries, with emphasis on smaller scale enterprises and more highly skilled workers, has increased concern. Innovative approaches to strengthening literacy skills are encouraged by governments but rarely resourced.

Many practitioners draw a distinction between adult literacy learning programmes in industrialised and developing countries, asserting that the former are not dealing with 'initial literacy' but only with 'post-literacy'. But all agree that there are many people in both settings who 'cannot perform the literacy-related tasks needed to function fully at home, at work and in civic life' (Benton 1996: 95) and that the aim of their literacy programmes is to help these people.

Most of the ground work is being undertaken by non-governmental organisations (NGOs), often using government money and materials but, at times, developing more locally appropriate materials and resources, and apparently being more effective. There is an emphasis in developing countries on literacy for women and rural literacy programmes; and, in industrialised countries, on literacy for workers.

SOME KEY ISSUES

Debates relating to adult literacy tend to focus on a number of issues.

Campaigns for learning literacy

The belief that illiteracy should and can be eradicated through a time-bound one-off learning programme (usually spoken of in terms of a military or health campaign) is still strong, despite the experience of failure in the last fifty years or more. Governments and major international donors normally organise and support these campaigns.

The independent role of NGOs is threatened by their dependency on these bodies for resources. In countries such as South Africa and Nicaragua, NGOs involved in adult literacy programmes formed the focus of opposition to oppressive governments. With political change, the programme promoted by these NGOs became government policy, with donor funds passing to the new government.

Structural adjustment is affecting adult literacy programmes, especially at national level. Most countries have cut resources for adult literacy; and, even in those industrialised countries where there is increased provision, the concentration tends to be on younger adults or adolescents. Some countries have turned their adult literacy agencies into parastatal bodies.

The issue of centralisation versus localisation of programmes remains a major problem. Governments see national campaigns as essential to their international image; and many national campaigns are best regarded as political activities. While locally developed initiatives have been shown to be more effective, these are less often supported by governments whose main concern is with national literacy statistics.

There are, however, no generally agreed ways of measuring literacy achievements (see also Verhoeven's review, this volume). Most countries take their standards from primary school (eg Grade IV), but the relevance of this approach for adults has been challenged by workers in the field (Benton, 1996). A good deal of research has been undertaken into the criteria of success in adult literacy. Benton (1996), for instance, draws attention to more sophisticated methods of measurement including performance tasks (USA), the use of literacy in daily tasks (Canada), and key skills (France). Efforts have been made most recently in South Africa to establish alternative forms of accreditation more appropriate to adults, but none of these has achieved even local recognition. Employers still prefer national forms of accreditation of the skills of potential employees.

Debates related to literacy learning often focus on motivation. Almost all literacy programmes are based on the assumption that adults (like children) need to be motivated to learn. Therefore, part of any adult literacy learning programme is advocacy for the benefits of being able to read and write.

This advocacy often results in exaggeration. Illiteracy is seen as depriving the non-literate populations not only of effective means of communication, but also of ways of thinking and reasoning (Ong, 1982). The assumption is often that great economic, social and personal benefits will automatically flow from learning to read and write, despite much evidence to the contrary (Rogers, 1994).

Two main drives seem to move adults to participate in literacy learning programmes – the wish to learn to meet direct instrumental needs (to read or write letters, keep accounts etc), and the wish to join the 'educated group' ('People treat you as stupid if you cannot read and write'). While there is little research into such motivation, recent fieldwork in India and Bangladesh undertaken on behalf of the UK-based Education and Development indicates that the drop-out rate among the status seekers is higher than among the instrumental learners.

A third motivation is often alleged: the desire to learn basic skills in order to gain access to further and more formal education at primary and eventually secondary level. There is a widespread debate about ways of helping adults (especially women) to enter what is, in some countries, called continuing education. However, it is unlikely that such a drive motivates more than a small number of younger adults. Nor it is always possible to maintain motivation: it would seem that drop-out rates from learning centres remain high.

There is also heated discussion as to whether learning literacy should be through the language normally used for oral communication or through the language in which the most commonly available materials are written, whether the vernacular or the local language of power or international language should be used (see Agnihotri's review of 'Sustaining Local Literacies, this volume).

There is a great deal of rhetoric about adult literacy and empowerment (especially of women), but measures for assessing increased empowerment are uncertain. The gender gap in all forms of education and in the spread of literacy skills is remarkable and persistent (Ballara, 1991; Stromquist, 1990; and Egbo, this volume), despite several years of special attention to the literacy needs of women. Effective methods of dealing with this gap are elusive.

A major issue which faces all adult literacy learning programmes is the selection, preparation and support of 'teachers' (facilitators, tutors, animators, etc). Many programmes find this their main problem; people who are chosen or who volunteer to work as teachers of adults often lack training and confidence and therefore fear to engage in more innovative approaches to teaching.

Despite this, there is growing concern for more participatory ways of developing teaching-learning materials for literacy programmes. Most primers are prepared by 'experts' (educationalists, journalists etc), though writers' workshops have been developed by several agencies (DSE 1993; ACCU 1992; ODA 1994). New ways of involving village level teachers and even student learners in writing their own learning materials (learner-generated materials) are a feature of some programmes.

Using literacy skills

The New Literacy Studies seek to redefine literacy in terms of using rather than learning skills. The argument is that learning literacy alone never benefited anyone; it is only in the use of literacy skills in real situations that the social and economic benefits will arise (Rogers, 1994). But the transfer of skills learned in the adult learning centre into daily life is one of the weakest points of modern adult literacy programmes. This issue is being addressed in countries such as Nepal (Tuijnman, 1996: 76), but is proving very difficult; and the lack of use of these skills, once acquired, has sometimes resulted in substantial relapse. Countries like Ethiopia and Tanzania which recorded major advances through national campaigns have since lost their relative advantage.

For this reason, provision for 'post-literacy' (a term which several writers on literacy find unacceptable) is a feature of all literacy campaign programmes today. Most post-literacy programmes consist of further learning activities, using specially prepared follow-up or supplementary materials, and aimed at a substantially smaller target group than the initial literacy learning programmes. However, new approaches to post-literacy, seen as the provision of community-based assistance to all those who have limited literacy skills and experience, are now being advocated (ODA, 1994).

Adult literacy and national development

The assumption that increased literacy brings social and economic change (Bown, 1990; Lind & Johnston, 1990; Arnove & Graff, 1987) is commonly asserted. The literacy needs of special groups, in particular, immigrant communities, minorities and refugees and displaced populations, is also of major concern to literacy agencies. But the widespread view that 'literacy is the entry point to development' is now being challenged (Olson, 1996: 76). A 'literacy comes second' approach (Rogers, 1994) in which the development of literacy skills follows from, and is based on, other development activities is advocated in place of 'literacy comes first' (see the review by Egbo in this volume).

Although there are many statements about the ability of 'neo-literates' to overcome their poverty (in China, a new programme has been launched under the title 'learn literacy and grow rich'), there is no real evidence that adult literacy programmes lead to any poverty relief, a fact which has led several agencies to abandon their adult literacy classes in favour of primary education or direct poverty relief. There are few programmes where the participants have been able to use their newly developed literacy skills to enhance their income at all significantly (Rogers, 1994). In developing countries, income generating skills are taught separately and are often more popular than literacy enhancement programmes. In industrialised countries, programmes are concentrated on unemployed persons (mainly youth) and on school drop-outs, aimed at helping them to secure employment.

The current pressure by international donor agencies on developing countries to introduce forms of multi-party democracy as a pre-condition for aid is also encouraging greater stress on adult literacy programmes. As Lind & Johnston (1996: 227) point out, "It is obviously not easy to democratise society if large sections of the population are illiterate".

THE FUTURE

It is not easy to see the future of adult literacy. There is unlikely to be any decline of interest in this area in industrialised countries but, in many developing countries, the chief focus will probably remain primary education for children. The gap between rich and poorer countries in terms of literacy as well as economic development is still wide. In industrialised countries, adult literacy is likely to be even more closely linked with work-based learning needs rather than with social justice, and with more emphasis on certification than in the past.

The interest in the cultural approach to literacy is likely to grow, and may lead to newer forms of provision. Research into literacy practices (Baynham, 1995) will almost certainly continue to grow, but it is not yet clear how such research will lead to better learning programmes. Work-based programmes (often supported by trade unions), context-specific with customised curricula and based on learner-needs, are being developed, but as Benton (1996: 95) indicates, "although it is possible to point toward some particularly compelling experiments, no single strategy has gained a solid reputation for effectiveness".

New approaches to enhancing adult literacy skills through technology and through inter-generational approaches (e.g. family and work-place literacies) are providing encouraging results (Wagner, 1995; see also Auerbach this volume) but alternative trends such as television and videos may lead to a greater polarisation of society into those who have very effective reading and writing skills and those whose skills are minimal.

The transfer of government resources to primary schooling raises the question as to where the support for NGO adult literacy programmes into the next millennium will come from. It is to be regretted that the international networks of NGOs which began to emerge with International Literacy Year 1990 have to some extent disappeared.

University of Reading, England

REFERENCES

Asian Cultural Centre for UNESCO (ACCU): 1992, *New Guidebook for Development and Production of Literacy Materials*, ACCU, Tokyo.

Archer, D. & Cottingham, S.: 1996, *Regenerated Freirean Literacy through Empowering Community Techniques: experiences of three REFLECT pilot projects in Uganda, Bangladesh and El Salvador*, ODA Education Research Report 17, Overseas Development Administration, London.

Arnove, R.F. & Graff, H.J. (eds): 1987, *National Literacy Campaigns in Historical and Comparative Perspective*, Plenum Press, New York.

Ballara, M.: 1991, *Women and Literacy*, Zed Books, London.

Barton, D.: 1994, *Literacy: An Introduction to the Ecology of the Written Language*, Oxford: Basil Blackwell.

Barton, D. & Ivanič, R. (eds): 1991, *Writing in the Community*, Sage, Newbury Park, California.

Baynham, M.: 1995, *Literacy Practices: Investigating Literacy in Social Contexts*, Longman, London.

Benton, L.: 1996, 'Postliteracy', in Tuijnman (1996), 94–99.

Bown, L.: 1990, *Preparing the Future: Women, Literacy and Development*, Action Aid Development Report 4, London.

Deutsche Stiftung für Internationale Entwicklung (DSE): 1993, *Join us in a Participatory Approach to Teaching, Learning and Production*, Freire Frings A, Gacuchi D, Matiru B and Mueller J, ZED, Bonn.

Dubbledam, L.: 1994, 'Towards a socio-cultural model of literacy education', in L. Verhoeven, 1994, *Functional Literacy*, John Benjamins, Amsterdam and Philadelphia, 405–423.

Freire, P. & Macedo, D.: 1987, *Literacy: Reading the Word and the World*, Bergin and Garvey, South Hadley, Mass.

Goody, J.: 1975, *Literacy in Traditional Societies*, Cambridge University Press, Cambridge.

Gray, W.S.: 1969, *The Teaching of Reading and Writing*, 2nd edition, UNESCO, Paris.

Hunter, C. St J. & Harman, D.: 1979, *Adult Illiteracy in the United States*, McGraw Hill, New York.

Jones, P.W.: 1988, *International Policies for Third World Education: UNESCO*, Literacy and Development, Routledge, London.

Lind, A. & Johnston, A.: 1990, *Adult Literacy in the Third World*, Swedish International Development Agency (SIDA), Stockholm.

Lind, A. & Johnston, A.: 1996, 'Adult literacy in the third world', in Tuijnman, 1996, 221–228.

Olson, D.: 1996, 'Literacy', in Tuijnman, 1996, 75–79.

Ong, W.: 1982, *Orality and Literacy: The Technologising of the Word*, Methuen, London.

Overseas Development Administration (ODA): 1994, *Using Literacy: A New Approach to Post-Literacy*, ODA Education Research Report 10, Overseas Development Administration, London.

Oxenham, J.: 1980, *Literacy: Writing, Reading and Social Organisation*, Routledge and Kegan Paul, London.

Rogers, A.: 1994, *Women, Literacy, Income Generation, Education for Development*, Reading.

Street, B.V.: 1984, *Literacy in Theory and Practice*, Cambridge University Press, Cambridge.

Street B.V. (ed.): 1993, 'Cross-Cultural Approaches to Literacy', Cambridge University Press, Cambridge.

Street, B.V.: 1995, *Social Literacies: Critical Approaches to Literacy in Development, Ethnography and Education*, Longman, London.

Stromquist, N.P.: 1990, 'Women and Illiteracy: the interplay of gender subordination and poverty', *Comparative Education Review* 34(1), 95–111.

Tuijnman, A.C. (ed.): 1996, *International Encyclopedia of Adult Education and Training*, second edition, Pergamon, Oxford.

UNESCO: 1976, *The Experimental World Literacy Programme: A Critical Assessment*, UNESCO, Paris.

Verhoeven, L.: 1994, *Functional Literacy*, John Benjamins, Amsterdam and Philadelphia.

Wagner, D.A.: 1995, 'Literacy and development: Rationales, myths, innovations and future directions', *International Journal of Education and Development* 15(4), 341–362.

Willinsky, J.: 1990, *The New Literacy: Redefining Reading and Writing in the Schools*, Routledge, London.

SUSTAINING LOCAL LITERACIES

Most discussions of literacy in this volume focus on standard official languages in general and English, in particular. This emphasis disguises the astonishing diversity of local literacies throughout the world. There is often an assumption that the move towards standardization is a necessary condition for development and the spread of literacy. However, such assumptions need to be scrutinised most carefully.

Scholars have started to examine different dimensions of local literacies only in relatively recent times (see, for instance, Barton, 1994); they have, however, identified a number of key issues which will form the focus for the present discussion. This review will attempt to define the characteristics of local literacies; the problems and difficulties associated with attempts to promote them; and the lessons which can be learned in developing new models for local literacies.

WHAT ARE LOCAL LITERACIES?

As Narasimhan (1991) argues, literateness should be seen as a continuum with no rigid polarization between orality and literacy (see also reviews by Verhoeven and Street, this volume). Any system of knowledge – oral or written – that involves reflective behaviour and symbolization and constitutes a part of a community's identity should be regarded as a local literacy, as distinguished from the overwhelmingly powerful mainstream literacies. Local literacies would include not only marginalised writing and counting systems but also systems of local art, poetry, music, dance, drama and architecture.

Sometimes, local literacies use the mainstream script while drawing on a lexicon and a syntax that may be significantly different from the mainstream language. Alternatively, scripts may play a critical role in defining group identity. In South Asia in general and in India in particular, a striking paradox obtains between an oral culture and a multiplicity of scripts. As Masica (1996) points out, separate writing systems may function as identity markers for speech communities that speak closely related often mutually comprehensible languages.

India offers many examples of the bewildering complexity of local literacies, both during the freedom struggle and after. Gandhi and others used 'Hindustani' as a lingua franca to mobilize people across the country

V. Edwards and D. Corson (eds), Encyclopedia of Language and Education,
Volume 2: Literacy, 173–179.
© *1997 Kluwer Academic Publishers. Printed in the Netherlands.*

speaking mutually incomprehensible and genetically unrelated languages. This local literacy first developed to fight the British empire now unites the nation as the medium of Hindi films. On the other hand, during the freedom struggle and after, groups of the low-caste and downtrodden have realised that the leadership of the national movement was in the hands of a select Brahmanical elite and that they needed to return to their local literacies for their liberation, be it in Telangana in the south, Bodoland in the east or Jharkhand in the centre (see the review by Agnihotri on 'Literacy teaching in India', this volume).

The notion of local literacies is developing ever broadening connotations. We also need to appreciate, for instance, the fact that, in the context of ruthless forces of globalization and free market economy with which prestigious languages such as English are inextricably associated, mainstream literacies in Nicaragua, Sri Lanka or Bangladesh can be seen as local literacies.

PROBLEMS AND DIFFICULTIES

Most people see a contradiction between processes of standardization, on the one hand, and those of sustaining local literacies on the other. It is suggested that standardization and homogenization can only be achieved at the cost of losing a rich heritage of regional and ethnic literacies of different kinds. Though there is some truth in this proposal – and though there is also often substantial historical evidence to support it – this is not necessarily the case.

In multilingual and multicultural countries such as India, heterogeneity is the norm and variability facilitates rather than hinders communication (see, for instance, Pandit, 1969; 1972). Sustaining local literacies is not an asocial or apolitical question; if the people and powers that be so desire, new languages, local and standard, flourish even as the old ones disappear. Sanskrit is dead but it lives in every Indian language, Indo-Aryan or Dravidian; even as young people find their native varieties functionally diminished, they create new mixed codes in the urban metropolis. Yet the threats of globalization and market economy may indeed destroy many literacies, if we fail to take action. More often than not, local literacies die because of the asymmetrical and exploitative power structures obtaining in a given society.

The standard argument against local literacies is that mainstream literacies will help the learners in occupational mobility and economic prosperity. As Heath (1986: 16–17) shows, with convincing historical evidence, time-honoured beliefs about a positive correlation between mainstream literacy and occupational mobility are highly suspect; yet local literacies are ignored without compunction. A careful rethinking of local literacies in the context of a new social order is absolutely necessary before we give in to the overwhelming pressures of mainstream literacies and join UNESCO in its drive to eradicate illiteracy by the year 2000. As Heath (1986: 18) points out,

> Generalisations about oral and literate modes of thought and their causative links to abilities in hypothetical reasoning, abstract thinking, or logical organization of ideas have not been borne out in cross-cultural studies of literacy. Literacy acquisition is often a function of society-specific tasks, which are sometimes far removed from those of formal schooling, and are not conceived of as resulting from effort expended by "teacher" and "learners".

Local literacy is also seriously threatened by various attempts at 'Sanskritising' languages of the common people to the extent that speakers become strangers to their own languages (Agnihotri, 1977; Mukherjee, 1992). As Lankshear (1987, 216) argues, it is imperative for us to make a distinction between proper and improper literacies:

> Proper literacy comprises practices of reading and writing which enhance people's control over their lives and their capacity for making rational judgements and decisions by enabling them to identify, understand and act to transform social relations and practices in which power is structured unequally.

The most striking example of the dangers of failing to contextualise struggle, past or present, may be seen in Mexico (King, 1994). In spite of following Freire and his generative word (palabra generation) method (Freire & Macedo, 1987), literacy compaigns among communities such as the Nahualt, Maya and Tzeltal could achieve very little. The idea was to provide literacy in the languages of these communities as a bridge towards mainstream literacy in Spanish. Once again we notice a minimization of goals and demeaning of local literacies. Results were largely predictable. It was found 'that the bilingual Indians registered in the literacy courses were learning to read and write in Spanish but did not necessarily comprehend what they read' (King, 1994: 127). The monolingual Indian, of course, fared much worse.

We may also note that it is societies with grassroot multilingualism such as India, China and Africa that exhibit highest levels of social disparities and economic differences (see also the review by Egbo, this volume). It is in these societies that corruption and exploitation are endemic and child labour, high infant mortality rate, diseases and gender bias more common. Once again it is for this reason that a local literacy agenda that is not a part of a holistic social programme is likely to have very little impact on either sustaining local literacies or social transformation.

This became abundantly clear even in the Native Language (e.g. Cree and Ojiwbe) Teaching Programmes organised by such Universities as Lakehead (Thunder Bay, Canada) for the American Indians in North America. Or, consider King's (1994) study of language and literacy in Mexico.

She shows how the collaboration of the Summer Insititute of Linguistics
(its primary objective being propagation of the gospel) with the mestizo
(of mixed Spanish and Indian ancestry) Mexican government discouraged
and frustrated the growth of any local literacy. Alphabetization of Mexican
Indian Languages was simply to act as a bridge to the eventual teaching of
Spanish, the language of the dominant group and culture to which minority
ethnic groups must assimilate.

FUTURE DEVELOPMENTS

The agenda for sustaining local literacies could possibly avoid the pitfalls
that have affected most mainstream literacy programmes. We should, for
instance, stop talking of 'literacy' and switch, as several researchers have
now argued, to 'multiple literacy' models (see the review by Street, this
volume). Multiple literacies would include not only mainstream language,
but also local languages; the most critical aspects of this approach would
be understanding and sustaining local systems of knowledge. A literacy
programme that is not embedded in a vision of global social transformation
is not likely to survive.

Just learning to read and write should satisfy neither the learner nor the
instructor or the evaluator. One must be able to read with understanding
and one must be familiar with the whole dynamics of the written mode of
communication (see the review by Verhoeven, this volume).

All activities associated with literacy programmes must involve some
degree of reflective and critical behaviour and, in addition, the relationship
between literacy and empowerment should be clearly spelt out without
any romanticization. Local literacies are not to be preserved as objects
of wonder; and mainstream literacy goals are not to be stated in such a
minimalist format that they constitute an insult to human intelligence. It is
imperative that mainstream literacies be acquired to fight forces of oppression and authoritarianism; it is equally imperative that local literacies be
sustained to make that struggle possible. The human resources, methods
and materials required for such an enterprise will not be imposed from
above in hierarchically organised structures but will be generated in close
collaboration with the community in question.

If we wish to struggle for a socially just multiple literacy model of sustaining local literacies, we need to carefully examine multilingual societies
such as India. As Pandit (1969; 1972; 1988) and Khubchandani (1983;
1988 and see the reviews by Khubchandani in Volumes 1 and 5) among
others have shown, multiplicity of languages does not by itself constitute
a barrier in communication; rather it may in fact facilitate communication,
language maintenance and development of new speech varieties. Children
and adults can learn several literacies simultaneously with equanimity
when the objectives and functions of each are clearly understood, when

the input is rich, complex and contextualised (Krashen, 1981; 1982) rather than segmented and graded, and when the motivation to learn is high.

Most programmes in local literacies come to an end too soon on the ground that learners themselves are more eager to master mainstream literacy. This is indeed critical. We first belittle the significance of local literacies rendering them dysfunctional and stigmatised and then blame their users for rejecting them. As Illich (1981: 30) pointed out,

> We must shamelessly spend enormous amounts of money to standardise languages at the cost of ethnic languages telling our children and students how to speak, and then spend token amounts to teach the counterfeits of ethnic languages as academic subjects.

Lankshear also shows how, in spite of the near elimination of its native people by the Spaniards and subsequent American Contra war and support to terrorists, the Nicaraguan literacy crusade created conditions for the development of proper literacy. The goals were not defined in a minimalist fashion. Rather, rudimentary literacy skills were located in political awareness, critical thinking, research in health and agriculture, economic and political participation and, most of all, in an active interest in local literacies including local history, art and culture. A major part of the theory and practice of the literacy agenda was predicated on the history of the Nicaraguan revolution. Most literacy programmes across the world have failed to capitalise on this rich resource; rarely if ever have struggles for liberation constituted the content of literacy programmes. And, to that extent, these programmes have failed to elicit any lasting community level involvement.

There are also lessons to be learned from the Nicaraguan approach to teaching materials and teacher training. Literacy materials consisted of meaningful dialogues and pictures rather than isolated letters and words. Considerable preparations were made before (and not after) the crusade was launched in training teachers and preparing primers and teachers' guides. Every teacher was supplied with a portable blackboard and adequate supply of chalks.

Strategic planning was also crucial in a campaign marked by speed, intensity and preparation for post-literacy work in the early stages. Primary education, adult education, special education for the disadvantaged and the handicapped and the details of the crusade itself were all examined and fine-tuned collectively. In fact, once the revolutionaries were ready to launch the crusade, all educational institutions were closed for a period of six months to involve school and college students and teachers. Finally, massive financial inputs, local or foreign, were neither available nor sought. Once the revolutionary context of the literacy crusade was made explicit, volunteer help was readily forthcoming.

In order to sustain local literacies it is necessary to discard the monolin-

gual mode of teaching which in a variety of ways insults and undermines
the literacies and cultures which learners bring to various formal learning situations. A whole new theory and practice of multilingual teaching
is now beginning to take shape (see, for instance, papers in Heugh et al
1995). One is no longer concerned with teaching 'a language' or 'a subject'; journeys across disciplines are more important than the boundaries
that separate them. The multilingual and multicultural diversity of the
classroom (which more often than not is the norm rather than a deviation)
is seen as an asset rather than an obstacle (see also the reviews by Viv Edwards in this volume for discussion of the same phenomenon in a western
setting). Teachers become participant learners who help formulate cogni-
tively challenging tasks that motivate learners to talk with and learn from
each other. Local literacies are not just tolerated; they are actively used in
the process of all learning and therefore begin to command respect.

University of Delhi, India

REFERENCES

Agnihotri, R.K.: 1977, 'Choice of styles in Hindi: A pilot study', *Papers in Linguistic Analysis* 2, 43–52, University of Delhi.
Barton, D. (ed.): 1994, *Sustaining Local Literacies, special issue of Language and Education* 8(1) & 2.
Freire, P. & Macedo, D.: 1987, *Literacy: Reading the Word and the World*, Bergin & Garvey: Mass, USA.
Heath, S.B.: 1986, 'The functions and uses of literacy', in S. de Castell, A. Luke and K. Egan (eds), *Literacy, Society, and Schooling*, Cambridge University Press, Cambridge, 15–26.
Heugh, K. et al. (ed.): 1995, *Multilingual Education for South Africa*, Heinemann, Johannesburg.
Ilich, I.: 1981, 'Taught mother tongue and vernacular tongue', in D.P. Pattanayak (ed.), *Multilingualism and Mother Tongue Education*, Oxford University Press, Delhi.
King, L: 1994, *Roots of Identity: Language and Literacy in Mexico*, Stanford University Press, Stanford, California.
Khubchandani, L.M.: 1983, *Plural Languages, Plural Cultures*, East West Centre, University of Hawaii, Hawaii.
Khubchandani, L.M.: 1988, *Language in a Plural Society*, Motilal Banarsidass, Delhi.
Krashen, S.: 1981, *Second Language Acquisition and Second Language Learning*, Pergamon Press, New York.
Krashen, S.: 1982, *Principles and Practice in Second Language Acquisition*, Pergamon Press, Oxford.
Lankshear, C.: 1987, *Literacy, Schooling and Revolution*, The Falmer Press, New York.
Masica, C.: 1996, 'South Asia: Coexistence of scripts', in P.T. Daniels & W. Bright (eds), *The World's Writing Systems*, OUP, New York.
Mukherjee, A.: 1992, 'Planning Hindi for mass communication', *The Administrator* 37(4), 73–80.
Narasimhan, R.: 1991, 'Literacy: its characterization and implications', in D.R. Olson & Nancy Torrance (eds), *Literacy and Orality*, Cambridge University Press, Cambridge, 177–197.

Pandit, P.B.: 1969, 'Parameters of speech variation in an Indian community', in A. Poddar (ed.), *Language and Society in India*, Indian Institute of Advanced Studies, Shimla.
Pandit, P.B.: 1972, *India as a Sociolinguistic Area*, University of Poona Press, Pune.
Pandit, P.B.: 1988, 'Towards a grammar of variation', in L.M. Khubchandani (ed.), 40–49.
Street, B.: 1994, 'What is meant by local literacies? 'in D. Barton (ed.), 19–30.

CHRIS ABBOTT

IT AND LITERACY

The impact of the typewriter on literacy was wide-reaching and pervasive for over a hundred years. However, its impact can scarcely be compared with that of the computer. Information technology (IT) has become an essential tool for literacy, offering new avenues for writing and publishing, and opening new lines of communication between the literate peoples of the world. Computers enable people to express, re-draft, print and communicate their thoughts, ideas and aspirations. The convergence of telecommunications technology with IT in the mid- and late-1990s has made telematics an indispensable part of modern literate life. This development has been mirrored in classrooms and is further reflected in pedagogical research.

EARLY DEVELOPMENTS

As information technology developed ever closer relationships with literacy, particularly within education, so researchers began to investigate the nature and dimensions of these relationships. Unfortunately, there was little or no research into the drill-and-practice programs which were bought in large numbers by schools in the early 1980s. Such programs were used as storage devices for activities reminiscent of prior technological advances, such as audio pages, Language Masters and taperecorders. This was doubly unfortunate, for not only were computers used ineffectively, but teachers often made the mistake of assuming that this was their only function. Focused research at this time would have been helpful in establishing the limitations of this kind of software.

Much early research also revolved around wordprocessing and the way in which it differed from previous tools for writing. Development within IT often led to associated research developments. When it became possible, for example, to track all the key-presses made by a user and thus to log corrected errors as well as finished product, a whole body of research grew up to investigate this area (Sharples, 1991). More recently, the focus has shifted from what happens at the keyboard to the nature of collaborative writing and the way in which writers interact with technology.

Much of the early work on writing was concerned with psychological and cognitive processes, and many of the researchers were indeed psychol-

V. Edwards and D. Corson (eds), Encyclopedia of Language and Education,
Volume 2: Literacy, 181–188.
© *1997 Kluwer Academic Publishers. Printed in the Netherlands.*

ogists (see, for example, Hartley, 1992). The needs of bilingual writers were another focus of interest, and the development of one of the first multilingual word-processors, Allwrite, at the Inner London Educational Computing Centre (ILECC) in the 1980s led to considerable international interest and activity (see also Edwards' review of *Writing in multilingual classrooms*, this volume).

MAJOR CONTRIBUTIONS

In a wide-ranging and authoritative volume, Hartley (1992a) looked at the effect of modern technology on writing in four areas: at school, with the disabled, with electronic texts and in the future. Included in this volume are various important contributions to the literature. Hartley (1992b) himself provides a useful summary of the research to date on writing and computers, much of which is useful to the student of literacy. Daiute (1992), for instance, building on her earlier seminal work (Daiute, 1985), examines the area of collaborative writing. An article by Zvacek (1992) also offers a view of the uses of word-processing which is firmly grounded in classroom practice. She links the move towards a process model of writing to the strategies that writers adopt when they have access to technology.

Hawkridge & Vincent (1992) and Singleton (1994) deal with the impact of information technology in a wide range of contexts on learners with special educational needs, especially in the area of dyslexia. In his authoritative study of the computers and the history of writing, Bolter (1991) goes well beyond a discussion of pedagogy, but makes many points which are relevant in the context of education. His analysis of 'electronic writing' is placed in the context of arguments about the forthcoming demise of the printed book as a primary text artefact.

> All forms of writing are spatial, for we can only see and understand written signs as extended in a space of at least two dimensions. Each technology gives us a different space. For early ancient writing, the space was the inner surface of a continuous roll. For medieval handwriting and modern printing, the space is the white surface of a page, particularly in a bound volume. For electronic writing, the space is the computer's video screen (Bolter, 1991, p. 11).

Bolter's discussion of picture writing and pictorial space was published in 1991 and thus predates much of the current activity in that area. Nonetheless, his comments have proved to be far-seeing.

Various authors have provided overviews of the field. Holt & Williams (1992), for instance, build on Chandler and Marcus' (1985) earlier summary of computers and literacy, particularly from a psychological and cognitive perspective. In her volume on *Computers and Language*, Monteith

(1993) brings together a number of British writers who deal with literacy and computers from the perspective of activities within classrooms. Marcus (1993) contributes a summary of hyper and multimedia from an American perspective and covers much of the ground which was to be explored by researchers in the mid 1990s as the tools which he describes moved from the universities to schools. He reminds his readers of the essential newness of multimedia writing and explains the ways in which it is much more than just another form of writing:

> Hypertext systems, while often sophisticated in their way, are still, relative to their potential, primitive . . . it is not unreasonable to expect that hypertext – and hypermedia – environments will have a major effect on education (Marcus, 1993, p. 20).

Selfe (1994) also presents a picture of IT and literacy in the USA, while Snyder (1993; 1994) has studied the effect of computers on the context in which classroom writing takes place, and the changes in student writing that accompany the use of word processors.

Abbott (1995) discusses twenty-three statements concerning IT support for literacy and numeracy which have emerged from the National Literacy and Numeracy Project set up in the UK by the National Council for Educational Technology (NCET). Far more of these statements affect literacy than numeracy, and this is, in part, an indication both of the greater use of the technology for that purpose and the clearer understanding of its benefits.

WORK IN PROGRESS

In a report on the use of computers to support reading, Lewin (1995) examines the relatively recent development of computer-assisted reading software, and, in particular, what are usually known as talking books. She relates the development of these products to theories of how children learn to read, starting from an assumption that a synthesis of alternative theories may be appropriate. She contrasts existing software with the more recent development of talking books and talking word processors, now widely used in the UK and the USA. Lewin offer a critique of previous evaluations and indicates some apparent contradictions which will become more important as the technology develops:

> Recent innovations in technology, such as speech synthesis, have ensured that computer assisted reading software has tangible benefits when compared to other classroom reading activities. However, it is not clear that the educational theories underpinning reading acquisition and the context in which reading is taught have been considered in the design of these teaching tools (Lewin, 1995, p. 9).

There is considerable interest in the rapid development of CD-ROM titles and the possibility that new forms of reading will develop as these become more widely used and more familiar to teachers and students. In the UK, for instance, on-going projects include MENO (Multimedia Education and Narrative Organisation) based at the Open University which is currently exploring the forms and functions of narrative in interactive media (see http://www-iet.open.ac.uk/iet/MENO/meno-home.html for further information).

Another emerging concern is that skimming and searching strategies developed for paper texts may not be transferable to electronic information sources. For instance, the Interactive Media in Primary Schools (IMPS) project based in the Department of Typography & Graphic Communication at the University of Reading in the UK is placing particular emphasis on design and navigational features of CD-ROM and the ways in which they differ from those found in the print media.

Teachers are in fact rapidly expanding their view of reading from print to interactive media. The UK National Curriculum, like that in Denmark and Finland, requires the use of IT across the curriculum, and mentions the forms of reading that should be developed:

> Pupils should be taught how to find information in books and computer-based sources by using organisational devices to help them decide which parts of the material to read closely. They should be given opportunities to read for different purposes, adopting appropriate strategies for the task, including skimming to gain an overall impression, scanning to locate information and detailed reading to obtain specific information (DfEE, 1995, p. 14).

Further dimensions have been added to research into literacy and computers with the development of talking and symbol processors. These tools enable writers to receive aural or pictorial feedback as they write, or to add to the message which is being communicated. Very little research is taking place into this area at the moment.

Some countries are in the process of establishing large-scale research projects into changing forms of literacy in their schools. In Denmark, the five year 'Literacy across the Curriculum Project' is designed to investigate the evolution of literacy in the classroom. Andresen (1996, p. 80) sees three ways in which IT is central:

> First, since education involves the acquisition of knowledge and skills, IT can have a key role in education in the communication of knowledge. ... Secondly, the use of IT as a means of communication should provide an instructional method which places the responsibility for learning on the student. ... Third, IT integration across the curricula will change the role of the teacher.

Perhaps the most exciting development in the area of writing and computers has been the rapid growth in the middle 1990s of the Internet as a site for writing and publishing. Always a potential site for writing, the Internet expanded with startling rapidity after the appearance of the World Wide Web in 1993. The combination of a seductively simple interface, almost free software and a low learning curve for the coding required to publish, led to many tens of thousands of students not only writing for new audiences, but publishing directly to many millions of others with Internet access around the world.

Many authors including Turkle (1996) have dealt with the question of identity and the Internet, and there is now increasing focus on the World Wide Web as a site for literacy. One focus for research is the developing forms of language used by young student writers on the Internet, both in the form of synchronous communication and in longer and more complex texts that form part of World Wide Web personal home pages. Early results (Abbott, 1996) indicate a heightened awareness of audience and a sophisticated understanding of publishing on the part of young people and a willingness to embrace this new form which is often lacking in established and published writers.

PROBLEMS AND DIFFICULTIES

Much of the research that has been undertaken on the pedagogical uses of information technology has been bedevilled by the apparent mismatch between the theory of the high-tech classroom and the practice of ten year old computers which a school can often ill afford to maintain. In the USA, centres of excellence such as the Apple Classrooms of Tomorrow (ACOT) have attracted some interest, but the validity or generalisability of research based on resourcing of this exceptionally high quality is open to question.

There has always been a problem in IT and education research with regard to the ever-onward march of technological progress. Manufacturers are far more interested in funding research for their most recent or forthcoming products than they are in establishing why the older, cheaper and possibly less profitable tools might be still of great value.

There is also a political dimension to some research which may not always be helpful. The British government, through the Department for Education and Employment (DfEE), has funded three years of research into Integrated Learning Systems following a fact-finding visit to the USA. The results of the first and second year (Avis, 1996) appeared inconclusive; some of the titles evaluated were incomplete or not fully developed, but the political interest and impetus ensured that the work continues.

A further difficulty with a political dimension is the place of national languages within world literacy. World languages and, in particular, English are powerfully entrenched in the new technologies. Very little is available in the languages of many of the smaller countries of the world. This, together with the associated perception by young people of English as the language of the future and of all that is technological, has led many to question the future of other languages. This was a particular concern of Palsson (1996), speaking at a conference in Denmark.

> [By using CD-ROMs in English] ... those Icelandic children ... were being given a silent but unquestionable message. ... The language of your parents may well be a noble central language which has been spoken for centuries, and may well have its uses for collecting out-of-date and unexciting information about things which happened in the past – but if you want to know about modern things, those things which are presented by the most up-to-date technology, then you are going to have to turn to other languages (Pálsson, 1996, p. 112).

Luke's review in this volume discusses still further political dimensions associated with the challenges of new technologies.

FUTURE DIRECTIONS

Talking and listening must form a major focus of interest for the future. It is unlikely that the use of computers in the classroom will ever be the same again once teachers and students start to control a computer with speech, see their words appear on the screen as they dictate or ask the computer to say their words. Research will be needed into the effects of different kinds of speech controls, the implications for traditional orthography and the nature of the collaborative writing process when instant transcription of discussion becomes an everyday matter.

Speech recognition in general seems likely to change the nature of the relationship between the human – a lifelong learner in the eyes of many national governments – and technology. No longer sited in only one computer, the group of technologies "owned" by a user may be available at a number of different sites, especially if the predicted Network Computer (NC) revolution takes place. It will no longer be necessary for texts to be reconciled between home and office variants; with any NC a communications call will link up to the same package at the same remote site.

Far greater in its effect than any of these, however, is the astonishing success of the Internet as a site for publishing, linked to much greater home ownership of PCs. Students already write and publish texts from their homes as well as from school; schools can become publishers of the work produced by their students, and vast audiences can have access to all these products. It will be essential to explore this area with care and to establish the nature of the writing process when publishing is in the hands of the author. What we are seeing is nothing less than a radical shift in the author-publisher-reader relationship, a vital area for future research.

King's College, London, England

REFERENCES

Abbott, C. (ed.): 1995, *IT Helps: Using IT to Support Basic Literacy and Numeracy Skills*, NCET, Coventry.

Abbott, C.: 1996, 'Young people developing a new language: The implications for teachers and for education of electronic discourse', Euro Education 96, Aalborg, Denmark, 97–105.

Andresen, B.B.: 1996, 'Literacy of the future: Knowledge, skills and attitudes', Euro Education 96, Aalborg, Denmark, 79–87.

Avis, P. (ed.): 1996, *ILS: A Report of Phase II of the Pilot Evaluation of ILS in the UK*, NCET, Coventry.

Bolter, J.D.: 1991, *Writing Space: The Computer, Hypertext and the History of Writing*, Lawrence Erlbaum Associates, Hillsdale, NJ.

Chandler D & Marcus, S.: 1985, *Computers and Literacy*, Open University, Milton Keynes.

Daiute, C.: 1985, *Writing and Computers*, Addison-Wesley, London.

Daiute, C.: 1992, 'A case-study on collaborative writing', in J. Hartley (ed.), *Technology and Writing: Readings in the Psychology of Written Communication*, Jessica Kingsley Publishers, London, 39–44.

Department for Education and Employment (DfEE): 1995, *The National Curriculum*, Department for Education and Employment, London.

Hartley, J. (ed.): 1992a, *Technology and Writing: Readings in the Psychology of Written Communication*, Jessica Kingsley Publishers, London.

Hartley, J.: 1992b, 'Writing: A review of the research', in J. Hartley (ed.), *Technology and Writing: Readings in the Psychology of Written Communication*, Jessica Kingsley Publishers, London, 18–35.

Hawkridge, D. & Vincent, T.: 1992, *Learning Difficulties and Computers: Access to the Curriculum*, Jessica Kingsley Publishers, London.

Holt, P.O.B. & Williams, N. (eds).: 1992, *Computers and Writing: State of the Art*, Intellect Books, Oxford.

Lewin, C.: 1995, *"Test Driving" CARS: Addressing the Issues in the Evaluation of Computer Assisted Reading Software*, Open University, Milton Keynes.

Marcus, S.: 1993, 'Multimedia, hypermedia and the teaching of English', in M. Monteith (ed.), *Computers and Language*, Intellect Books, Oxford, 21–43.

Monteith, M. (ed.): 1993, *Computers and Language*, Intellect, Oxford.

Pálsson, H.: 1996, 'Multimedia and the language of the Vikings', Euro Education '96, Aalborg, Denmark, 107–114.

Selfe, C. & Hilligoss, S. (eds.): 1994, *Literacy and Computers: The Complications of Teaching and Learning with Technology*, Modern Language Association of America, New York.

Sharples, M. (ed.): 1991, *Proceedings of the Fourth Annual Conference on Computers and the Writing Process, Computers and Writing Association*, Computers and Writing Association, Brighton.

Singleton, C. (ed.): 1994, *Computers and Dyslexia: Educational Applications of New Technology*, Dyslexia Computer Resource Centre, Hull.

Snyder, I.A.: 1993, 'The impact of computers on students' writing: A comparative study of the effects of pens and word processors on writing context, process and product', *Australian Journal of Education* 37(1), 5–25.

Snyder, I.A.: 1994, 'Writing with word processors: The computer's influence on a class-room context', *Journal of Curriculum Studies* 26(2), 143–162.

Turkle, S.: 1996, *Life on the Screen: Identity in the Age of the Internet*, Weidenfield & Nicholson, London.

Williams, N.: 1993, 'Post writing software and the classroom', in M. Monteith (ed.), *Computers and Language*, Intellect Books, Oxford, 114–124.

Zvacek, S.M.: 1992, 'Word-processing and the teaching of writing', in J. Hartley (ed.), *Technology and Writing: Readings in the Psychology of Written Communication*, Jessica Kingsley Publishers, London, 57–64.

Section 4

Focus on Selected Regions

DANIELLE BECHENNEC &
LILIANE SPRENGER-CHAROLLES

LITERACY TEACHING IN FRANCE

For well over a century, interest in both reading standards and methods of teaching of reading in France has been high. It is interesting, however, to note that this interest has been more at the level of political polemic than actual research. In this overview, attention will be paid to the French education system and its implications for the organisation of literacy learning; the different approaches used in teaching children to read; and the ongoing debate on standards.

THE ORGANISATION OF FRENCH EDUCATION

The history of formal schooling in France can be traced back to the late eighth century when Charlemagne decided that state agents should deliver his orders in writing. Later, during the Middle Ages, children were taught to read and count in 'les petites écoles' (little schools). The sixteenth century marked the advent of religious schools run by priests. By 1802, there was a division of responsibility between state and Church, with primary schools falling under the aegis of the Church and secondary schools under state control.

With the passsing of the Jules Ferry laws in 1881–1882, education was made free, non-religious and compulsory for children between the ages of six and 11. Subsequently, the school leaving age was raised first to 12, then to 14 and finally, in 1959, to 16. Today there are four distinct phases of education: nursery or kindergarten (two to five years of age), primary or elementary (six to 11), 'collège' (12–15), and 'lycée' (16–18), at the end of which children take the 'baccalauréat', a school leaving and university entrance examination.

Until quite recently, specific lessons for the teaching of reading and writing were reserved for the first year of primary school, between the ages of 6 and 7. Children whose progress in reading was unsatisfactory had to retake this first year. However, in 1992, increasing dissatisfaction with this arrangement, on the part of both parents and teachers, resulted in the reorganization of the primary years into three different stages:
- Stage 1 ('cycle des apprentissages premiers'), nursery (2–4 years of age)
- Stage 2 ('cycle des apprentissages fondamentaux'), from the last year of kindergarten to the end of grade 2 (5–7 years of age).

V. Edwards and D. Corson (eds), Encyclopedia of Language and Education,
Volume 2: Literacy, 191–198.
© 1997 Kluwer Academic Publishers. Printed in the Netherlands.

- Stage 3 ('cycle des approfondissements') from grade 3 to the end of grade 5 (8–11 years of age).

These new arrangements are designed to reflect more faithfully children's natural development. They also have the effect of extending the amount of time in which children receive formal reading instruction by three years, to the age of 8.

APPROACHES TO LITERACY TEACHING

Methods for teaching reading have been the subject of debate in France (see Chartier & Hébrard, 1989, 1990) since at least the 1880s when the Jules Ferry laws made school attendance compulsory for children up to the age of 11. There was general agreement at this time that children needed to become more efficient readers, able to understand what they were reading. Traditional alphabetic approaches which required children to name letters (see Thompson, and Hagtvet & Lyster, this volume) gave way to newer methods in which letter sounds were learned in the context of syllables and words.

In the early twentieth century, two figures were particularly influential in literacy teaching in the French-speaking world. The first, Ovide Decroly, worked with children with learning difficulties. In 1907, he opened a school (l'Ecole de l'Ermitage) in Brussels where he developed a revolutionary new approach to the teaching of reading. Children first built up a sight vocabulary of words or expressions presented to them on flash cards. These words were then broken down into syllables and letters. Learning did not take place in isolation but was always related to children's own interests or work already taking place in class.

Madame Rouquié introduced Decroly's approach into France in 1920 as the 'global method' (Chartier & Hébrard, 1989; 1990). Over a period of time, the original ideas were modified in significant ways outlined later in this review. Aspects of Decroly's global method have, however, had a considerable impact on the teaching of reading in France, particularly the tendency to start with a whole text which is then analyzed into words, syllables and letter sounds before building up new words from specific letter sounds.

Célestin Freinet was another influential player during the same period in France. His 'natural method' has much in common with the language experience approach (see Thompson, this volume). Lessons begin with an informal discussion; the teacher then focuses on a sentence (and, later in the year, on a short passage) written on the blackboard and read back by the whole group. Then, the text is printed out in the classroom and given to each child. The 'natural approach', even at the peak of its influence in the 1960s, was only ever used in a small number of schools. However, some of the ideas associated with this approach have had a long-lasting impact, for example, the pattern of starting a reading lesson with stories dictated by the children themselves.

The French Department of Education gives only very general guidelines on the teaching of reading and no specific reading method has ever been officially prescribed. On the contrary, government directives emphasize the autonomy of individual teachers in this area. Hébrard (1988), in a review of one hundred years of official recommendations relating to the teaching of reading, indicates that the current philosophy has remained consistent for at least the last four decades. In January 1958, for instance, the Cabinet du Directeur (Minister of Education) commented as follows:

> Which method is the most appropriate in the early stages: 'syllabic', 'global' or mixed? Research has shown that for 6-year-olds of average ability, results are identical irrespective of the method. We therefore do not advocate any one approach.

A Directive on the teaching of French in primary school published by the Department of Education and distributed to all teachers in December 1972 makes similar observations:

> Methods of teaching reading have been the subject of fierce debate, though we have gradually been moving towards a greater consensus. Experience shows that there can be no single approach either to segmenting words into syllables and letters or to building up words syllable by syllable. ... Teachers should be on their guard against the problems associated with monolithic approaches, even when they are using commercial materials which claim to be using a mixture of methods.

A Department of Education directive issued almost a quarter of a century later in February 1996 sums up the situation thus:

> There can be no single approach to the teaching of reading. Any method is acceptable, providing it meets the needs of the child. Only the teacher is equipped to make decisions about which approach is the most suitable in a given situation.

The current situation

While the Department of Education sets out guidelines for the minimum amount of time to be spent on formal reading instruction (nine hours out of 26), the teacher has some degree of freedom. It is also noteworthy that the Department of Education has never prescribed, or even recommended, specific basal readers or reading schemes (materials designed specifically for the teaching of reading), even though these materials are supplied to the children on loan. Nevertheless, two schemes out of a total of more than 50 commercially available have proved extremely popular in primary schools in the 1990s and account for about half of all sales:

- *Ratus* (Guion & Guion, 1987). In the early stages, this method has elements of both the 'global method' (using key words and short texts) and the 'analytical' approach (focusing on simple vowels and consonants in nonsense syllables and in words).
- *Au fil des mots* (As words go by) (Debayle, Touyarot, Giribone & Vitali, 1990). This method draws on the 'global method' (words, sentences and short texts) for approximately the first two months. For the next three weeks, the exclusive emphasis is on synthesis, followed by a mixture of synthesis and analysis. Like *Ratus*, vowels are introduced in words at an early stage, but there is no study of nonsense syllables.

The sales figures for commercial schemes give an indication of what is actually taking place in French classrooms. This information is supplemented by two recent questionnaire surveys (Fijalkow & Fijalkow, 1996, Robillard, 1995). The Fijalkow & Fijalkow study is based on responses to questions about teaching methods provided by over 1000 teachers. The findings suggest that the methods presently in use can be classified into two main groups. The first, more traditional approach stresses decoding skills; the second, more recent approach stresses meaning. Fijalkow & Fijalkow conclude that most teachers strongly rely on traditional time-tested practices and have a cautious attitude to new approaches which they feel have not been scientifically tested.

In a typical lesson, children are presented with a simple text and accompanying illustration, for instance 'Julien est chez Sophie. Il a apporté une voiture et une moto' (Julien is at Sophie's house. He has brought a car and a motorbike). The class then undertakes a series of analytical activities, focusing first on words within the sentence, next on syllables in words and finally on letter-sounds in syllables. For example, they might be presented with an illustration of a car labelled 'voiture' and showing [y], the phonetic form of the letter *u*, as well as the upper case, lower case and manuscript versions.

In the next stage, the emphasis is on synthesis: children blend letter-sounds together in order to read words or nonsense syllables. For instance, they might be required to blend the 'u' with the other letter-sounds in *une, voiture, Julien* and *tu*. Finally, they reread the whole sentence.

Reading is a whole class activity in which children are usually asked to read aloud in front of their peers. If necessary, they will be set work to do on their own while the teacher spends time with individual children.

SPECIAL EDUCATION

In 1990, the Chief Inspector of Schools, Louis Baladier, wrote: 'The integration of children suffering from a physical handicap or learning difficulties remains a national priority and must continue to be so.' Children with special needs are, wherever possible, educated in the mainstream. This is achieved partly through the RAS (Réseau d'Aides Spécialisées): initially, an educational psychologist and specialist teachers offer individual help to children experiencing difficulties in nursery and primary schools; if necessary, these specialist teachers continue work for a further year in transition classes of 15 or fewer pupils with the aim of returning children as quickly as possible to the mainstream. French state education makes no separate provision for dyslexics or for children with specific language difficulties. Educational psychologists can alert parents or confirm their concerns about their child's reading or language related problems. It is then the parents' responsibility to arrange for a doctor's referral to a speech therapist, though any course of treatment is subsidised by the Department of Social Security.

READING STANDARDS

Ever since the early nineteenth century, the general perception has been that French reading standards are quite low and certainly worse than they used to be. For example, in 1820 the president of the Commission for Public Instruction wrote, 'We must admit that we have sometimes received written communication from individuals with the baccalauréat whose writing style and spelling reveal a shameful ignorance'.

The facts actually show that widespread anxieties about standards have little substance (see also the reviews by Clay, Goodman and Raban, this volume, in relation to reading standards in English speaking countries). The results of reading tests for conscripts to the armed forces show that between 1880 and 1975 the number of illiterates decreased from over 13 per cent to less than one per cent (Dumazedier & De Gisors, 1984; but see also Rogers, this volume for discussions of the difficulties of defining literacy). The public perception of falling standards also emerges from a recent international comparison of reading (Elley, 1992). Interestingly, in France and just two other countries, more than 44 per cent of the students who took part claimed to be average or not very good, when their actual performance was above average.

The study in question was undertaken on behalf of the International Association for the Evaluation of Educational Achievement and was based on the reading of narrative prose, expository prose and documents in approximately 30 countries around the world. Two age groups took part in the study: 9 year olds and 14 year olds. The mean student scores in all domains for the younger group and older groups place France in fourth and second places respectively.

Elley (1992) also throws interesting light on the findings of Postlethwaite & Ross (1992) that children's reading performance is affected by a range of social variables. When scores were adjusted using a Composite Development Index (the aggregation of six indicators highlighting national differences in economics, health, and literacy) both groups of French children performed better than predicted, suggesting that social factors were less important than aspects of school organisation.

The particular focus for the Postlethwaite & Ross (1992) study mentioned above is the cross-national comparison of schools which are effective in the teaching of reading. In the French context, they show that teachers in the more effective schools have more years of teaching experience (nine years), devote more time to reading in class, and spend more time assessing lower order reading skills and hearing children read aloud than those in the less effective schools. There is a wider range of reading material in effective schools, and the principals in these schools indicated that they pay more attention to staff appraisal, even though, strictly speaking, this is not allowed in France. The study also indicates that there was room for improvement in France in the number of public libraries, circulation of newspapers and the economic status of teachers.

In spite of evidence to the contrary, the debate about falling standards continues unabated. Since 1989, in an attempt to provide more objective measurements of reading achievement, annual national assemments have taken place in French and Maths at the beginning of the third year of primary school and the first year of secondary school. Results suggest that at the end of primary school most children are able to decode, although less than half of them are able to answer questions requiring higher order reading skills (Thelot, 1992; Robillart, 1995).

FUTURE DIRECTIONS

The teaching of reading has always been a matter of interest in France. Nevertheless, for a considerable period, there was very little research on this area. The widespread assumption that children learned to read in the same way irrespective of the language which they spoke was probably responsible for the heavy reliance on the findings of the vast research literature in English. However, it has gradually become clear that language differences may well have an impact on the acquisition of literacy (for Italian, see Cossu, Shankweiler, Liberman & Gugliotta, 1995; for German, Wimmer & Hummer, 1990; for a comparison between French, English and Spanish, see Goswami, Gombert & Fraca de Barrera, 1997).

The fact that sound-symbol correspondences in French are more regular than in English (see Catach, 1980) may well have implications for literacy acquisition. As suggested by Share (1995) in an overview of studies on reading acquisition (predominantly) in English, phonological recoding might be a self-teaching mechanism, the *sine qua non* of reading acquisition (see also Tunmer, this volume). This phenomenon has also been observed with French-speaking children (see Leybaert & Content,

1995; Sprenger-Charolles & Casalis, 1995; Sprenger-Charolles, Siegel & Béchennec, 1997; Share, 1995). However, the lack of comparative studies makes it difficult to verify to what extent the regularities of sound-symbol correspondence influence literacy acquisition. There is therefore an urgent need for continuing work in the area of inter-language differences for literacy learning and teaching.

Institut National de Recherche Pédagogique, France
Université René Descartes, France

REFERENCES

Catach, N.: 1980, *L'Orthographe Française: Traité Théorique et Pratique*, Nathan, Paris.

Chartier, A.M. & Hébrard, J.: 1989, *Discours sur la Lecture (1880–1980)*, Editions du Centre Georges Pompidou, Paris.

Chartier, A.-M., & Hébrard, J.: 1990, 'Méthode syllabique et méthode globale: Quelques clarifications historiques', *Le Français Aujourd'hui* 90, 100–110.

Cossu, G., Shankweiler, D., Liberman, I.Y. & Gugliotta, M.: 1995, 'Visual and phonological determinants of misreadings in a transparent orthography', *Reading and Writing: An Interdisciplinary Journal* 7, 235–256.

Debayle, J., Touyarot, M., Giribone, C. & Vitali, D.: 1990, *Le Nouveau Fil des Mots (Lire au CP)*, Nathan, Paris.

Dumazedier, J. & De Gisors, H.: 1984, 'Français analphabètes ou illettrés?', *Revue Française de Pédagogie* 69, 13–20.

Elley, W.B.: 1992, *How in the World do Students Read?* International Association for the Evaluation of Educational Achievement, The Hague.

Goodman, K.S.: 1976, 'Reading: A psycholinguistic guessing game', in H. Singer & R.B. Ruddell (eds.), *Theorical Models and Process of Reading*, International Reading Association, Newark.

Goswami, U, Gombert, J.E. & Fraca de Barrera, L.: 1997, 'Children's orthographic representations and linguistic transparency: Nonsense word reading in English, French and Spanish', in C. Perfetti, M. Fayol & L. Rieben (eds.), *Learning to Spell*, Erlbaum, Hillsdale, NJ.

Guion, J. & Guion, J.: 1987, *Ratus et ses Amis (Méthode de Lecture, CP)*, Hatier, Paris.

Foucambert, J.: 1976, La Manière d'être Lecteur: Apprentissage et Enseignement de la lecture de la Maternelle au CM2, SERMAP, Paris.

Fijalkow, E. & Fijalkow, J.: 1996, 'Enseigner à Lire et à Ecrire au CP: Etat des Lieux', in C. Garcia-Debanc, M. Grandaty & A. Liva (eds.), *Didactique de la Lecture*, Regards Croisés, Presses Universitaires du Mirail, CRDP Midi-Pyrénées, 75–100.

Hebrard, J.: 1988, 'Apprendre à Lire à L'Ecole en France: Un Siècle de Recommandations Officielles', *Langue Française* 80, 111–128.

Leybaert, J. & Content, A.: 1995, 'Reading and spelling acquisition in different methods', *Reading and Writing: An Interdisciplinary Journal* 7, 65–88.

Lundberg, I. & Linnakyla, P.: 1992, *Teaching Reading Around the World*, International Association for the Evaluation of Educational Achievement, The Hague.

Postlethwaite, T.N. & Ross, K.: 1992, *Effective Schools in Reading: Implication for Educational Planners*, International Association for the Evaluation of Educational Achievement, The Hague.

Robillard, G.: 1995, *L'Apprentissage de la Lecture à l'Ecole Primaire*, Bilan et Perspectives, Inspection Générale de l'Education Nationale, Paris.

Share, D.L.: 1995, 'Phonological recoding and self-teaching: Sine qua non of reading acquisition', *Cognition* 55, 151–218.

Sprenger-Charolles, L. & Casalis, S.: 1995, 'Reading and spelling acquisition in French first graders: Longitudinal evidence', *Reading and Writing: An Interdisciplinary Journal* 7, 39–63.

Sprenger-Charolles, L., Siegel, L. & Béchennec, D.: 1997, 'Learning to read and spell in French: Longitudinal studies', in C. Perfetti, M. Fayol & L. Rieben (eds.), *Learning to spell*, Erlbaum, Hillsdale, NJ.

Thélot, C. (ed): 1992, 'Que sait-on des connaissances des élèves?' Special issue of *Les Dossiers Education et Formation* 17, 1–120.

Wimmer, H. & Hummer, P.: 1990, 'How German speaking first graders read and spell: Doubts on the importance of the logographic stage', *Applied Psycholinguistics* 11, 349–368.

LITERACY TEACHING IN INDIA

According to the 1991 census, the total population of India (including the projected population of Jammu and Kashmir, where the census could not be held) is 845.30 million. In order to calculate literacy rates, only those aged seven years and over were taken into account, yielding a total of 359.28 million literates, i.e. approximately 52 per cent of the total population in that age group. The literacy rate among females was 39.29 per cent, as against the male literacy rate of 64.13 per cent; again, the rural literacy rate was 44.69 per cent, as against the urban literacy rate of 73.08 per cent. The drop-out rate from class I to V in primary school was estimated at approximately 50 per cent. (For all the above details, see National Institute of Adult Education, 1993).

After nearly fifty years of independence, this is indeed a dismal picture. Approximately half the population aged seven years and above is illiterate on the government's own admission, and the condition is much worse in rural sectors and among women. Notice that this is the case when we accept government's minimalist definition of literacy as someone who can read, write and count with some understanding in any language. It is obvious that, if we were to define literacy as the ability to understand and produce written texts which in some sense would empower the individual and open up new areas of investigation, the literacy rate would drop dramatically, possibly to less than a quarter of the population aged seven and above.

What has brought us to this impasse? Judging from the rhetoric of the manifestos of different political parties, the country has not been lacking in declared political will. The support from voluntary agencies already engaged in similar or related work has always been forthcoming (see also Rogers, this volume). The government has often set aside substantial parts of its educational budget for literacy and primary education. The support from international agencies such as UNICEF, World Bank and IMF has also intensified considerably in recent years. A major breakthrough was expected with the launching of the National Literacy Mission (NLM) in 1988 and the establishment of the National Literacy Mission Authority as an autonomous wing of the government vested with full financial and executive powers. The objective of NLM was to bring functional literacy to all the adults in the 15 to 36 age group. These Total Literacy Campaigns (TLCs) were expected to be area specific, time bound, result oriented and

V. Edwards and D. Corson (eds), Encyclopedia of Language and Education,
Volume 2: Literacy, 199–206.
© *1997 Kluwer Academic Publishers. Printed in the Netherlands.*

undertaken with a spirit of sacrifice and volunteerism. More recently the District Primary Education Program (DPEP) has taken several states of India by storm. Yet we do not see any tangible results forthcoming. There is only a sense of desperate hurry.

EARLY DEVELOPMENTS

Some of the earliest notable attempts at literacy were associated with social reform movements of the Christian missionaries, though we know today that the motivation for these projects was not entirely innocent. For example, the Andhra Evangelical Church in Guintur, founded in 1848, organised several educational and literacy related activities, in addition to its primary task of spreading Christianity. Almost as a defensive reaction to the activities of the missionaries, Brahmo Samaj (1857), Prarthana Samaj (1867), Arya Samaj (1875), Indian Social Conference (1887), Rama Krishna Mission (1897) and several other organisations launched social reform movements in which literacy and education became an integral part. The library movement also gained momentum with the support of people like T. Madhav Rao in rural areas of Baroda, and gradually spread to Bombay and Madras.

Developments of this kind provided an authentic context for literacy. Learners were highly motivated and engaged in reformist activities. They wanted to learn to read and write with understanding and to be able to communicate their ideas to other people. Yet for all these movements, literacy was a peripheral issue and there was no long term agenda for literacy programmes. Moreover, most of these literacy efforts were spearheaded by an elite deeply rooted in the Indo-Aryan religious and cultural tradition predicated on an absolute faith in the Vedas (the most celebrated of the ancient Indian scriptures) and Upanishads (the metaphysical and philosophical commentaries on the Vedas); there were, of course, rare voices of dissent such as that of Jotiba Phule who exposed the economic exploitation and cultural domination of the low-caste shudras by the upper-caste brahmins and started schools for the untouchable children as early as 1870s in Maharashtra (see Omvedt, 1995: 18–24).

Meaningful literacy related activities also emerged clearly as a part of the struggle for independence. It soon became clear to the leaders of the national movement that non-co-operation with British rule could not succeed without a solid foundation of grassroots reconstruction. The period 1920–1940 is marked by intense literacy and political awareness related programmes which were implemented through summer schools for political education, literacy classes and literacy campaigns, library movements, extension lectures and a variety of other socially relevant activities. For example, the school started by Lala Lajpat Rai in 1920 in Lahore focused not only on reading and writing but also on political education and social awareness. Several state governments, including those of Panjab, Bengal, Bombay and Uttar Pradesh, took keen interest in literacy programmes and set aside budgets for adult education. A large number of non-government organisations sprang up in almost every major city of the country, and night schools, literacy classes mobile libraries and extension lectures were a common phenomenon. Christian missionaries invited the American educator P.C. Laubauch who participated actively in the national literacy effort and helped prepare primers in several Indian languages. The country witnessed a remarkable increase of seven per cent in the literacy rate during the decade 1930–41.

Two great leaders of the twentieth century, Tagore and Gandhi, noted the immense importance of literacy for the freedom struggle and national reconstruction. Both also noticed that literacy, as it is generally understood, could only be the beginning and not the end of education. For Tagore, all education had to be rooted in nature; for Gandhi it had to be rooted in a definite socio-economic order. Gandhi believed that students must pay for their education; they should learn a craft, e.g. spinning, weaving, sandal-making, and produce goods that the government would willingly buy. In a series of articles written between 1937 and 1938 in *The Harijan*, Gandhi elaborated his concept of Basic Education in considerable detail. In the Harijan of 9 October 1937, for instance, he says:

> I am a firm believer in the principle of free and compulsory primary education for India. I also hold that we shall realize this only by teaching the children a useful vocation for cultivating their mental, physical and spiritual faculties. Let no one consider these economic calculations in connection with education as sordid or out of place. There is nothing essentially sordid about economic calculations. True economics never militates against the highest ethical standard, just as true ethics to be worth its name must, at the same time, be also good economics (Bose, 1950, p. 292).

Tagore, for his part, was convinced that national unity and international harmony could not be achieved without universal education. As he points out in his 1924 'Talks in China',

> Our endeavour has been to include this ideal of unity in all the activities in our institution, some educational, some that comprise different kinds of artistic expression, some in the shape of service to our neighbours by way of helping the reconstruction of village life (cited in Das, 1996: 612–613).

For Tagore, all education must be located in a harmonious interaction between the learner, community and nature. It was common for renowned artists to visit Tagore's educational institutions and mix freely with learners sharing their ideas and work. Tagore himself would translate a play from English into Bengali, share the process and product of translation with school inmates who would then perform the play. Tagore's vision of adult education included not only rural reconstruction in terms of cottage industries, co-operative banking, rural health and hygiene, but also poetry, painting and music. As Mohsini (1993) points out, Tagore's Institute of Rural Reconstruction at Sriniketan

> started a number of night schools in the villages around Srinike-
> tan with the help of student volunteers or the village teacher
> engaged on a meagre honorarium. The schools were opened in
> the houses provided by the villagers. In 1923, the institute had
> seven night schools and their number rose to 12 in 1932. The in-
> stitute also had a Rural Circulating Library with only 200 books
> for providing support to literacy work. In these night schools
> were also organised lectures with the help of magic lantern shows
> on agriculture. ... The night schools, accordingly, also organ-
> ised some sessions of story-telling and Ravindra Sangeet [an
> Indian musical tradition]. Fortnightly, a news bulletin was also
> published and distributed to the neoliterates

The 1940s and 1950s was a period of consolidation and institutionalisation of literacy efforts in India; it was also a period during which the limitations of enthusiastic small scale campaigns became increasingly evident. The University of Jamia Millia Islamia was deeply inspired by Gandhi's idea and under the able guidance of its Vice-Chancellor Dr. Zakir Hussain (later President of India), had already established the Jamia Institute of Adult Education in the 1920s. It was, however, in 1939 that it launched a literacy campaign in Delhi based on Laubach's idea of 'Each one, Teach one'. Similar programmes were started in Bombay and Mysore.

Again, it was in 1939 that the Indian Adult Education Association was created and in its 1942 meeting it recommended the formation of an Adult Education Department. This association also launched several literacy programmes and did some pioneering work in the areas of material production, teacher training and field level surveys. Not only were these programmes short-lived, but they failed to even remotely approximate to the success achieved during the struggle for freedom.

Since the kind of zeal that originates from a Tagore or a Gandhi or a desire to free oneself from slavery was missing, the time and money invested in materials and eliciting pledges produced limited results. Illiterates saw no point in learning to read and write and were certainly not willing to go to literate adults in their working hours; the literate adults, on the other hand, wanted to fulfil their pledge to 'teach one' only when they were free. As metanarratives such as the struggle for national independence became scarce, the literacy agenda took on a minimalist aspect. The teaching materials were no longer informed by issues of national importance and consisted largely of meaningless, boring and unnatural texts which aimed at teaching alphabets and a small set of words in a linear and additive fashion. Such an enterprise could hardly prove to be a fertile ground for innovative teaching materials. This was functionalism at its worst: a limited amount of curriculum and materials to be transacted in a few weeks to produce quantifiable results. You were generally declared literate if you could write your name and address, read a few sentences and count upto 10.

AFTER INDEPENDENCE

This approach to literacy continued to flourish during what may be described as the Nehru era. For Nehru, the key to progress was industrialisation and other development activities, a vision of India which was significantly different from that of Tagore or Gandhi. His pace was also much quicker. Adult Education gave way to social education; literacy became the most neglected aspect of the rural Community Development Programmes that dominated this period. The most unfortunate part of this project was that the little money and few resources earmarked for education were appropriated by the relatively rich segments of rural population. The literacy levels among the deprived and underprivileged did not witness any significant improvement. Bordia and Kaul (1992), among others, have shown how, in spite of adult education centres working for over 25 years in certain areas, the literacy rate has not improved significantly as compared to other villages without an adult education centre, and most of the neoliterates easily relapse into illiteracy. As in other periods, the most outstanding and rewarding feature of this era was the multiplication of a large number of small scale literacy and development projects (see Mohsini, 1993: 50–53) including those started in Madras (1946), Etawah (1948), Nilokheri (1949), Kanpur (1945) and Resulia (1951). For example, Dey's Nilokheri experiment showed how over 7000 displaced refugees from Pakistan could be rehabilitated and made self-sufficient. A variety of educational and cultural activities became an integral part of this project.

A variety of literacy programmes has been launched in recent times e.g. the Farmers Functional Literacy Project (1967), the National Adult Education Programme (NAEP, 1978) and the National Literacy Mission (NLM, 1988). The constitution of India (Article 45) stipulated in 1950 that, within a period of ten years, free and compulsory education for all would be provided until the age of 14. The country should have been fully literate by 1960. Although that target has not been achieved and does not seem achievable, the government announces almost every decade a new national literacy programme often accompanied only by cosmetic changes. Both NAEP and NLM had promising starts, particularly in terms of environment building, community participation and some innovations in the development of learning materials and teaching methods. None the less, these programmes failed to have any lasting impact because of inherent structural drawbacks, rigid implementation strategies, inflexible and boring curricula, minimisation and instrumentalization of literacy goals, desire to declare villages and districts literate in a short period, inadequate financial resources and, most of all, absence of a driving force and a vision.

The intervention of national and international agencies, even in collaboration with the local non-government organisations (NGOs), to juxtapose vocational training, rural development and literacy has not produced any significant results, no doubt because these efforts have often been motivated only by pseudo-Freirean adult education programmes (Kidd & Kumar, 1981; Ramabrahman, 1988, 1989; see also Rogers, this volume). Long-term programmes of literacy cannot be created without a vision of social change; further, these programmes must elicit the active participation of all sections of society. In order to decide the nature of curriculum for a set of learners, we cannot take shelter in the received principles of curriculum development. We need to engage in an active social dialogue in which teachers, learners and their community, and not just academics and pedagogues, are fully respected participants (Kumar, 1987).

In the late sixties and early seventies, the slogan was: we should teach them what they need. It was stressed that we should first identify the needs of illiterates and then plan our literacy programmes accordingly. This argument on the surface looked so compelling that the whole country was carried away by functionalist slogans. Literacy must be instrumental, i.e. learners should be able to read bus numbers, fill in different kinds of forms at the railway station or post office, understand measures and counting money, so that they are not cheated and so on. This perspective only further narrowed what counts as literacy and gave a false sense of achievement to both the learners and the evaluators. Functionalism in literacy has had far more disastrous consequences than in any other domain. It legitimised what was effectively a narrow delimitation of the essential agenda of education.

CAMPAIGN-BASED LITERACY PROGRAMMES

It should be clear from the above short history that literacy has had its moments of glory only when it was undertaken as a part of a larger social cause, be it the freedom struggle or the vision of a Gandhi or a Tagore. Very little can be achieved in hierarchically organised centre-based programmes.

There is a sense in which campaign-based literacy programmes may be regarded as a compromise between centre-based programmes and more local initiatives. The three most important ingredients of a campaign-based approach are: mass participation, voluntary workers and environment building through a variety of community based socio-cultural activities. This model has emerged clearly in Kerala (Athreya, 1991), in particular in the Ernakulam total literacy project, where the Kerala Sastra Sahitya

Parishat (KSSP), a well-known voluntary organization, has been engaged for years in bringing about social change among the rural people. It was also tried out with considerable success in Pudukkottai, Tamil Nadu (Athreya & Chunkath, 1996) and in Ambedkar Nagar (Agnihotri, 1994).

The campaign-based Kerala model should be seen in context. As Agnihotri (1994) argues, it is built on the solid base of a tradition of voluntary social work, the ability to generate and mobilize local resources and effective networking with governmental and voluntary agencies. It should be seen in the context of Kerala which has the highest literacy rate and lowest infant mortality rate in India and a long tradition of socially sensitive political work. It is also important to keep in mind Kerala's strategic geographical location on the ocean facing the Middle East, its largely matrilineal structure which assures economic security for women, the role of Christian missionaries, timely rainfalls, the influence of leftist governments and, most of all, the role of KSSP.

It is thus a convergence of social, political, historical, geographical and cultural factors that made the campaign-based approach succeed in Ernakulam. The dangers of attempting to transplant a model of this without appreciating context are becoming increasingly apparent. Social volunteerism is not created overnight through organising street plays or painting competitions, and is difficult to sustain without a minimal level of economic security, particularly when the context is not one of political revolt. One is therefore not surprised that Athreya and Chunkath (1996: 274) treat the success story of Pudukkottai with guarded enthusiasm:

> Even in a non-revolutionary social milieu, it is possible to initiate and carry out with some degree of success a mass literacy campaign because there is a tremendous reserve of innate goodness and volunteer spirit among the people, which can be catalysed, despite an overwhelming ambience of cynicism, if a critical minimum core of committed activists and governmental support are present. Sustaining the process, however, is a far more difficult challenge.

It is now clear that most of the campaign-based literacy programmes hardly if ever transcend their initial enthusiasm (see, for instance, Saxena, 1992).

FUTURE DIRECTIONS

Campaigns are by definition transient and can hardly provide solutions for a country of 900 million people, approximately half of whom have yet to be introduced to the possibilities of written language as a tool in their struggle against corruption and oppression. The situation deteriorates as international funding accelerates the speed of these campaigns and co-opts whatever little talent was engaging itself with critical literacy. This history of literacy efforts in India clearly shows that centre-based approaches prove counter-productive; it also shows that success stories are closely associated with visions of social struggle and change. Let us not dismiss idealism as is the fashion. Literacy in a country like India is an invitation to struggle for those who can still muster the courage to dream.

University of Delhi, India

REFERENCES

Agnihotri, R.K.: 1994, 'Campaign-based literacy programmes: The case of the Ambedkar Nagar experiment in Delhi', *Language and Education* 8(1-2), 47–56.

Athreya, V.B.: 1991, 'The Kerala model: How to extend the literacy drive', *Frontline* V (May 25–June 7), 97–98.

Athreya, V.B. & Chunkath, S.R.: 1996, *Literacy and Empowerment*, Sage Publications, New Delhi.

Bordia, A. and Kaul, A.: 1992, 'Literacy efforts in India', *Annals* (Aapss), 520, 151–162.

Das, S.K. (ed.): 1996, *The English Writings of Rabindra Nath Tagore*, Vol II, Sahitya Akademi, New Delhi.

Kidd, R. and Kumar, K.: 1981, 'Co-opting Freire: A critical analysis of pseudo-Freirean adult education', *Economic and Political Weekly* 15(1): 27–36.

Kumar, K.: 1987, 'Curriculum, psychology and society', *Economic and Polical Weekly* 22(12), 507–512.

Mohsini, S.R.: 1993, *History of Adult Education in India*, Anmol Publication, New Delhi.

National Institute of Adult Education: 1993, *Statistical Database for Literacy*, New Dehli, National Institute of Adult Education.

Omvedt, G.: 1995, *Dalit Visions*, Tracts for the Times Series. No. 8, Orient Longman, New Delhi.

Ramabrahman, I.: 1989, 'Literacy missions: Receding horizons', *Economic and Political Weekly* 24(17), 2301–2303.

Ramabrahman, I.: 1988, *Adult Education: Policy and Performance*, Gian Publishing House, Delhi.

Saxena, S.: 1992, 'Myth of Total Literacy in Narsingpur', *Economic and Political Weekly* 27(45), 2408–2410.

PIETER REITSMA

LITERACY TEACHING IN THE LOW COUNTRIES

The Low Countries roughly constitute the northern part of the Kingdom of Belgium and all of the Kingdom of the Netherlands. Although other languages, such as Frisian, are also spoken, the main language is Dutch or Nederlands. This review offers some historical perspectives on the development of spoken and written Dutch; discusses the social context of literacy in the Low Countries; and presents information on the teaching of reading at the various stages. Finally possible directions for future research are considered.

THE HISTORICAL DEVELOPMENT OF DUTCH

The Holland dialect spoken in the areas around the cities of Amsterdam, The Hague, Rotterdam and Utrecht, forms the basis of the standard language of today. Other dialects are still very much alive in both home and community, but the dialect of the provinces of Holland and Utrecht is used in official and more formal communication and is also the basis of standard written Dutch.

Dutch is written with the roman alphabet adapted to accommodate phonemes which did not occur in Latin. In earlier times, variation which reflected dialect differences was common. Gradually, however, there was a move towards a greater uniformity in both spelling and grammar. Important factors in the standardization process were the invention of printing in the fifteenth century, the political unification of the 'Low Countries', and the influence of formal education. A major landmark in this process, which continued rather longer in the case of Dutch than certain other European languages, was the publication of the Siegenbeek's first official rules for spelling in 1804. Since this time, there have been several other spelling reforms the most recent of which was accepted in 1995 by both the Dutch and Belgian Governments.

Sound-symbol correspondence in Dutch is very regular, although there is no perfect one-to-one relationship (Booij, 1995). Departures from regular phonemic mapping on to the orthography are motivated by morphological or etymological considerations. The rule of congruence or uniformity prescribes that the root form must be spelled in the same way as in derivatives; for example, whereas the final *d* in *goed* is pronounced as /t/ the letter *d* is used, reflecting its relationship with derivatives such as *goede*

V. Edwards and D. Corson (eds), Encyclopedia of Language and Education,
Volume 2: Literacy, 207–213.
© *1997 Kluwer Academic Publishers. Printed in the Netherlands.*

and *goedig*). The rule of analogy also stresses morphological or syntactic relationships between words. For example, the verb forms *ik vind* and *hij vindt* (I or he finds) are pronounced the same, but the different spellings reflect different syntactic functions (Assink, 1985). A third principle is that of etymology. For example, the letters q, x, c, y, reflect the Latin origin of words; the digraph *th*, pronounced as /t/ as in *thee* (tea), is retained in some loan words. Generally, however, the pronunciation of most native Dutch words can be derived by applying the basic rules of grapheme-to-phoneme correspondences (Reitsma & Verhoeven, 1990).

SOCIAL AND CULTURAL ASPECTS OF LITERACY

As John Edwards (this volume) points out, discussions of literacy need to take into account not only factors relevant to the acquisition of skills and strategies, but also the ways in which this knowledge is applied. Various studies in the Low Countries address these issues. Piek (1995; 1996), for instance, points to differences in reading habits between and within different age groups. She reports that about a quarter of the population above the age of 12 never read books, papers or magazines, whereas approximately half had read at least one book during the month prior to questioning. In contrast, 8 per cent of children between the ages of 7 and 12 report that they never read a book in their leisure time, while about 60 per cent of children in this age range read one book or more every week.

Data is also available on reading habits at home which indicate gender differences. Research using diaries and questionnaires with children between 6 and 16 years of age reveals that children read at home for 25 minutes a day on average; equal amounts of time are spent on reading books and reading magazines, etc. (Piek, 1995). However, girls spend more time reading than boys – about 30 minutes a day, compared with 20 minutes. No significant relationships have been found between the amount of time devoted to literacy activities and social background, except that there is a tendency for ethnic minority children to read less at home (Verhoeven, 1994).

Another variable which has been considered is the influence of television on reading habits. Koolstra (1993) establishes a relationship between the frequency of reading and television viewing: children who watch television more often tend to read less frequently.

Our understanding of reading habits can be illuminated by statistics on the use of public libraries (Piek, 1995). In 1992, approximately 30 per cent of the total Dutch population were members of a public library, borrowing 171 million books in that year. However, a much higher proportion of children regularly visits libraries: 90 per cent of the eight to 11 years olds and 72 per cent of the four to seven year olds. Interestingly, use of libraries is positively related to ownership of books: those children who have more books at home also visit the library more often.

Information on book sales also throws light on reading patterns (Piek, 1995). In a population of almost 15 million, annual children's book sales number 4.6 million (in 1995). It was recently estimated that, on average, two books per year are bought for each child below the age of 12. The actual distribution of these books is, of course, variable: in the region of 14 per cent of children own more than 50 books, while fewer than 5 per cent have no books at all. Again, it would appear that ethnic minority parents (mainly of Turkish or Moroccan origin: see the review by Kroon in Volume 5) buy fewer books than indigenous Dutch parents (Peeters & Woldringh, 1993).

THE TEACHING OF READING

The discussion of the teaching of reading can be conveniently divided into three main issues: pre-school activities; literacy teaching in the early years; and reading for meaning.

Pre-school literacy activities

The teaching of literacy does not take place in isolation but builds on children's previous experiences and interests as well as their knowledge of language and books (see Thompson, this volume). Literacy socialization in the family is therefore considered to influence both the development of literacy skills and attitudes towards the written word (see Auerbach, this volume).

As in many other countries, there is a growing interest in the Low Countries in emergent literacy. Van Lierop (1992), for instance, drawing on interviews with 537 children, shows that most parents read to their children, often every day. Nearly half of the parents start reading stories when their children are as young as one year old, although many stop sharing books as soon as children can read on their own. The quality of the relationship between parent and child seems to be an important factor influencing the interaction and dialogue during story reading (Bus & Van IJzendoorn, 1988).

Literacy events are also an important feature of day-care centres and nursery schools where professional carers and teachers report that they read stories frequently. In fact, this is a daily practice in nearly 88 per cent of such settings. However, it is not common practice for adults to spend time talking to children about what they have been reading.

Literacy teaching in the early years

Dutch children normally start school at the age of four. During the first two years, children may be introduced to a variety of pre-reading activities, such as word games which help to develop phonemic awareness, and print conventions such as left-right, though there is no clear picture of how widespread these activities may be. As part of the national PRIMA-cohort study, researchers investigated the pre-reading skills of kindergarteners in some 270 schools. An important finding of this study was that there were significant differences between ethnic groups (Driessen, 1996).

Formal literacy teaching starts after the summer holidays in the third year (mean age 6: 5). A number of commercial schemes are currently used in the teaching of reading in the first grade. Perhaps because of the regularity of sound-symbol relationships in Dutch, approaches to initial reading instruction place a heavy emphasis on phonics. Children are expected to learn the basic structure of written language and appreciate the close correspondence between graphemes and phonemes. Instructional strategies (set out in the teacher's manual) and exercises for children in workbooks and worksheets focus simultaneously on the 'structural' elements of both speech and writing, which are considered to be inter-related language skills. Children are required to relate letters to sounds in decoding the written words and sounds to letters when encoding spoken language. Both processes are therefore taught together.

The most popular schemes emphasise both phonic skills and reading and writing for meaning. Schemes also include suggestions for monitoring and recording children's development and diagnostic tests which make it possible to keep track of individual pupils' progress and alert the teacher to specific problems or delays. In addition, there are materials and suggestions for remedying given problems and differentiating instruction within first grade groups.

In Grade 1, an average 265 minutes a week is devoted to the teaching of reading (van der Pluijm & van Dongen, 1992). The emphasis on decoding lasts for 4 or 5 months. By the second half of the first year of formal teaching, most (but not necessarily all) children are able to decode simple, regular Dutch words. At the end of this year, the goal is for children to be able to correctly read aloud approximately 20 sentences (comprising about a hundred one and two-syllable words) within two minutes. Of course, not all children achieve this goal.

There would also seem to be a relationship between the choice of teaching materials and reading performance (Hol, de Haan & Kok, 1995). Schools using the most popular method (*Veilig leren lezen* – Learning to read safely), which is currently found in more than 60 per cent of schools, produces the lowest proportion of children that do not attain this goal.

Reading for meaning

Whereas reading instruction in the first year focuses on decoding skills, it is important to encourage children to make meaning of the text (see reviews by Thompson and Raban, this volume). Teaching activities specifically oriented toward the development of reading comprehension and higher order reading skills receive more attention as children make their way through school. Weterings & Aarnoutse (1986), for instance, report a study of reading comprehension lessons in 12 fourth grade classes in elementary schools. The most frequent activity taking up a quarter of the time was found to be the assessment of children's reading responses, usually by asking questions about the text. Other common activities included discussing background information, listening to the students reading aloud and assistance with exercises and assignments. Direct instruction in reading comprehension took place only four per cent of the time and focused in the main on the explanation of word meanings. Similar findings have been reported (Reitsma & Sliepen, 1992) for children in special education.

Direct instruction of reading comprehension has received increasing attention in recent years. Several small scale studies indicate that explicit teaching of metalinguistic awareness and comprehension strategies tends to increase pupils' understanding of what they read (see, for instance, Walraven & Reitsma, 1993; Reitsma, 1994, 1995). Various commercial approaches which build on these findings have been published in recent years. These stress the notion that reading involves making meaning of the text: the reader is seen as engaging in an internal dialogue with the writer. Activities are designed to help children draw on relevant background knowledge. Children are explicitly taught strategies, for example, for drawing inferences or finding the main idea in a text, which are modelled by the teacher. Exercises provide practice in the skills which form the focus for the lesson. Finally, children are given the opportunity to apply the new skills in other settings.

The PRIMA-cohort study revealed that less than half of teachers in Grades 5 and 7 use more recent methods for teaching reading comprehension (Overmaat, 1996). However, teachers who do use the newer approaches were found to be more satisfied with their methods and materials than those who use more traditional approaches. It is also noteworthy that, although commercial approaches advocate the organization of teaching groups according to ability, in practice whole class teaching is the norm.

FUTURE DEVELOPMENTS

Current Dutch research on literacy leaves no doubt that literacy development is a lifelong undertaking. Against this background, an obvious direction for future research is remediation and early interventions in literacy problems (eg the 'Reading Recovery' approach – see Clay's review, this volume – adapted to the sociocultural and educational context of The Netherlands) in an attempt to counter possible 'Matthew effects' (Stanovich, 1986) whereby initial problems in decoding can lead to later comprehension or motivational problems. Research activity in this direction will, of course, be in line with international interest in the remediation of reading problems and developmental dyslexia (see reviews by Clay and Béchennec & Sprenger-Charolles, this volume).

There is clearly scope for considerably more research in the area of reading comprehension. A number of studies currently in progress, including one directed by Dr. C. Aarnoutse of the University of Nijmegen, address the long term effects of direct teaching of comprehension strategies, and optimal ways of grouping of students.

Finally, increasing attention is being focussed on the use of multimedia technology in literacy education (see also Abbott, this volume). Technological developments are already producing new initiatives in the teaching of reading and writing, as well as opening up exciting new possibilities for sharing information and for communication.

Vrije Universiteit Amsterdam, the Netherlands

REFERENCES

Assink, E.M.H.: 1985, 'Assessing spelling strategies for the orthography of Dutch verbs', *British Journal of Psychology* 76, 353–363.
Booij, G.E.: 1995, *The phonology of Dutch*, Oxford University Press, Oxford.
Bus, A.G., & IJzendoorn, M.H. van: 1988, 'Mother-child interactions, attachments, and emergent literacy: A cross-sectional study', *Child Development* 59, 1262–1272.
De Geus, W.C. & Reitsma, P.: 1994, 'Cognitive components that explain item difficulty of functional reading tasks', in C.K. Kinzer & D.J. Leu (eds.), *Multidimensional Aspects of Literacy Research, Theory and Practice*, NRC, Chicago, pp. 101–111.
Donaldson, B.C.: 1983, *Dutch: A Linguistic History of Holland and Belgium*, Martinus Nijhoff, Leiden.
Driessen, G.: 1996, *Allochtone ouders te optimistisch over onderwijskansen eigen kind'* (Ethnic minority parents are too optimistic about their children's educational perspectives). PRIMA-cohortonderzoek 1994/1995. Didaktief, Den Haag.
Hol, G.G.J.M., de Haan, M., & Kok, W.A.M.: 1995, *De effectiviteit van methoden voor aanvankelijk leesonderwijs* (The efficiency of methods for initial reading instruction), ISOR, Utrecht.
Koolstra, C.M.: 1993, *Television and Children's Reading: A Three Year Panel Study*, Doctoral dissertation, University of Leiden.
Lierop, W.L.H., van: 1992, *Ik heb het wel in jouw stem gehoord* (I heard it in your voice), Eburon, Delft.
Overmaat, M.: 1996, *Oefening en instructie in vaardigheden is nog weinig systematisch* (Practice and instruction in skills is far from systematic.) PRIMA-cohortonderzoek 1994/1995, Didaktief, Den Haag.

Peeters, J. & Woldringh, C.: 1993. *Leefsituatie van kinderen tot 12 jaar in Nederland* (Social context of children under 12 in The Netherlands). ITS, Nijmegen.

Piek, K.: 1995, *Lezen – Zoveel lezen we (niet)* (Reading – what we do and don't read), Stichting Lezen, Amsterdam.

Piek, K.: 1996, 'Onderzoek naar leesvaardigheid in Nederland en Vlaanderen, een overzicht' (Research on reading ability in The Netherlands and Flanders, a review), *Leesgoed* 23(2), 59–64.

Pluijm, J. van der, & Dongen, D. van: 1992, *Verbreding van het vormingsaanbod in het basisonderwijs* (Broadening educational provision in elementary education), Katholieke Universiteit Tilburg, Tilburg.

Reitsma, P. & Verhoeven, L.: 1990, 'Acquisiton of written Dutch: an introduction', in P. Reitsma & L. Verhoeven (eds.), *Acquisition of reading in Dutch*, Foris Publications, Dordrecht, pp. 1–13.

Reitsma, P. & Sliepen, S.E.: 1992 'Developments in strategic reading instruction: effects of a training of teachers', in T. Plomp, J.M. Pieters & A. Feteris (Eds.), *European Conference on Educational Research* 2, University of Twente, Enschede, pp. 875–878.

Reitsma, P.: 1994, 'Instructional approaches to problems in reading comprehension of dyslexics', in K.P. van den Bos, L.S. Siegel, D.J. Bakker, & D.L. Share (eds.), *Current Directions in Dyslexia Research* Swets & Zeitlinger, Lisse, pp 269–286.

Reitsma, P.: 1995, 'Forderung des Textverstehens bei Kindern mit Leseschwierigkeiten', in H. Brugelmann, H. Balhorn & I. Fussenich (eds.), *Am Rande der Schrift – Zwischen Sprachenvielfalt und Analphabetismus*, Libelle Verlag, Lengwil am Bodensee, pp. 160–172.

Stanovich, K.: 1986. 'Matthew effects in reading: Some consequences of individual differences in the acquisition of literacy', *Reading Research Quarterly* 21, 360–406.

Verhoeven, L.: 1994, 'Linguistic diversity and literacy development', in L. Verhoeven (ed.), *Functional literacy: Theoretical Issues and Educational Implications*, Amsterdam/Philadelphia: John Benjamins, pp. 199–220.

Walraven, A.M.A., & Reitsma, P.: 1993, 'The effect of teaching strategies for reading comprehension to poor readers and the surplus effect of activating prior knowledge', in D.J. Leu & C.K. Kinzer (eds.), *Examining Central Issues in Literacy Research, Theory, and Practice*, NRC, Chicago, pp. 243–250.

FEMALE LITERACY AND LIFE CHANCES IN RURAL NIGERIA

Much has been written about the material, social and psychological benefits accruing to beneficiaries of literacy. Yet illiteracy remains a major and socially sustained problem in Sub-Saharan Africa. In Nigeria, for instance, the estimated illiteracy rate in 1990 was barely 50 per cent. Of this figure, almost two thirds were women (UNESCO, 1993). Part of the problem may be that, despite the battery of claims and the extensive coverage of the problem in the academic literature, there is a paucity of research on the links between women, literacy and individual well-being on the micro level, both in Sub-Saharan Africa and in many other parts of the developing world.

This review provides an overview of a recent study of the socio-psychological and economic impact of literacy on two groups of women in rural Nigeria. The findings underscore the unfortunate consequences of persistently excluding women from access to literacy. The study also offers valuable insights into the problems of literacy research in Sub-Saharan Africa.

EARLY DEVELOPMENTS

Western-style literacy came to Nigeria as a result of Christianity and colonial domination. To facilitate the teaching of the bible, early missionaries needed to teach their converts to read and write. Later, as colonial rule began to expand, so, too, did the literacy teaching required to provide indigenous clerical support staff. Regrettably, the western culture that accompanied colonialism also carried rigid gender ideologies which aided and supported exclusionary practices against women (Amadiume, 1987; Mba, 1982). This was in accordance with the prevailing Victorian belief that women's roles in society were best confined to the private sphere (Callaway, 1987). In consequence, the early beneficiaries of literacy teaching were male Nigerians. As the nation's economy began to shift from its agrarian base to a 'modernizing' one, women found themselves still further devalued. Western capitalist economic ideology became the national goal, with its attendant emphasis on the individual and accumulation of material wealth (values that were incompatible with traditional African culture).

V. Edwards and D. Corson (eds), Encyclopedia of Language and Education, Volume 2: Literacy, 215–223.
© *1997 Kluwer Academic Publishers. Printed in the Netherlands.*

Women who were still predominantly illiterate were edged out from the entire process of development and nation building.

This exclusionary practice has persisted even though there is no shortage of evidence concerning the practical benefits of literacy for women in Sub-Saharan Africa and other developing countries (see Rogers, this volume). These include: improved health-related practices, such as increased use of contraception and subsequently reduced fertility rates; participation in the formal wage sector; improved agricultural productivity; improved maternal behaviour resulting in reduced infant and child mortality rates and overall well-being (Blumberg, 1995; Stromquist, 1990; United Nations, 1991; Cochrane, 1982; LeVine 1982; Caldwell, 1979; Comings et al., 1994; Okojie, 1983). All of these benefits, of course, culminate in sustainable development (Browne and Barrett, 1991; United Nations, 1991). Unfortunately, contemporary literacy trends in Sub-Saharan Africa continue to show significant gender disparities.

PRESENT TRENDS

Nigeria's National Policy on Education (henceforth NPE), the blueprint for current educational practices which was adopted in 1977 and revised some four years later (Federal Government of Nigeria, 1981) advocates equal educational opportunities for all citizens. Implicit in its supposedly gender neutral approach is the assumption of a national policy of equity and social justice. However, while the NPE pays only cursory attention to the education of women, a number of activities indicate some progress in this direction. Since 1986, for instance, Women's Education units have been created, the Nigeria Association of Women in Science, Technology and Mathematics (NAWSTEMS) has been launched, and 'Blueprint on Womens Education in Nigeria', which is currently the closest thing to a national philosophy of women's education, has been adopted. Other government interventions include the creation of women's education centres to teach basic and functional literacy and the reduction of entry requirements for secondary schools (Osinulu et al., 1994; see also Rogers and Verhoeven, this volume).

Despite these efforts and despite the fact that Nigeria has significantly expanded overall educational provision since independence, women still lag behind. Available statistics show, for instance, that, at the time of independence in 1960, girls comprised 37 per cent of primary school enrollments, while the figures for 1993 and 1994 are 43.7 per cent and 44.1 per cent respectively. Similarly, female adult literacy enrollments over a five year period (1986–1990) averaged 37.5 per cent (Federal Government of Nigeria 1995; 1990).

Profound cultural, religio-social and attitudinal factors, particularly in traditionally more conservative rural settings, undoubtedly reduce the status of women. Although these attitudes originate predominantly within the private domestic sphere (Etta, 1994), they are tacitly institutionalized by government through inaction. Ultimately, such attitudes reduce parental motivation to educate the girl child.

More recently, the international economic system, in alliance with the Nigerian state, has exacerbated the problem through such stringent fiscal policies as Structural Adjustment Programmes (SAPs), forcing parents to make difficult choices vis à vis the education of their children and reversing the post-independence educational gains made in the 1970s and early 1980s. Further, because these choices are often detrimental to girls, there is a strong possibility illiteracy among women in the nation will increase. Paradoxically, denying girls and women access to education significantly retards overall social progress.

THE CASE STUDY

The study reported below explores the living conditions and life chances of literate and non-literate women in rural Nigeria, and is based on their own accounts (Egbo, 1996). It attempts to identify the factors which help or hinder progress towards literacy in two groups of women within the same rural setting. It also explores the links between access to literacy and the empowerment of women, particularly within a rural context.

Data for the study were collected over a period of three months through in-depth one-to-one interviews, focus group interviews and participant observation. The informing philosophy was critical realism, a philosophical perspective recently advanced by Roy Bhaskar, a British philosopher (see Bhaskar, 1986, 1989; Corson, 1993, 1997). Critical realism assigns considerable importance to the personal accounts of participants in the research process, thereby giving a voice to the voiceless, a major goal of the present study.

Nigeria is a relatively large country. In 1988 the estimated population was 112 million people, more than two thirds of whom lived in rural areas. Two rural communities in South-Western Nigeria were chosen for the study: Onitcha-Ugbo and Ebu in the Aniocha local government area of Delta state. Both communities are located a few kilometres from Asaba which is the capital of the state, about 700 kilometres from Lagos, the commercial centre of the country. Both towns have an estimated population of approximately 8,000 speakers of a language belonging to the West-Niger Igbo group.

The study focused on thirty-six respondents, aged between the ages of 23 and 52: 18 literates and 18 non-literates all of whom have lived in rural communities for most of their adult lives. All the participants share a similar socio-cultural background.

The analysis of individual and focus group interviews, as well as field and observations notes, revealed some significant findings in the areas of income generation, health, children's education and welfare, self-perception and participation in adult literacy programmes.

Income Generating Activities

Virtually all the literate respondents reported significantly higher monthly income than the non-literate participants. All but one were engaged in the formal wage sector. In addition to other income generating activities, the average monthly income for this group was 2500 Naira, a sum which is considerably higher than the average of 700 Naira reported by the non-literate group. Some of the literate participants also reported having access to credit facilities because their monthly salaries were often accepted as collateral and ability to repay.

The non-literate group were predominantly engaged in labour-intensive subsistence farming and reported the sale of surplus farm produce as their major source of income. Only three of the non-literate participants were employed in the formal wage sector as non-skilled menial labourers.

Health Related Practices

The study focused on three particular areas of health related practices: female circumcision, the use of contraception and the immunization of children.

Female circumcision is still quite prevalent in certain parts of Nigeria, including the study area. 78 per cent of the non-literate group reported circumcising their daughters, in comparison with only 39 per cent of the literate group. In addition, most of the literate group who circumcised their daughters said they would not in future. For both groups, the main reason for circumcising their daughters was adherence to cultural traditions. The reasons cited for not circumcising female children included religious grounds, the influence of government eradication campaigns, the print media (literate group only) and family tradition.

67 per cent of the literate group reported either using or having used birth control methods, in comparison with only 11 per cent of the non-literate participants. All the women, however, appeared to have adequate knowledge, and were aware that contraceptives were quite readily available at nearby family planning centres. When asked why they did not use such methods, many of the non-literate participants (89 per cent), cited fear of possible adverse after effects.

Again there is a clear difference between the use of birth control methods in the two groups. Although there is a need for further in-depth study, the findings of this study would seem to support those of other researchers who suggest a positive relationship between education and the use of contraception (see Smock, 1981, Cochrane, 1982; LeVine, 1982).

A related and perhaps the most significant finding of the study was that the average number of children was 6.3 for non-literate participants and 4.7 for the literate group, suggesting an inverse relationship between education and the desire to have many children.

The final health-related focus for the study was immunization. All the participants with the exception of four non-literates, reported having immunized their children. Most cited government campaigns and advice from nurses at post-natal clinics as the reasons for doing so. Reasons for not immunizing children included religious grounds and fear of potential health risks.

Children's Education and Welfare

There was no correlation between the desire to educate children and literacy. All respondents reported valuing education highly. Indeed, all rated education as the single most important factor in their children's socio-economic advancement and upward mobility. However, participant observation and reports from one-to-one interviews revealed that children were engaged in different kinds of after-school activities. While the children of the literate participants appeared to take part more in school-related activities, those of the non-literate participants appeared to engage more in domestic activities. This often included helping their parents on the farm on a daily basis. Thus, while the desire to educate their children may be high among the non-literate group, the very stringent living conditions may have negative consequences on the quality and level of education of their children. This may in turn, have a negative impact on their life chances.

Self-perception

A good number of the literate respondents reported feeling quite positive about themselves, particularly their relative financial independence and the élite status which they seem to enjoy within their communities. The non-literate group, on the other hand, often referred to their lack of literacy as a state of 'blindness'. They seemed quite aware of the advantages of literacy perhaps because most of them (72 per cent), were married to literate men. Illiteracy, they reported, limited their potential.

Participation in Adult Literacy Programmes

According to the findings, a majority of non-literate adult women would prefer immediate economic solutions to attending literacy classes. Although many indicated willingness to attend, they reported that realistically they could not, even if such programmes were available, because of time constraints and more urgent matters of survival (see also, Rogers, this volume).

PROBLEMS AND DIFFICULTIES

One of the greatest challenges literacy researchers in Sub-Saharan Africa face is the paucity of previous related research. This is the result of inadequate funding of educational research in the region. It is therefore often difficult to find adequate background material. Also related to the lack of previous research is the difficulty in accessing statistical data. Even when available, the figures are often disparate and conflicting. While these problems may not necessarily prevent research, they do create additional burdens.

The logistic and infrastructural constraints involved in conducting research in the region are considerable (see also Smock, 1981; Ndongko, 1994). In rural Nigeria and elsewhere in the region, lack of reliable modes of communication means that all arrangements, including the selection of participants and scheduling of interviews, have to be made through personal contacts. The problem is further compounded by lack of public transportation systems in rural towns and villages.

Another significant problem literacy researchers may encounter, is the reluctance and apprehension of potential participants, particularly non-literates who may view researchers' motives as suspect.

A workable knowledge of local languages is clearly a prerequisite for literacy research in the region. Researchers who cannot speak local languages often require the assistance of translators which, in itself, creates a range of problems. Translators may, for instance, have inadequate knowledge of the research process even after some training. There is also the possibility of misinterpreting questions and responses.

Different but also related to the above is the question of 'cultural and semantic sensitivity' particularly when dealing with non-literate groups. Asking personal questions often demands tact and answers to such questions may sometimes have to be elicited indirectly. Intrusion into people's private lives is not a common phenomenon in rural Sub-Saharan Africa.

A final limitation for researchers in the region involves the difficulties encountered in trying to get information from related government agencies

(Ndongko, 1994). As is often the case in developing nations, the prevailing political climate does not favour criticism of government policies by government employees.

FUTURE DIRECTIONS

Even in the 1990s, the life chances of the girl child in Sub-Saharan Africa continue to be marginal: limited educational opportunities invariably result in deprivation, poverty and the diminution of her status. This has significant implications for future literacy research, practices and policies in the region.

A major implication of the findings of the study described above is that effective literacy policies for women in the region should be tied to micro-economic policies. Further, policies should be designed to encourage the education of girls, on the one hand, and to sustain the interests of adult female learners, on the other. Such economic policies – which I refer to as femanomics – thus become the cornerstone of attempts at eradicating female illiteracy.

'Femanomics' essentially advocates the following:

- The notion that the fundamental way of combatting female illiteracy is to significantly increase investment in girls' education (early intervention), since they eventually become adult illiterates;
- The creation of tangible reward systems for adult female learners. This involves the provision of funds for adult women who are enroled in literacy classes or who would like to do so, either through direct remuneration or as capital for income generating activities.

An important assumption of femanomics is that, unless new and drastic strategies are created, the eradication of female illiteracy by the year 2000 and beyond as advocated by the UN and other donor agencies, will remain an illusion. The evidence suggests that female non-literates would like to participate in literacy programmes, but only if they have guaranteed sources of income.

Given the importance of the prudent use of limited funds, a useful direction for literacy research in Sub-Saharan Africa might be to determine which age cohort would benefit most from literacy programmes. Also in urgent need of investigation is the number of years of literacy instruction required for tangible results, such as access to formal employment. As Wagner (1992) points out, current global trends suggest that, as basic literacy becomes more widespread, its 'purchasing power' is diminishing correspondingly.

Finally, parental perception of the value of the education of girls quite often influences whether or not they attend and, most importantly, remain in school (Etta, 1994). However, the relative importance of economics, on the one hand, and the traditionally higher value placed on the male child as a result of patrilineal lineage system, on the other hand, is not at all clear. There is a need to further investigate this attitudinal factor. Findings of such research could have significant policy implications in the region.

University of Windsor,
Canada

REFERENCES

Amadiume, I.: 1987, *Male Daughters, Female Husbands*, Zed Books, London.

Bhaskar, R.: 1986, *Scientific Realism and Human Emancipation*, Verso, London.

Bhaskar, R. 1989, *Reclaiming Reality: A Critical Introduction to Contemporary Philosophy*, Verso, London.

Blumberg, R.L.: 'Engendering wealth and well-being in an era of economic transformation', in R. Blumberg, C. Rakowski, I. Tinker, & M. Monten (eds.), *Engendering Wealth & Well-Being*, Westview Press, Boulder.

Browne, A. & Barrett, H.: (1991). 'Female education in sub-Saharan Africa: The key to development?', *Comparative Education* 27, 275–285.

Caldwell, J.: 1979, 'Education as a factor in Mortality Decline: An examination of Nigerian data', *Population Studies* 33, 395–413.

Callaway, H.: 1987, *Gender, Culture and Empire: European Women in Colonial Nigeria*, MacMillan Press, London.

Cochrane, S.: 1982, 'Education and fertility: An expanded examination of the evidence', in G. Kelly & C. Elliott (eds.), *Women's Education in the Third World: Comparative Perspectives*, State University of New York Press, Albany, 1982, 311–330.

Comings, J., Smith, C., & Shrestha, C.: 1994, 'Women's literacy: The connection to health and family planning', *Convergence* 27, 93–101.

Corson, D.: 1993, *Language, Minority Education and Gender: Linking Social Justice and Power*, Multilingual Matters, Clevedon.

Corson, D.: 1997, 'Critical realism: An emancipatory philosophy for applied linguistics?', *Applied Linguistics* 18, 166–188.

Egbo, B.: 1996, *Variability in The Quality of Life of Literate and Non-Literate Rural Women: A Nigerian Case Study*, PhD thesis, University of Toronto.

Etta, F. E.: 1994, 'Gender issues in contemporary African education', *Africa Development* 19, 57–84.

Federal Government of Nigeria: 1981, *National Policy On Education* (Revised Edition).

Federal Government of Nigeria: 1990, *Statistics of Education in Nigeria 1985–1989*, Federal Ministry of Education, Lagos.

Federal Government of Nigeria: 1995, *Statistics of Education in Nigeria 1990–1994*, Federal Ministry of Education, Lagos.

LeVine, R.: 1982, 'Influences of women's schooling on maternal behaviour in the third world', in G. Kelly and C. Elliott (eds.), *Women's Education in The Third World: Comparative Perspectives*, State University of New York Press, Albany.

Mba, N.: 1982, *Nigerian Women Mobilized: Women's Political Activity in Southern Nigeria, 1900–1965*, Institute of International Studies, University of California, Berkeley.

Ndongko, W.A.: 1994, 'Social science research and policy-making in Africa: Status, issues and prospects', *Africa Development* 19, 71–90.

Okojie, C.: 1983, 'Improving the quality of life for rural women in Nigeria: The role of education and technology', in U. Igbozurike & M. Raza (eds.), *Rural Nigeria: Development and Quality of Life*, ARMTI Seminar Series 3, 130–145.

Osinulu et al.: 1994, 'Women education [in Nigeria]', in O.O. Akinkugbe (ed.), *Nigeria and Education: The Challenges Ahead, Proceedings and Policy Recommendations of the 2nd Obafemi Awolowo Foundation Dialogue*, Spectrum Books Limited, Ibadan, 1994, 185–190.

Smock, A.: 1981, *Women's Education in Developing Countries: Opportunities and Outcomes*, Praeger Publishers, New York.

Stromquist, N.: 1990, 'Women and illiteracy: The interplay of gender subordination and poverty', *Comparative Education Review* 34, 95–111.

UNESCO: 1993, *World Education Report*, Unesco Publishing, Paris.

United Nations: 1991, *Women: Challenges to the Year 2000*, United Nations New York.

Wagner, D.: 1992, 'World literacy: Research and policy in the EFA decade', in D. Wagner & L. Puchner (eds.), *World literacy in the year 2000*, The Annals of The American Academy of Political and Social Science. Vol. 520. Sage Publications, Newbury Park, 1992, 12–26.

BENTE E. HAGTVET & SOLVEIG-ALMA H. LYSTER

LITERACY TEACHING IN NORWAY

Historically, the driving forces behind literacy education in Norway have been the church and the state. Compulsory literacy education was introduced indirectly in 1736 as part of the preparation for the Confirmation ceremony. Widespread literacy was not achieved, however, until the beginning of the twentieth century. The major teaching tools throughout this period were alphabet books, in conjunction with phonologically-based methods. More recently other approaches, such as language experience and emergent writing, have been gaining ground.

Literacy research has focused on a number of areas, including the different approaches to the teaching of reading and writing; reading difficulties, the role of writing in literacy development; and the relationship between oral language abilities and literacy development. A school reform reducing the age of admission to school from seven to six from 1997 has also had the effect of greatly stimulating research.

EARLY DEVELOPMENTS

In very early times, there were two overlapping literacy traditions. The first, based on the runic alphabet, goes back to 200–600 but was also in general use during the middle ages, particularly in trade and business (Vannebo, 1994). The second tradition, based on the Latin alphabet was associated first with the court and clergy following the introduction of Christianity around 1030, and later with the education of children of the wealthy.

The various Nordic countries launched their first literacy campaigns at different times between 1680 and 1740. The legal basis for literacy instruction in Norway was the Confirmation Ordinance of 1736. The ordinance demanded, at least indirectly, compulsory education for all children and, in 1739, the Royal School Ordinance required schooling for all children from the ages of six or seven until they were 'at least able to read without hesitation from a book and know their catechism' (Tveit, 1991). If reading was not of the required standard, it was not possible to be confirmed, to have a marriage licence, land or a permanent job, or to enlist in the armed forces. These constraints often had tragic consequences but, in terms of advancing literacy development, the linking of reading and civic status was 'a stroke of genius' (Tveit, 1991).

V. Edwards and D. Corson (eds), Encyclopedia of Language and Education,
Volume 2: Literacy, 225–233.
© *1997 Kluwer Academic Publishers. Printed in the Netherlands.*

The first stage of the literacy campaign, then, was inspired by the Church; it was intended primarily to further religious education and stressed the reading of texts already learned by heart. The main impetus for literacy teaching passed from the Church to schools around 1850. Now there was an emphasis on writing, in addition to reading, and the aim of education was to produce children who could read not only religious works, but also texts from 'real life'.

It was not, however, until the first decade of the twentieth century that widespread literacy was achieved. Even then, language minorities such as the Sámi continued to experience low levels of literacy. The same is true today of many more recently arrived immigrants from the Third World (Vannebo, 1994).

MAJOR CONTRIBUTIONS

Any discussion of teaching methods needs to take into account two key facts. The first is that Norwegian children have always started school in the year of their seventh birthday. The second is that sound-letter correspondences in Norwegian are relatively regular – more regular, for instance, than in English and Danish, but less regular than Finnish and Italian. This latter observation may well explain why phonic methods have always had a strong hold in Norway (see parallel arguments for French and Dutch writing systems in the reviews by Béchennec & Sprenger Charolles, and Reitsma, this volume).

In addition to a heavy emphasis on sight recognition, the early teaching of reading was based largely on the alphabetic method (see also Thompson, and Sprenger-Charolles & Béchennec, this volume). For instance, in the 1830s beginning readers would spell a word aloud using letter names: 'S-U-N says /sun/'. Later more stress was gradually put on phonology. At this stage, writing skills were developed largely through copying exercises; these gradually gave way after 1850 to retelling, dictation, letters and essays (Dokka, 1989; see also Hall, this volume).

From 1922, a national curriculum strengthened the position of the mother tongue through the teaching of Norwegian as a subject and stressed that phonics should be used in the early phases of literacy teaching. These recommendations, supported by a range of alphabet books approved by the Department of Education, have served as the main guidelines for teachers for most of this last century. None the less, the principle that individual teachers should have the right to choose teaching methods has been defended throughout this period.

The single most important individual contributor to literacy education has probably been Nordahl Rolfsen who fostered increased awareness of the need to interpret reading as something much broader than simply decoding. He produced a series of five text books, the first of which was published in the early 1890s; the books were still in use in many schools as late as the 1960s. They covered a broad variety of subjects and set out to encourage an enjoyment of reading, thus heralding a new era in the teaching of literacy. They contained drawings by famous Norwegian artists designed to stimulate children's imagination and bring the text to life. The language was simple compared with earlier text books and closer to the spoken language familiar to children.

Other than Rolfsen, few individuals have had a national impact on the teaching of literacy. A notable exception is Gjessing (1986), who is well known for his work on reading and spelling difficulties. Gjessing stressed the need for early identification and intervention, and offered guidelines on remedial teaching. He also helped to raise awareness of dyslexia and the fact that even children of normal intelligence may experience reading problems.

Skjelfjord (1987) has also made an important contribution to the teaching of reading. Drawing on empirical data, he emphasises the importance of children's ability to segment speech sound by sound in a sequential way for the teaching of reading and spelling, and argues that phonemic analysis proceeds mainly on an articulatory basis' (Skjelfjord, 1987: 82; see also Thompson, this volume). Results from a study conducted by Lie (1991) support Skjelfjord's findings: first grade children who were offered practice in breaking up words into articulatory units were found to develop more advanced literacy skills during the first grade than children following a phonologically-based program with no focus on the links between phonemes and their ariculatory realisation.

In addition to the contribution of a small number of individuals, various broad movements have emerged over the years. In the 1970s, for instance, the emphasis on the importance of the child's own dialect emerged as a challenge to the longstanding use of alphabet books. In Sweden, Leimar (1974) stressed the importance of language experience – the use of texts composed by children and dictated to the teacher as the material for reading (see also Thompson, this volume). This approach, with its focus on the children's own language and interests, has also had a considerable influence on Norwegian teaching practices in the last two decades. However, while the language experience approach has been widely accepted in many classrooms, attention continues to be paid to phonics. Although academic debate on the merits of different approaches continues to be heated, most teachers use a mixture of methods. Children's own texts are used alongside alphabet books, phonologically-based strategies modified to accommodate different dialects, and the sight reading of certain high frequency words.

During the last decade there has been increasing interest in the role of writing in the development of literacy and learning (see, for instance, Smidt, 1993). The concept of 'emergent literacy' has also gained ground as, too, has the notion that reading and writing may be discovered in the preschool in play-oriented and informal activities.

RECENT RESEARCH ON LITERACY

Recent and ongoing research on literacy can be divided into three main areas: early literacy, writing and spelling, and evaluation studies.

Early writing

Recent interest in early reading and writing has been stimulated in part by international research (Read, 1986 and see the review by Raban in this volume). The decision to lower the age of admission to school from seven to six in 1997 has also invited an interest in this area. Until the mid-1980s, there was a reluctance among both kindergarten teachers and parents to encourage interest in reading and writing before the start of formal schooling.

There has, however, been a shift in opinion in recent years. Drafts of the new curriculum for 1997 place great emphasis on the teaching of literacy at age six, but through play-oriented and creative activities and with great emphasis on oral language and informal teaching situations which prepare children for more formal reading and spelling instruction.

A number of researchers have contributed to the growing body of knowledge about the development of literacy with six-year olds. Inspired by the work of Leimar (1974), Lorentzen (1991), for instance, discusses ways in which texts or 'stories' dictated to an adult by the child act as a bridge between oral and written language. Hagtvet (1989) shows how activities aimed at developing children's (oral) language awareness through role play writing in everyday activities helps early reading and spelling development. Elsness (1991) describes developmental aspects of children's early writing and emphasises the importance of creative writing for literacy development.

Influenced in the main by English and Scandinavian research (e.g. Bradley & Bryant, 1983; Lundberg, Frost & Petersen, 1988), various studies have focused on the relationship between preschool oral language abilities and later literacy development. Results from a study conducted by Lyster (1995) show that both phonological and morphological awareness training in the pre-school were beneficial for the development of reading and spelling in first grade (see also Thompson, this volume). The phonological awareness program, however, proved most effective for children with less experience of literacy prior to formal schooling.

Qualities associated with 'good' child-adult interaction are identified by Olaussen (1992) in a study of mother-child interaction during book reading.

Finally, the focus of ongoing longitudinal studies of children between the ages of two and eight at the Institute of Special Education of the University of Oslo (Hagtvet et al, 1992; Hagtvet, 1994; Lyster, 1995) is on preventing literacy problems. One issue which has already emerged as important is the identificaton of oral language precursors of reading ability in children of dyslexic parents.

Writing and spelling

Over the last ten years there has been a growing interest in the quality of children's writing and the role of writing in literacy development, particularly in relation to older children and students (see Smidt, 1993, for an overview). The quality of written work has been analyzed with reference to the time at which it was written, the age of the writer and genre. Topics which have received attention include the effects of the cultural and social characteristics of high school students on writing; the linguistic characteristics of 'good' and 'poor' essays produced by high school students and university students; the linguistic characteristics of narrative and expository texts; and cohesion and coherence in texts (see Evensen, 1992 & Smidt, 1993).

There has also been a growing interest in both the process of writing and the social psychology of writing. The observation that written texts are influenced by other students – as well as other texts – has led to an increased awareness of the interaction between literacy and personality development, and also between writing and learning in other school subjects (Dysthe, 1993). Group writing has also received attention, in particular the social planning of writing and the feedback given by response groups (e.g. Hoel, 1996). Teaching guidelines have been developed at college and university levels (Hertzberg, 1995).

Both Thygesen (1992) and Wiggen (1992) investigate the relationship between spelling mistakes and dialect variation (see the review by Corson in Volume 6). In Wiggen's study, spelling mistakes are interpreted as correlates of oral language. In a similar vein, Thygesen finds that children who speak a dialect that differs significantly from the written norm, make more spelling mistakes than children who speak a dialect which corresponds more closely to writing.

Bråten (1994) studies spelling strategies used by beginner and more experienced readers, and also develops a program for use with poor spellers. He suggests that different spelling strategies should be used with different spelling problems and at different stages in development.

Writing also implies motor activity. Søvik and co-workers have studied handwriting in normal and deviant populations with dysgraphic problems, and also the relationship between handwriting, spelling and reading (Søvik, Arntzen & Thygesen, 1987).

Evaluation studies

Literacy levels in Norway were assessed as part of the last international study on literacy conducted by the International Association for the Evaluation of Educational Achievement (Elley, 1992; Høien, Lundberg & Tønnessen, 1994). The study included children at ages nine and fourteen. Although Norwegian nine-year olds as a whole scored above the international mean, the bottom 25 percent performed less well than the comparable group in most other countries. Further, fourteen-year-olds, scored consistently below the international mean on all tests after national economic, health and literacy differences had been controlled. Such results invite increased attention to the teaching of literacy with older children. They also raise questions as to the wisdom of leaving the school entrance age as late as seven. The IEA results have caused some worry among politicians as well as school authorities. Drafts of curriculum plans for the 1997 reform draw attention to a number of variables which IEA results suggest may have an impact on literacy development.

PROBLEMS AND DIFFICULTIES

One reason why the IEA results may have come as such a surprise is the scarcity of standardised testing in Norwegian schools in recent decades. This policy may well be associated with late assessment and lack of intervention for children with specific learning difficulties. For this reason, the Department of Education has charged the Centre for Reading Research to develop reading tests as part of a large-scale evaluation project (Kirke-, Utdannings- og Forskningsdepartementet/ Senter for leseforskning, 1996).

Another area of concern is the difficulties involved in assessing the writing of older children. Berge (1996) found that inter-marker reliability in the assessment of high school exam essays was astonishingly low. He related discrepancies to the different criteria used by markers when describing the characteristics of good and poor essays. These findings may be related, in part at least, to the traditional autonomy of teachers in the Norwegian education system.

Drafts of the 1997 curriculum indicate that the Department of Education intends to exert more influence on classroom practice than has previously been the case. The recommendations, however, are very general and might be difficult to interpret. There is relatively little research on curriculum implementation in the classroom, though there are indications that text books and examination requirements – rather than centrally issued guidelines – determine what happens in the classroom. It would appear that teachers interpret directions differently, stress different areas of the curriculum in different ways and use different approaches to literacy development. Central figures and organizations in the field of literacy, such as the Norwegian

Dyslexia Association, question whether methods and theory related to the teaching of literacy receive sufficient attention in initial teacher education. They argue that theoretical and practical issues around literacy development should have a much higher profile in the future.

FUTURE DIRECTIONS

The 1997 school reform is undoubtedly one of the most important developments in education in this century. Since 1959 Norwegian children have had nine years of compulsory education beginning in August of the year of their seventh birthday. When formal schooling begins one year earlier in 1997, they will have ten years of compulsory education before entering either the upper secondary school or the labour market.

The Department of Education in conjunction with the Norwegian Research Council is planning a broad-based research programme on 'Education, competence and the formation of values for the period 1996 to 2001'. Researchers are invited to focus on factors which help or hinder learning and development, on teaching approaches and organization. Factors related to special education are also included. Although literacy forms one small area of this program, the Department of Education has indicated that some of the projects should be related to topics such as the quality of literacy teaching and the evaluation of literacy development.

The draft of the new curriculum stresses that listening, reading with understanding and reading aloud are central elements in the stimulation of literacy. Teachers themselves have placed particular emphasis on the pivotal role of the parents in developing literacy skills. Many teachers and schools have introduced projects involving parents in reading activities at home and have also initiated 'book weeks' and special reading sessions, where all children are involved in extra reading activities for at least fifteen minutes every day. Most schools have some kind of a school library, but the size of these libraries and whether they are run by a full-time librarian or a part-time teacher, differ not only from area to area but from school to school.

University of Oslo, Norway

REFERENCES

Berge, K.L.: 1996, *Norsksensorenes tekstnormer og doxa*, doctoral thesis, University of Trondheim.

Bradley, L. & Bryant, P.: 1985, *Rhyme and Reason in Reading and Spelling*, Ann Arbor, University of Michigan Press.

Bråten, I.: 1994, *Learning to Spell. Training Orthographic Problem-Solving with Poor Spellers: A Strategy Instructional Approach*, Scandinavian University Press, Oslo.

Dokka, H.J.: 1989, *En skole gjennom* (The school through 250 years), Universitetsforlaget, Oslo.

Dysthe, O.: 1993, *Writing and Talking to Learn. A Theory-Based, Interpretive Study in Three Classrooms in the USA and Norway*, doctoral thesis, University of Troms.

Elsness, T.F.: 1991, '"Meningsfylte tekster" og den grunnleggende lese- og skriveopplæringen' (Meaningful texts and the basic teaching of reading and writing), in: I. Austad (ed.), *Mening i tekst. Teorier og metoder i grunnleggende lese- og skriveoppl*, Cappelen, Oslo.

Elley, W.B.: 1992, *How in the World do Students Read? IEA Study of Reading Literacy*, Hamburg: The International Association for the Evaluation of Educational Achievement.

Evensen, L.S.: 1992, 'Emerging peaks, turbulent surfaces: advanced development in student writing', in A.M. Langvall Olsen & A.M. Simensen (eds.), *Om språk og utdanning*. Festskrift til Eva Sivertesen, University Press, Oslo.

Gjessing; H.J.: 1986, 'Function analysis as a way of subgrouping the reading disabled: Clinical and statistical analyses', *Scandinavian Journal of Educational Research* 30, 95–106.

Hagtvet, B.E.: 1989, 'Emergent literacy in Norwegian six-year-olds. From pretend writing to phonemic awareness and invented writing', in F. Biglmaier (ed.), *Reading at the Crossroads*, Conference proceedings, the 6th European Conference on Reading. Berlin, 31 July–3 August, 1989.

Hagtvet, B.E., Horn, E., Lassen, L. & Lyster, S.A.H.: Prosjekt for å redusere lese-og skrivevansker (A project aimed at preventing literacy problems). *Dyslektikeren* 5/6.

Hertzberg, F.: 1995, 'Uttalte og uutalte normer for vitenskapelig skriving' (Implicit and explicit norms for scientific writing), in E.B. Johnsen (ed.), *Virkelighetens forvaltere*, Universitetsforlaget, Oslo.

Hoel, T.L.: 1995, *Elevsamtalar om skriving i vidaregåande skole. Responsgrupper i teori og praksis* (High school students' discussions about writing), doctoral thesis, University of Trondheim.

Høien, T., Lundberg, I. & Tønnessen, F.E.: 1994, *Kor godt les norske barn?* (How well do Norwegian children read?), Stavanger, Senter for leseforsking.

Kirke-, utdannings- og forskningsdepartementet/ Senter for leseforskning: 1996, *Kartlegging av leseferdighet*, Prøver for 1, 2. og 6. klasse (Assessment of reading competence for grades 1, 2 and 6), Oslo, Nasjonalt læremiddelsenter.

Lie, A.: 1991, 'Effect of a training program for stimulating skills in word analysis in first grade children', *Reading Research Quarterly* 26, 234–250.

Leimar, U.: 1974, *Läsning på talets grund* (Reading on the basis of oral language), Liber forlag, Lund, Sweden.

Lorentzen, R.T.: 1991, 'Skriftspråkstimulering i førskolealder' (Stimulating the written language in preschool), in: I. Austad (ed.), *Mening i tekst. Teorier og metoder i grunnleggende lese- og skriveopplæring*, Cappelen, Oslo.

Lundberg, I., Frost J. & Petersen, O.P.: 1988, 'Long term effects of a preschool training program in phonological awareness', *Reading Research Quarterly* 28, 263–284.

Lyster, S.A.H.: 1995, *Preventing Reading and Spelling Failure: The Effects of Early Intervention Promoting Metalinguistic Ability*, doctoral thesis, University of Oslo.

Olaussen, B.S.: 1992, *Barns språk og lesing* (Children's language and their reading), doctoral thesis, University of Oslo.

Read, C.: 1986, *Children's Creative Spelling*, Routledge & Kegan Paul, London.

Skjelfjord, V.: 1987, 'Phonemic segmentation. An important subskill in learning to read. I og II', *Scandinavian Journal of Educational Research* 31, 41–58, 81–98.

Smidt, J.: 1993, 'Ny skriveforskning i Norge' (Research on writing), Program for utdanningsforsknings småskrifter, NFR, 3.

Søvik, N., Arntzen, O. & Thygesen, R.: 1987b, 'Writing characteristics of "normal", dyslexic and dysgraphic children', *Journal of Human Movement Studies* 13, 171–187.

Thygesen, R.: 1992, *Språknormkonflikt og skrivevansker. En empirisk studie av sammenhengen mellom tale -skriftsprŒkdiskrepans og utvikling av ortografiske skrivevansker* (Children's spoken language and their spelling failure), doctoral thesis, University of Trondheim.

Tveit, K.: 1991, 'The development of popular literacy in the Nordic countries. A comparative Historical study', *Scandinavian Journal of Educational Research* 35, 241–252.

Vannebo, K.I.: 1994, 'Alfabetiseringen av Norge' (Reading and spelling development in Norway), in B.E. Hagtvet, F. Hertzberg, & K.I. Vannebo (eds), *Ferdigheter i fare?*, Ad Notam Gyldendal, Oslo, 13–25.

Wiggen, G.: 1992, *Rettskrivings-studier II. Kvalitativ og kvantitativ analyse av rettskrivingsavvik hos ¿stnorske barneskoleelever* (A study of spelling development and spelling failure in the eastern part of Norway), doctoral thesis, University of Oslo.

SUBJECT INDEX

academic literacy 135, 138
acquisition of writing xi
adult education 146, 148, 201–203
adult literacy 163–171
Adult Literacy Programmes 220
Africa 175
African-American community 50, 108
African-Americans 110
aliteracy 120
alphabetic approaches 192
alphabetic literacy 62
Alphabetic Method 9, 10
alphabetic principle 13–15
alphabetic scripts 65
alphabetic systems 60
alphabetic writing 62
alphabetical order 66
alphabetization 176
analogy 208
Ancient Greeks 70
analytical activities 194
Analytical Phonics 12
anglocentricism xv
aspects of teaching 9
assessment 130, 159, 230
attention deficit disorders (ADD) 40
attention deficit hyperactivity disorder
    (ADHD) 40, 41
au fil des mots (as words go by) 194
authorial capabilities of children 71
authorship 69–76
autonomous model of literacy 63, 128,
    133–139

background information 211
ball point pens 101
Bangladesh 174
basic literacy 128
basic skills development 125
beginning readers 30, 31
Belgium 207–213
bilingual children 100
bilingual programmes 47
bilingual support 52
bilingualism 48, 51, 107, 108
biliteracy 51, 65, 109
biliterate children 81

biliterate development 48
book sales 209
books 52
brain damage 40
brain dysfunction 38, 40
brain processing 41
broad-nibbed pen 100

campaign-based literacy programmes 204
campaigns for learning literacy 166
capitalism 148, 215
capitalist countries 149
campaigns for literacy 166–168
CDROM 184
child-adult interaction 228
child-centredness 25
childhood 71
children 69, 77
children's authorial capabilities 71
children's education 219
children's experiences of the world 22
children's literacy development 23, 24
children's literacy skills 19, 20, 22
child-tested methods of teaching 163
China 175
Chinese literacy 51
choice of language 130
Christian missionaries 200, 201, 205
class 150
classification of writing systems 61
classism 65
classroom activities 78
classroom research 83
classroom writing 78
classroom writing curriculum 82
clinical syndrome 38
colonialism 215
common underlying proficiency 108
communicative competence 129
Community Development 203
community literacies 159
competence-based approach 130
complexity of reading 121
composing processes 79, 81
composition 70, 78, 107
comprehension strategies 2, 211, 212
compulsory education 225, 231

235

NAME INDEX

243

TABLE OF CONTENTS

VOLUME 1: LANGUAGE POLICY AND POLITICAL ISSUES IN EDUCATION

TABLE OF CONTENTS

TABLE OF CONTENTS

VOLUME 3: ORAL DISCOURSE AND EDUCATION

Section 3: Oral Language and the Curriculum

TABLE OF CONTENTS

VOLUME 4: SECOND LANGUAGE EDUCATION

TABLE OF CONTENTS

TABLE OF CONTENTS

VOLUME 5: BILINGUAL EDUCATION

TABLE OF CONTENTS

VOLUME 6: KNOWLEDGE ABOUT LANGUAGE

TABLE OF CONTENTS

TABLE OF CONTENTS

VOLUME 7: LANGUAGE TESTING AND ASSESSMENT

TABLE OF CONTENTS

TABLE OF CONTENTS

VOLUME 8: RESEARCH METHODS IN LANGUAGE AND EDUCATION

TABLE OF CONTENTS

Encyclopedia of Language and Education

Set ISBN Hb 0-7923-4596-7; Pb 0-7923-4936-9

1. R. Wodak and D. Corson (eds.): *Language Policy and Political Issues in Education.*
    1997   ISBN Hb 0-7923-4713-7
                                                       ISBN Pb 0-7923-4928-8

2. V. Edwards and D. Corson (eds.): *Literacy.* 1997   ISBN Hb 0-7923-4595-0
                                                       ISBN Pb 0-7923-4929-6

3. B. Davies and D. Corson (eds.): *Oral Discourse and Education.* 1997
                                                       ISBN Hb 0-7923-4639-4
                                                       ISBN Pb 0-7923-4930-X

4. G.R. Tucker and D. Corson (eds.): *Second Language Education.* 1997
                                                       ISBN Hb 0-7923-4640-8
                                                       ISBN Pb 0-7923-4931-8

5. J. Cummins and D. Corson (eds.): *Bilingual Education.* 1997
                                                       ISBN Hb 0-7923-4806-0
                                                       ISBN Pb 0-7923-4932-6

6. L. van Lier and D. Corson (eds.): *Knowledge about Language.* 1997
                                                       ISBN Hb 0-7923-4641-6
                                                       ISBN Pb 0-7923-4933-4

7. C. Clapham and D. Corson (eds.): *Language Testing and Assessment.* 1997
                                                       ISBN Hb 0-7923-4702-1
                                                       ISBN Pb 0-7923-4934-2

8. N.H. Hornberger and D. Corson (eds.): *Research Methods in Language and Educa-*
    tion. 1997   ISBN Hb 0-7923-4642-4
                                                       ISBN Pb 0-7923-4935-0

KLUWER ACADEMIC PUBLISHERS – DORDRECHT / BOSTON / LONDON